A M ODYSSEY

To Chris.

Hope you enjoy!

Malcolm

Malcolm Anderson

First Published 2008

ISBN 978-0-9683158-2-8

Library and Archives Canada Cataloguing in Publication

Anderson, Malcolm, 1961-
     A marathon odyssey / Malcolm Anderson.

ISBN 978-0-9683158-2-8 (pbk.)

     1. Anderson, Malcolm, 1961-. 2. Marathon running. I. Title.
GV1065.A54 2008   796.42'52   C2008-907297-9

Published by The Experience Publishers
www.experiencebooks.ca
Ottawa, Ontario, Canada
1-877-755-5155
michelle@experiencebooks.ca

Cover Design by Jacqueline Vinkle
Cover Image Credits
Stopwatch: © icefront | Stockxpert.com,
Baikal Beach: © sumnix www.sxc.hu/profile/sumnix,
Acropolis: © Konstantinos Dafalias
Inside Image Credits
Cork board: © Pietro Romeo | dreamstime.com
Thumb tacked note: © Willeecole | dreamstime.com
Thank you to Coenraad Groenewald and Dave Major
for providing some of the images from our time in Athens

Odyssey – a series of wanderings;
a long adventurous journey

The Concise Oxford Dictionary

Tell me, O Muse, of that man who travelled far
and wide after he had started training ...

Acknowledgements

There have been many people that have made this odyssey possible. First, I'd like to express a special thanks to Michelle Bronsema for her wonderful comments, review and support as this book evolved. A special thanks also to Dave Major for opening my eyes and supporting this odyssey of mine, and for his friendship and wide-ranging insights into the marathon world. Another big thanks also to Jeff Hagen, another friend, from whom I've learned so much about distance running. And thanks to Karen for making me laugh and sharing the distance.

I'd also like to thank the following people who in different, diverse ways also helped to make this book see the light and who put a smile on my face and a skip in my stride. Thanks to you all: Paul Adams, Sue Adams, Callum Anderson, Jack Anderson, Fred Anderson, Michelle Atkins, Robyn Bassett, Roger Biggs, Rich Benyo, Bill Bronsema, Jack Brooks, Martin Brule, Jeff Busschaert, Nigel Compson, Amy Crawley, John Flynn, John Dawson, Bob Dolphin, Lenore Dolphin, Steve Edwards, Teresa Edwards, Matthew Evans, Bob Fickel, Jeff Galloway, Dan Graham, Sue Greene, Coenraad Groenewald, Gavin Goodwin, Alan Goodwin, Joyce Hagen, Joe Henderson, Ian Johnston, Rhonda Kelly, Lorne Knutson, Juergen Kuhlmey, Linda Major, Jim Mundy, New

Zegon, Troy Norris, Ray O'Connor, Dave Penfold, Horst Pre-
isler, Sherri, Shirley and Mike, Karen Raddon, Phil Roberts,
Bill Rogers, George Russell, Michaela Sanders, Selina Da
Silva, Bev Sinclair, Scott Umpleby, Liz Vinkle, Rob Vinkle,
Gord Warner, thanks mate, Patty Warner, and all my family in
New Zealand, which would require another page.

On the production side I'd like to thank Barbara Bell for her
editing and overall suggestions for improving the book. Very
much appreciated. Thanks also to Jacqueline Vinkle who is
responsible for the 'look' of the book; its design from cover
to cover and everything in between. Thanks also, to Allan
Graphics in Kingston for the printing and support.

Finally, a very warm thanks to everyone I met during this
odyssey. Although in some ways it's over, in many ways it's
only just begun.

I hope the book does justice to the enthusiasm, support and
interest shown by everyone – my family, old friends and new
friends – in this project. It's been a great run.

Malcolm Anderson.

TABLE OF CONTENTS

Chapter 1: In the Beginning 1

Chapter 2: After In the Beginning 4

Chapter 3: A Movement 10

Chapter 4: Before In the Beginning 14

Chapter 5: Before Before In the Beginning 18

Chapter 6: Some Numbing Numbering Context 26

Chapter 7: The Attraction Of Running 32

Chapter 8: Place and Space 39

Chapter 9: Gearing Up 42

Chapter 10: Here Goes 52

Chapter 11: The Odyssey to Athens begins 57

Chapter 12: The 1896 Athens Marathon 66

Chapter 13: Onward Goes the Odyssey 71

Chapter 14: The Speedsters 80

Chapter 15: Still Onward 82

Chapter 16: Of Mice and Men 88

Chapter 17: Immersion 98

Chapter 18: Slowing Down and Gearing Up 102

Chapter 19: Athens Bound 112

Chapter 20: A Lot Of Hype 119

Chapter 21: Growth... 123

Chapter 22: I'm here, Where Am I?.. 129

Chapter 23: Why Is There A Transformation?.......................... 211

Chapter 24: And Now For The Cayman Islands Marathon 218

Chapter 25: What Am I Doing To My Body?............................ 231

Chapter 26: The Cayman Countdown 241

Chapter 27: History, Heat and Humidity.................................. 251

Chapter 28: Destination Marathons 258

Chapter 29: People, Peace, Pasta and All That Jazz.............. 270

Chapter 30: The Cayman Islands Melt Day 282

Chapter 31: Cayman R&R 296

Chapter 32: All Roads Lead To Disney.................................... 316

Chapter 33: It's Magical.. 332

Chapter 34: Running Marathons For A Cause.......................... 372

Chapter 35: End Of An Odyssey...Or? 379

Prelude

The first Olympic marathon held in Athens in 1896 was run over 25 miles, not the 26.2 miles famously associated with the marathon distance today. Only seventeen athletes competed in the first Olympic marathon, thirteen of whom were Greek. All the runners walked at some point in the race. One of them cheated. Just over 110 years later in January 2007, 11,000 competitors ran and walked in the Disney Marathon in Orlando, Florida. On the previous day 15,000 had completed the half-marathon, and other runs organized by Disney.

Those seventeen runners in Athens had no idea what would evolve over the next 100 years. Why would 11,000 people want to run a marathon at Disney World? Not a bad question. Especially when there are over 300 other marathons these folks could run in North America alone during the year.

The winning time for the very first Olympic race was 2:58:50 (remember, about 25 miles). The World Record for the longer 26.2 mile distance today is 2:04:26. In the United States, in 2006, there were 7,025 sub 3-hour finishers (10.7% of all finishers).

At 2pm on April 10 1896, the runners set off from a bridge in Marathon after hearing the Starter's speech. They'd been taken to Marathon the night before; some of them had competed in other Olympic events the previous day. At Disney World, most of the 11,000 competitors arrived in darkness at the starting location between 3:00am and 5:00am on the morning of the race. Before most birds are even contemplating what to do with the day, a live rock band was performing at a huge parking lot while a merchandise store was open to keep runners entertained and purchasing as they waited to race. Jumbotron video screens blasted music and interviews with runners and officials. At 6:00am, after the American national anthem, a rousing and welcoming speech from Mickey Mouse and his friends, and fireworks, the 11,000 competitors began the race, high-fiving Mickey and his colleagues at the start-line.

Mickey was nowhere to be seen at the Athens race. In fairness though, he wasn't even conceived then. While the 1896 competitors ran over a rough stony road to the legendary Panathinaikon Stadium in Athens – itself about one kilometre from the Acropolis – competitors at Disney's marathon ran through the Magic Kingdom, MGM Studios, the Epcot Centre and the Animal Kingdom (where there are not actually that many animals). The 1896 runners were cheered along the way by the local communities. So too were the Disney runners, giving high-fives, hugging and taking photos with Goofy, Donald Duck, Snow White, Peter Pan, and the many other Disney characters. In Athens, each competitor had a bicycle attendant to provide refreshments and support.

Disney competitors drank and ate at Aid stations strategically placed at regular intervals along the route. Many ran with their own food and drinks and gels and gu in fanny packs or specially designed 'fuel belts' so they could consume these any time they wanted during the run. Many took their cameras, cell phones and music on the run.

While awards were presented only to the first and second placed runners in Athens, everyone who completed the marathon at Disney received a huge Mickey Mouse Medal. The 1896 Olympic marathon was an all male affair. Women did not get to run in the Olympic marathon until 1984, almost 90 years later. In the Disney marathon, 5,156 finishers were women.

Something has happened in the 110 years between Athens and Disney. More of us run. We are older. We are comprised of both genders. We have better gear. We know more about running the distance. We recognise, appreciate and maybe thrive on the strong social side of running; we make long lasting friendships. We know the benefits of the training. We are not out to win. We're willing to spend a lot of money. We are consumers in an expanding and increasingly competitive marketplace.

We are a social movement.

1

In the Beginning

My calf muscles felt like they'd just been pounded with a hammer, there was an angry alien trying to get out of my left knee, and someone was playing the cello with my Achilles tendon. The lungs once filled with air seemed to have simply given up. A strained contorted smile appeared on my face, indicating that an acupuncturist had put 26.2 pins inside my mouth. I couldn't go any further. It was the best of times. It was the worst of times. I'd started training.

'Training' is a bit of a stretch. But there I was. The image still sends shivers through the bone fragments in my left knee. A beach in New Zealand. February, 2006. The sun streaming down, because it would look strange going in any other direction. Waves crashing upon the shore as the cool Pacific breeze, well, alright, gale actually, was doing everything to knock me down. People walking their dogs, smiling at me with a touch of pity in their eyes. Their owners were doing the same.

Had they realized I'd just run the entire length of the country? That would've been nice. Truth was I'd just taken an extremely long and painful time to run a very short distance.

My first fifteen minute run in years. 'My God,' I thought. 'Has it come to this?'

Apparently it had. For someone so active in early life this was a hard message, but one I'd suspected was coming for a long time. Still gasping for air I checked my various body parts to discover that at least I wasn't seriously physically injured. Mentally I was a train wreck. I'd told myself before the run to take it easy, the world record would have to wait. I couldn't imagine what I'd feel like if I hadn't taken it easy.

That was the beginning of a thought process that several months later led to this book. I'd unknowingly set off on a journey of discovery, my own personal Homerian Odyssey. Along the way I've had the privilege of learning a lot about people, places, history, running marathons, airports, bonking, and myself.

As my running became less of a circus act, I sensed my body actually liked it even though it wouldn't admit it. I started thinking about the remotely possible. A marathon? Like most people, I felt that running marathons is what *other people* do. But I wanted a goal. I needed a goal. A marathon seemed on the outer fringe of the possible.

I ran a few more times in New Zealand, each time feeling a little bit better than the previous one. I made a point of running almost daily when I returned to Canada, with the thought, almost dream I suppose, that I could run a marathon if I kept this up. I began to immerse myself in the whole marathon 'gig' as my body continued to awkwardly put one foot in front of the other.

There was a fascinating story unfolding, which is what this book is about. It's a Tale of Three Marathons, an odyssey, and much more.

And it's not about me.

Well, maybe some of it is, but not the fascinating parts.

2

AFTER
IN THE BEGINNING

I started reading books on marathons and googling marathon related websites. I flicked through running magazines at the bookstores while trying not to spill cups of coffee all over them. I wanted to learn about where it all started and what's going on now in the world of marathons. I was enrolled in my own immersion class.

As interesting as all this was, and still is, what I really wanted to do was to experience it all. One night on the Internet I found the Athens marathon. I found *The Place* – Marathon – where the legend began. A short drive, well, long run, from Athens. Marathon is the site of the historic battle in 490 BC where it is said that *Pheidippides*, the messenger, immediately after the battle, but before cell phones, ran to Athens to announce that the 20,000 invading Persians had been defeated by the vastly outnumbered Greeks. Only 192 Greeks died, compared to 6,400 Persians.

That event, regardless of what actually happened, inspired a story, which centuries later led to a poem, that in turn begat some ideas, that begat some smooth talking, that in turn begat, well, anyway ... led to the original 1896 Olympic marathon; the same route used in 1896 was also used in the 2002 Olympics.

Well that's a little too brief, I guess. Here's the story.

The Persian plan had been to invade and capture Athens. It's the sort of thing that happened in those days. This was no friendly merger. Legend has it that Pheidippides was sent to Sparta to request Spartan help to repel the Persians; word was out they were on their way. He covered the distance of about 150 miles in two days without Nikes, gels, sports drinks or an MP3 player. The run is now commemorated with the annual Spartathon race each year.

Depending on which source you read, the Spartans either didn't want to help because of the festivals they were currently engaged in, or the Athenians couldn't wait for when the Spartans *would be* ready. With email down, Pheidippides ran back to Athens to pass the news on and immediately headed over to Marathon for his moment in history. The Athenians prepared for the worst – rape, pillage, plunder, murder, Paris Hilton, etc, and planned to evacuate the city once they had burnt it down so the Persians couldn't have it.

We'll have to wait for the definitive account of the actual event – the Hollywood Epic – but for now we do at least know, we think, that the Greeks strategically outsmarted and out-battled the Persians, on a Friday possibly, and claimed an outstanding and extraordinary victory. The Persians retreated, and Pheidippides, no doubt still feeling the effects of his brisk run to Sparta and back, was ordered to speedily return to Athens to share the breaking news before the folks set the place alight.

Pheidippides made it, as we know, and told the Athenians the battle had been won. He then dropped dead, the story goes, from exhaustion. Who wouldn't?

That's the sort of action, commitment and resilience that will get you into the history books. Well, not straight away. Legends take time. The Greek historian *Herodotus* made mention of Pheidippides' journey to Sparta and the Battle of Marathon but said nothing about the 'running-to-say-we've-won-now-I'll-drop-dead' story. *Plutarch*, another Greek writer, added this about 500 years later. He also mentioned other collapsing all-day runners (these were messengers – known as *hemeroromoi*). Then, not long after, *Lucian*, another writer, added the words to Pheidippides' arrival in Athens: "Rejoice! We are Victorious."

Even Pheidippides' name is up for dispute. Some scholars suggest his real name was Philippides, which in ancient Greek means "the son of a lover of horses." Doesn't sound too heroic does it, and you've got to wonder. The suspicion is that at some point in history his name was changed to Pheidippides.

Not much happened for hundreds of years as the world kept busy creating western history through wars, famines, wars, diseases, wars, arts and literature, wars, music, the invention of rugby, revolutions, colonialism, evolution, the renaissance period, wars, and that industrial revolution thing. Then in 1879, while the British and the Zulus fought in South Africa and the Pirates of Penzance was first performed, Robert Browning, the English poet, wrote the poem "Pheidippides", another work of fact and fiction.

Inspirational enough, however, to motivate Michel Breal, a French professor of languages, to propose and market to the 1896 Olympic planning committee that a race from Marathon be held. The sales pitch and lobbying worked, and the rest, as they say, is history.

So the story is never quite consistent and some basic facts still remain unknown – his name, if he was the same messenger as the one who made the Sparta journey, the words used upon arrival in Athens, and even the route he took (there's a shorter, more logical route inland to get from Marathon to Athens). Even the longer route he took is not 26.2 miles, but we'll come to that later. Is it possible he simply went the wrong way?

The marathon run of today, like in 1896, finishes in the famous Panathinaikon Olympic Stadium in the centre of Athens, a short stroll from the Acropolis. And so to run this route and immerse myself in the history and mystique seemed a perfect way to understand more about marathons, in addition to it being a tangible goal for my running.

At around the same time, a close friend and I found the Disney marathon on the Internet.

Disney? What's Disney doing with a marathon?

Well quite a lot as it turns out.

Disney is not just any marathon. We had discovered the *Goofy Challenge*. Walt Disney World hosts the Goofy Challenge – complete the half marathon around Disney World on the Saturday and you are awarded a Donald Duck medal. Finish the Full marathon on the Sunday and you get a Mickey Mouse medal. Complete both within specified times, and you receive a Goofy medal as well.

Three large, spectacular medals. How could we pass up on this opportunity? Almost on impulse, we registered for the Goofy Challenge.

The Walt Disney World Goofy Challenge epitomizes the transition of *'the marathon'* from legend and Olympic heroes to the worldwide social movement; marathon running becoming mainstream. It's estimated that about a million people now run a marathon somewhere in the world each year. The numbers are likely to keep increasing. It sounds like a lot, but it's not when you consider there are five billion potential marathoners living on the planet right now.

People of all ages, shapes and sizes run in marathons to participate in an activity – an experience – that has many, many benefits and can be a lot of fun. What started off in 1896 as an endurance event celebrating a legend in Greece is now a global social movement. People seem to have an unmet need – a need for 'something' and a marathon seems to provide it. People reshape their lives.

So there it was. The Athens Marathon in November and the Goofy Challenge in early January. Possible?

Something inside me snapped and it wasn't my ligaments. I had to experience retracing the historical steps of the Athens marathon and then a few weeks later run with Donald Duck, Mickey Mouse, Goofy and other famous Disney characters I don't even know.

For reasons I can't explain, or due to the moon's influence on the world's tidal pattern perhaps, I decided it would be even more interesting with another marathon tucked in between the two. *Destination Marathons* have become an increasingly popular segment of marathon running. They provide runners with an opportunity to run a marathon at the same time as taking a vacation. Doesn't sound like much of a vacation, does it? But it's a big growth area, especially in Europe. Remarkably, I found a marathon on the Internet that fit perfectly between Athens and Disney. It was meant to be. I registered for the Cayman Islands marathon.

So there it was: The Plan. Three marathons in two months. My body had little say in this, of course. Rightly or wrongly, I assumed it would follow the mind. But I now had a tangible goal. Not only to get into shape by training for a marathon, but to immerse myself in marathon running, be able to gain a first-hand look at what it's all about, and write a book about what I found.

Strangely, the Athens marathon was being run on the same day as the New York City marathon. I'd run one other marathon in my life – New York in 1985. Life sometimes pieces together in unpredictable ways.

I had no idea when I started this book how it would end. Could I do it? Perhaps... Possibly... Maybe.

Well I didn't know obviously. What you'll read here is what I did and how I felt over the training and travel period. Someone recently asked if I found what I was looking for. I said quite honestly that I hadn't realised I was looking for anything. But now, looking back, perhaps subconsciously I was; I just didn't know it at the time. What I did do over the time was keep absolutely open to any and all experiences. Looking back I see I found a lot of things.

3

A MOVEMENT

This book describes the changes that have taken place in marathon running over the past 110 years. I'm involved in this too, although I can't time warp myself to run in the races of yesteryear. What I can do, is take you on my own journey as I live the experience of marathon running from the vantage point of someone who doesn't know much about what he's doing. This is a significant bite to chew – there's a lot to cover in one book. I'm viewing the story of marathon running through the lens of someone – me – training for, travelling to, and running three marathons in a two-month period.

The book is about *movement* – my own pathetic and ungainly movement as I crash along the running surfaces, and my other movements, bowel excluded, as I take myself to different parts of the world to find out more about marathons, and, as it turns out, myself.

The book is also about a social movement. We're currently witnessing and experiencing a transformation. Despite the marathon distance – 42.2 kilometres, or 26.2 miles – being roughly the same over the past 110 years or so, running marathons these days is quite different from running them at any other point in history.

What *is* the transformation?

There are more people running marathons than ever before and the growth continues. The profile of these runners is changing as well. There are more marathon events than ever before, and the number of marathons continues to rise. Never before have we been able to run so many marathons in so many different places. It's no longer a question of *where can you run a marathon*, it's more a question of *where can you not run a marathon*, and those options are fewer and fewer each year.

There is an increasing amount of diversity in the type of marathon events being held. There is big money being spent, invested, donated, and committed to sponsorship for marathons, and that trend is increasing.

We know more about how to train for marathons than ever before. We know more about our bodies; what to do with them, what not to do with them and the consequences of both. We know more about how to minimise the risks involved in running long distances and the associated injuries that occur (all too easily). We run faster marathons now compared to the past, and we will likely get faster, but maybe not much faster.

There is more being written and discussed about marathon running than ever before. There is more technology being applied to marathon running than ever before, most of which is focused on making training and competing more effective, and easier for the marathon 'runner'. The very word 'competing' is associated less and less with marathon running as the new social movement unfolds with increasing numbers and diverse runners. We talk today of *completing* a marathon, *not competing* in a marathon.

In short, the marathon running world of today is much different from ten or twenty years ago, significantly different from fifty years ago, and almost unrecognizable compared to how it looked a hundred years ago. What was once seen as an endurance event of epic proportions for only the superhuman of us all is now increasingly associated with the words 'fun' and 'enjoyment' by everyone, including grandmothers, runners with disabilities, elite runners, people who like to dress up in costumes, people who may drag a tire behind them, and people with nothing better to do on a Sunday.

With some obvious exceptions, running marathons is becoming mainstream – a social movement – it's possible for almost anyone, like me for example, to run a marathon, especially if the right context is available and there is a commitment to a goal. It's exciting and empowering, and lies at the very heart of what we are witnessing. What satisfies the soul is no longer necessarily material possessions. People are looking increasingly inward – just glance at the self-help bookshelves these days – and running a marathon is fulfilling on so many dimensions.

Yet, for all these changes, the distance remains the same. It's still a long way.

Why then, are all these changes occurring? What compels us to run a marathon?

I wanted to answer these questions. I needed to read

about marathon running. I needed to talk to people. I needed to experience it for myself. I'm as much a poster child for the social movement as anyone else, even though my running style – my form – can make a drunk, one-eyed, limping gorilla with a nervous twitch strutting along a fashion runway look elegant and graceful.

What you're about to read, if you haven't given up already, or tossed back into the shelves or recycling bin, is part training log, part travel log, and part information gathering and synthesizing. Like any journey, or any marathon run, I'm not sure how it will go exactly, how it will end – it's a work in progress. I've set myself a goal and I'm writing about it. What you'll read is as it happened over a three-month period.

I found out a lot about myself in this time, and my faith in people rose substantially. The transformation in marathon running, in fact, has contributed to my own transformation, and I'm better for it. Without getting teary-eyed about it all, I can't imagine not running marathons. I'm hooked.

It's one thing to experience the transformation; it's another to write about it. Let's hope it works.

4

BEFORE
IN THE BEGINNING

A beach in New Zealand may sound like a long way to go to start training, and it is. But that's where I'm from originally and I was home visiting friends and family. I now live in Ontario, Canada. A run along a beach in a New Zealand summer, even a Dunedin beach, still beats running in 20 degree Celsius *below* along an icy road in the middle of a Canadian winter.

The plan was simple. Go home for two weeks to see everyone, and use some time to get out and run most days. There was no excuse for not doing this. I had to shake off bad habits and create new ones. New good habits, that is. It meant eating better and getting more sleep, and all those other obvious but seemingly difficult things to do these days.

But getting started was hard. I had to keep reminding myself that this was important. Essential really. If I failed to do the obvious and did not commit the time and effort required, I'd have to live with myself for, well, the rest of my life, which potentially could be a lot shorter if I didn't do something. I couldn't bear the thought of looking back years from now, perhaps after a critical medical event, and wishing I'd done something to prevent 'this' from happening.

And so I began running the long road.

I ran my first marathon in 1985. It was New York, 10:30am, October 27th. I remember it vividly because it had a fantastic sense of adventure and accomplishment. What a great way to see a city. Four weeks before the marathon the sports doctor told me I had Achilles tendonitis, most likely because I tried to cram too much training into a short amount of time. He advised me not to run again until the marathon, and to 'take it easy on race day, as you may not finish at all'. In those last desperate four weeks I didn't run at all, but trained daily on a stationary bike in the gym. My rear end still squirms when I think about it.

Eight of us piled into a rental van and drove from Ottawa to New York for the weekend. I was the only one running. While my friends were still sleeping I spent an hour of the pre-start build-up watching the world's largest row of porta-potties reach over-capacity, and runners of all shapes, sizes and genders disappear into the trees to respond to nature's calling. Some didn't bother with the trees. I missed the Expo but was smack dab in the middle of the expose.

With the injury ruling out my chances of winning, I decided instead to be the last runner to cross the start line. At the start-line I watched 18,000 runners begin their race and cross over the Verrazano Bridge ahead of me. Those who filled themselves up with too much pre-race liquid peed off the bridge, no doubt much to the surprise of people in the cars on the level below, wondering why it was raining on such a bright sunny day.

Years later I still take pride in telling others about the time I passed 6,000 people in a race. When I first told my boys they thought I was Mr Incredible. New York was also the last time I ran a marathon until now, over twenty years later.

My official 'starting day' for writing this book was also the day I did some spring cleaning of the house, possibly looking for an excuse for not writing. During the archaeological dig my shovel hit the tip of my 1985 New York Marathon poster. I hadn't seen it for years. In fact, I didn't even know I still had it. Filled with the 'wow' emotion, I pinned the poster on the wall in my office as a motivator. It's still there.

An hour later I had to take Fred – my two-year old yellow Lab – to the veterinarian because he had a lump on his head the size of a beach ball and wasn't telling me how he got it. I'd never met the vet before. We talked as Fred tried to vacuum the floor with his tongue. If you run, somehow conversations with strangers often end up on the subject of running. The vet, it turned out, had also run in that New York Marathon.

In this first day of writing I was thinking it was a bit crazy trying to run three marathons in just over two months. I was incredibly naïve. As I started writing, Dean Karnazes was running 50 marathons (the distance, not official marathons) in 50 days in 50 states (and then decided to run home when he was finished), and Sam Thompson, running before him in a very low-key, passionate way, had run 51 marathon distances in 50 days in 50 states. Exceptional endurance to say the least. Crazy is another word.

What I didn't know then but know now, is that there are some amazing extraordinary ordinary people running long distances. Compared to these people I'm like the toddler learning to walk by bouncing along the couch while the other kids are doing somersaults and riding bikes.

5

BEFORE BEFORE IN THE BEGINNING

I don't think I'm any different from any others who are part of this social movement. I realised at some point that the person who is going to be the most influential in improving my health is me. My guess was that if I focused on running, other parts of my life like eating properly, sleeping, less stress, working less hours and working fewer crazy early, early hours or late, late nights or both, would coalesce into making me feel better about myself, enjoying life in general, and be better at what I do do. Running is simple. Getting out there, doing it and being consistent, is the hard part.

I'm not lean and wiry, but I am a middle-aged man with less hair than I once had. That sounds sad, doesn't it? My two boys call me Baldy. It's not because they can't remember or pronounce my real name – Dad – it's to give me a hard time. The more people around when they say it, the funnier it is.

When I'm not falling off my chair laughing with them on

this point I'm standing at around 6ft. No doubt they will tell me I'm shrinking in the years to come. 'Dwarf-baldy' perhaps. When I stumbled my way along the New Zealand beach in February I weighed 95 kilograms. Now, in September, I'm 88 kilograms; the weight is coming mainly off the top of my head.

I am not known as a fast runner. In fact, I'm not even known as a runner. The only races I've won have been against competitors about thirty-five years younger. This is where experience and a long stride are useful. My two boys – Jack who is eight and Callum who is eleven, will run faster than me one day. But not today. Or tomorrow. Very soon though. No doubt laughing and screaming 'Baldy' as they fly by.

I was always active growing up, playing just about every sport possible. School interrupted the games, although it did enable a critical mass of kids to get together and burn up endless energy. When I got older I stopped being as active. Sports blurred into a very distant past, which is sad and pathetic.

My father died from a heart attack at the inconvenient age of fifty-two. I was eleven years old when he died. His younger brother died a few years later at age fifty. My two sisters and brother in New Zealand and their spouses are between thirteen and twenty-five years older than me and have amassed an impressive list of medical conditions that would take another book to describe. These include heart attacks, brain tumours, hip replacements, off the radar cholesterol and blood pressure, borderline diabetes, and cancer. I've probably missed a few things with that starter list partly because I'm not privy to it all, which is fine. I suspect there's a genetic predisposition for things to go wrong and I can't ignore it. As far as I know, I'm good on all fronts. But for how long?

I would have to be as bright as moose droppings not to take stock of these familial health signs and do something about my own health before it's too late. Especially with two young boys of my own. Ill health or dying young, or both, are not options. It simply doesn't make sense to start living healthier *after* you have developed a chronic illness or had a serious health event in your life.

My father broke his neck playing rugby in his late teens. My uncle and his friends were playing tennis at the time and joked as they saw the ambulance go by that it was probably my father. It was. Thanks to an eccentric doctor he survived. At the hospital he was put on a wooden board at a forty degree angle and sandbagged for several weeks. Then one day he was told to get up. He survived a broken neck but he didn't have good health after that, and I doubt running a marathon was up there on his things-to-do list.

The only running my mother did was around the neighbourhood trying to find me. From an early age I had wanted to travel. So I started small by always leaving – escaping – our house, and wandering the streets. The introduction of a seven foot gate was merely an invitation to a six-year old to climb over it and bask in the glory of another break for freedom.

I know of only one member of my family who has ever run. He's ninety now and not running too much, but still alive. No it's not my brother, despite what the photographs may suggest. It's my uncle, who used to run in cross-country events and mile races. He even started up a running club in 1946. But if there is a genetic predisposition for running then it has been a Da Vincian family secret locked in some Venetian vault for centuries.

Like most young boys, my body was beaten up and bashed around in various games and sports over the years. I have no major scars, body parts broken, out of alignment, or missing from these adventures. I still have a scar on my left knee from a serious scooter crash on gravel, winning respect and admiration from my friends which made it all worthwhile, and a scar just above my right eye from being kicked playing soccer, earning huge respect and admiration from rugby players who hadn't realized you could get injured like that playing a girls' sport.

My most serious injury and the one most relevant to running, aside from about one hundred sprained ankles, was losing the lateral cartilage in my left knee when I was 18 years old (1979). While my father was busy breaking his neck at the same age I instead wimped out, opting to simply lose a tiny piece of my knee.

I was playing tennis. My friend, but fierce competitor on any day, Ian, placed a low drop shot to the net. Seeing his cheesy smile, I stormed in with the elegance of a charging wild pig with its foot caught in a bucket, and managed to skilfully lob the ball gently back to him. Somewhat surprised, although he shouldn't have been, he instinctively hit it to the biggest empty space possible – my centre court. I ran to hit it back but my knee decided to stay at the net.

Barely able to walk, I heroically played on. I couldn't lose to my best friend, after all. Mathematically I calculated what movements would be possible to still win the game without lying down completely immobilised in centre court or be carried away on a stretcher. Unfortunately math is not my strong point. I played some more, thinking my knee would come right. Twenty-eight years later, things are finally starting to turn around. It's because I'm running.

My knee wasn't made any better at the time by our family doctor who decided the best therapy would be to do nothing with it. Weeks later, physiotherapists saw my knee and formed a lynching posse for the doctor, but by then it was too late. Several months and countless ultrasounds later, I was finally told my cartilage should be taken out. It was torn, not ripped as they'd guessed, which in those days was difficult to determine.

The night before I was due to go in for the operation I was tackled from behind by a boy in an Under 16 soccer team I was coaching. I went down like a bull in the rodeo. The soccer team didn't need to rope me because I wasn't moving anywhere. I now had a badly sprained right ankle that didn't work and a gamy left leg. So I then had a few weeks of recovery and rehab as my ankle transformed back to its usual size and shape, while my "good leg" waited for its turn on the operating table. Not even twenty years old and I was falling apart.

I don't remember too much about the operation to take my cartilage out. Unlike today when you can pretty much work on it alongside the surgeons or with the cleaning staff on rotation at the outpatient clinic, in those days I was 'put under' and knew nothing. I woke up pleased to see all my limbs were where I'd left them. For three nights I was given a shot of morphine as my bedtime snack. While visiting Nirvana each night my eyes would shut down completely until 5am the next morning when I resumed counting all the tiles and screws in the ceiling. These days once you've finished helping out with the arthroscopic surgery you'd be advised to maybe not run a marathon that evening.

I tell you this because back then in 1980, I was told with absolute certainty that I'd suffer from arthritis in 20-30 years' time. That comment has remained with me, just like my mother's insistence that I always eat plenty of marmite and that I keep my hair out of my eyes otherwise I would go blind. It's not stopped me from playing sports but it's tempered what I've thought has been possible. The arthritis comments, that is.

It seems that twenty-seven years later, I'm now 'due'. I don't hobble around like a one-legged pirate, but there is a little less flexibility in my left knee compared to my right. In part I've been responsible for that as I've very consciously made an effort to not let it limit what I do in my life. Trying to run these marathons is a good example.

So I'm very uncertain how my knee will cope with the sustained running. It may be a short book. There's only one way to find out. I'm convinced though that any physical pain from running will be way offset by all the other benefits I'll receive over these next few weeks.

Despite the knee aggravation, I've been gifted with the ability to put one foot in front of the other since I was very little. I'm not pretty to watch, and friends and neighbours will vouch for this, but at least my body usually moves in the direction I point it.

.....

Fast forward then, to 2006. When I started training in New Zealand, I also started eating better. I became more conscious of health-related things around me. I even read food labels, not fully understanding what it was I was reading, but reading it all the same. I avoided trans fats. I was becoming my own individual revolution. It felt great.

Back in Canada my friend Karen had also started running again. Like me, she had been very active years ago, and now had a life that was completely out of balance and was looking to turn things around. Over the spring we both kept running when we could, and talking, and talking some more. Before we knew it, conversation gravitated to marathons. It was *big feeling* talk for sure, but we developed a very tangible goal – the Goofy Challenge – that appealed to both of us on many different levels.

The thing about running a marathon is you can't fake it. It's not like an exam that we cram for the previous night. It's 42.2 kilometres – 26.2 miles. If we haven't trained we're in for a miserable time, serious injury, both, or worse. But by slowly building up with regular training we create the ability to do the distance and, I hope, enjoy it. And not injure ourselves. Marathon training imposes a level of discipline and requires ongoing commitment.

It's not hard to find a marathon on any weekend of the year. If you choose, and have sold the house, you can run a marathon in Antarctica, Mt Everest or the North Pole. You can run a marathon along the Great Wall of China. Run under a river in a German tunnel. Find a few marathons in the heart of Africa. Or run a marathon around your local High School track, or run around a garden in downtown London. Anything is possible, anywhere. My youngest son, Jack, ran 80 times around the porch – his own marathon. It wasn't the full distance of course, because the house is not that big, but he still got a medal for it and I got dizzy counting and watching.

So here I go. Three marathons that I felt were back-to-back, and seemed ambitious for me to say the least. A suspect knee with a best-before-date a few generations past, limited running experience, just one previous marathon run 21 years earlier, a non-existent budget, and a work-life for which there are simply not enough hours in the day to complete. As Sponge-Bob would say, "good luck with that."

While Sam Thompson and Dean Karnazes ran their 50 plus marathon distances in 50 states in 50 days, Dave Major in England and Dane Rauschenberg in the US were each running 52 official marathons in the year. Meanwhile Lance Armstrong, seven-time winner of the Tour de France, ran his first ever marathon in New York and probably got more media attention than Sam, Dean, Dane and Dave combined. Lance said it was the toughest thing he'd ever done. The only difference between Lance and me is that I chose to run the New York marathon first and will tackle winning the Tour de France seven times at a later date. At the time this book goes to press Dave will have run over 280 marathons, and has plotted the course to run his 300th marathon in December 2008.

But this book is not about numbers. It's about the transformation of marathon running and the people who run marathons as part of their way of life.

The book is about people like you and me. These are exciting times.

6

Some Numbing Numbering Context

There has been an enormous growth in marathon running over the past few years. In 1994 there were 277,000 runners who finished marathons in the United States. According to *MarathonGuide.com*, in the years 2000 and 2001 there were almost 300,000 finishers in the United States. By 2003 this figure had risen to 334,000.

By 2007 the total estimated number of finishers was 407,000. The numbers may have even gotten higher had there not been the extreme heat on the 5th of October, when several major marathons were being held; the one receiving the most attention was the Chicago marathon, where, due to health and safety concerns, about 8,000 runners were removed from the course as they were running the race and not allowed to finish.

We have seen a growth rate in the number of marathon finishers of over 25% in 7 years. In 2007 men accounted for 60.5% of all finishers in the US, and women 39.5%. This is a slight decline in the number of women finishing compared to 2006, when 39.9% of finishers were women. In 2005, 40% of 383,000 finishers were women. Nevertheless, the number of women finishing (and percent of all runners) has increased since 2000. In 2000 there were 112,125 women finishers (37.5%), compared to the estimated 160,765 women for 2007 (39.5%).

These data are based on 340 different marathons held in the US in 2007 alone (down from 350 in 2006). The 2007 *MarathonGuide.com* report notes that two-thirds of all the marathons held during the year showed growth. What is significant in 2007 is that the top 30 marathons accounted for 57% of all finishers, which is well down from the 71% they had accounted for the previous year. The top 8 marathons, unchanged from 2006, were New York (38,557 finishers), Chicago (est. 26,000), Honolulu (est. 24,000), Marine Corps (20,622), Boston (20,348), Los Angeles (20,016), the Rock 'n' Roll marathon (15,958), and Disney World (10,936).

Although some marathons have 'ceased to be' over time, there is still an increase in the number of possible runs each year, certainly in North America. Almost 80 new marathons began in the United States alone between 2005 and 2007 (28 in each of 2005 and 2006, and 21 in 2007). One of these new 21 in 2007 was the ING Georgia Marathon in which over 4,300 runners competed.

The vast majority of runners are between 20 and 55 years old. The average age of marathon runners in the US has remained fairly constant over the past few years. In 2007 the average age was 38.9 years. Male finishers are on average older (40.5 years) than female finishers (36.5 years). Sixteen percent of all male finishers are in the 40-44 age cohort and another 16% are in the 35-39 age range, compared to just under 15% of all females in the 40-44 cohort, and 16% in the 35-39 range. The largest cohorts for women are ages 25-29 (18.7%), 30-34 (16.1%) and 35-39 (16.3%).

Most marathoners finish a race in a time between 4 and 6 hours (60.6%). Just under 19% finish between 3:30 and 4 hours, while less than 10% finish under 3:30. Just 1.6% of all finishers (6,326) were under 3 hours in 2007. At the other end of the race, about 11% percent of runners finish in times of over 6 hours. These 2007 data are comparable with those for 2005.

And it's not just in North America that we're seeing a huge increase in the number of marathoners and marathons. Hundreds of thousands vie each year in a ballot system for the 30,000+ entry spaces into the London marathon. Over 40,000 runners entered the Berlin marathon, entries for which had been closed months before. In Japan, the Tokyo marathon scheduled for March 2009, had received over 226,000 applications for the 30,000 places by September 2008.

Unfortunately, for Canada, there are no longitudinal detailed data like that collected and reported on by *MarathonGuide.com*, but if you go to the trouble of collecting all the data from what's available over the Internet you find similar patterns.

In 2006, there were 22,558 finishers of 48 marathons held in Canada. Most of these are run in Ontario (12), British Columbia (7) and Alberta (7). The numbers are small in comparison to the US figures, with only two marathons having more than 3,000 runners (The BMO Vancouver International Marathon (3,586) and the ING Ottawa Marathon (3,236). Yet despite the smaller numbers, the profile of runners is essentially the same.

Using detailed data collected from the websites of twenty-one Canadian marathons (which represents 82% of the 22,558 finishers for all 48 marathons), we see that 61.9% of all finishers are male (38.1% female). Overall there is a younger group of female runners when compared to males. Thirty-four percent of females are in the 30-39 age cohort, with 31.2% in the 40-49 cohort and 20.8% in the 20-29 age cohort. For males, the largest group is age 40-49 (35%), followed by 30-39 (30.1%) and then 50-59 (18.7%).

Meanwhile, without wanting to stretch a point too much or make your eyes glaze over, Nico Kotze reports in a 2006 research paper that in the South African *Two Oceans* marathon events in 2005, 58.5% of runners were male in the half-marathon (41.6% female), while 78.5% were male in the 56km ultra (21.5% female). Those aged between 30 and 50 provided the bulk of the runners in both events.

So there is a relative consistency of marathon runners among the different regions.

And then, of course, there are the runners that have created their own unique, and sometimes unfortunate categories. Zhang Huimin, as reported in the media, is a marathoner who lives in southern China. Evan Osnos of the Chicago Tribune reports that the 8-year old second grader Zhang gets up every morning at 2:24am to train for another marathon. On the weekends she will run 26 miles or more before school, on top of the dozens of miles she runs before school during the week.

Why?

Zhang's father started running with her when she was

4-years old. At seven years of age she ran the Haikou marathon in a time of 3:28. Her father has her on a training plan that has the 2016 Olympics as the goal; in part because sporting celebrity and expertise is a way out of poverty in China. Unfortunately it may be completely misguided. Sports Medicine Experts and athletics coaches alike say this is not going to happen because if she continues like this, especially as her body is still growing, the overtraining will reduce bone density, damage cartilage joints, cause a number of orthopaedic problems, delay menstruation and stunt her growth. Even now, she is underweight.

Meanwhile a 4-year old boy, Budhia Singh, from Bhubaneswar, a city in Northeast India, ran 40 miles without stopping, and now lives in an athletics hostel with over one hundred other hopefuls who may 'make it' one day in their respective sports. Four years old?! Budhia's full story is both fascinating and tragic. It seems that we are in a heightened state of redefining what *the possible* actually is for running long distances. Budhia's story, like Zhang's, requires us to always understand the social context in which these stories emerge.

But for the most part we are not like Zhang or Budhia. I'm certainly not. The individuals you will meet in this book are not that extreme in their stories, but they are inspirational.

The point is that in today's social movement in marathon running there are people of all shapes and sizes, ages and different genders. The fact that in the US in 2007 there were over 160,000 women finishing a marathon must be a source of immense pride for someone like Kathrine Switzer, who, in 1967 became an overnight news sensation by running in the Boston Marathon.

Women back then were simply not allowed to run marathons. Kathrine didn't stop there, however, and was instrumental in establishing a women's marathon event in the Olympics – the first event being in 1984; again, not very long ago.

In her book *'Marathon Woman'* published in 2007, Kathrine Switzer commented that in 1981, immediately after the International Olympic Association announced it had voted to include the women's marathon in the 1984 Olympics, she had stated: "Nobody will really understand how important this is until the first woman comes through the tunnel and into the Olympic stadium in three years ... Then the world will be changed."

Today, there are travel agencies focused solely on tours to marathons. There are match-making dating services available on the Internet specifically for runners to meet other runners. I can go on to the Internet and sign-up with numerous training programs and be able to log my training runs on various websites. I can join blogs, mailing lists, download running articles on almost anything and I can join running clubs around the world. It's a small world, but the marathon distance is always 26.2 miles, no matter where you go.

7

THE ATTRACTION
OF RUNNING

The image of me standing naked in front of the mirror is a frightful one. Trust me, I know. It's made even more frightful when I think about what I could look like ten years from now if I don't do something. I'm not lean and wiry but I'm not grossly overweight either. I can see where the current contours might go. I'm not built like a runner. I don't look like a runner. I don't, right now, feel like a runner. But I do want to get fit and healthy and restore some balance in my life.

I've opened a secret door at Hogwarts. This world of running has so many benefits – so many evidence-based scientifically confirmed slam dunk benefits – I almost feel evangelical just writing about it. There is no Hogawarthian magic, except perhaps for the Kenyans. I'm no Kenyan.

Kathrine Switzer and Roger Robinson summarize the benefits of running in their beautiful 2006 book *"26.2 Marathon Stories"*. We don't have to make our eyeballs roll into the recesses as we read through scientific evidence. They simply synthesize the research to note that:

Running helps us by...

- Strengthening the heart and reducing the rate of heart disease.
- Enhancing creativity and problem solving by stimulating endorphins.
- Improving sexuality by maintaining strong blood flow and creating a positive self-image.
- Helping to maintain (or create) healthy sleep patterns by leaving your body fulfilled and tired.
- Reducing the incidence of many forms of cancer by pumping oxygen and antioxidants through your body, which fight against carcinogenic free radicals.
- Reducing toxins in your body by evacuating waste promptly.
- Burning out infection by raising body temperature to fever level on a daily basis.
- Eliminating toxins through the skin and air by stimulating sweating and increasing breathing exchange.
- Pushing disease-fighting white blood cells and immune substances through your system with the release of adrenaline.
- Reducing stress on the heart, joints, lungs and muscles and non-insulin dependent diabetes, by reducing weight and countering obesity.
- Reducing stress by stimulating endorphins.
- Countering depression by stimulating endorphins.
- Reducing the incidence of osteoporosis by strengthening bones.

Source: Switzer and Robinson (2006)

A review of epidemiological studies and clinical trials published in the *American Journal* of Cardiology and reported on in *Runners World* (June, 2006), concluded that burning 1,000 calories by running reduces cardiac risk almost twice as much as burning 1,000 calories by walking. They both have the same effect, however, for losing weight.

So just getting out the door and continually putting one foot in front of the other on a regular basis will improve our health. It also increases longevity and improves the quality of later life. Wow. Why wouldn't you run?

And then there's a welcoming, engaging spirit and friendliness associated with runners. Runners come together for a marathon with a common goal – to run the distance – but for different reasons, often with remarkable human stories of courage, resolve, tenacity, dedication, commitment – the list goes on. Running becomes a part of you, and you it. Talk to someone as you're both running a marathon and you may well end up being friends for life.

What I once thought was a ridiculously long run with a lot of pain turns out to simply be a ridiculously long run with a lot of pain. But there doesn't have to be pain, that's the secret. It's what we make it.

What is it about the distance? Give or take a few feet here and there, the odd stumble into other runners and the water stations, and the trip, well, alright, fall, down the embankment while you're trying to relieve yourself, runners will typically take somewhere between 30,000 and 50,000 steps when they run a marathon. I'm guessing I'll take 41,675 steps in Athens.

There is research literature out there that has looked at the motivations for why people run marathons. In the 1980s and early 1990s especially, there were several studies conducted and a validated standardized survey designed to accurately determine runners' motivations.

First though it's useful to reflect why people choose to run, let alone to run marathons. Tim Noakes, in the fourth edition of his book *The Lore of Running*, which is a 'must read' for anyone wanting to learn everything about running, including marathon running, has identified several reasons to run. Tim gave me permission to quote him liberally here and I do so because he is worth repeating. His comments are about himself, they come from his heart, are eloquent, thoughtful and engaging, and I'm sure resonate with runners around the world. He writes:

*"the point is reached [when running] when fatigue drives us back into ourselves, into those secluded parts of our souls that we discover only under times of such duress and from which we emerge with a **clearer perspective** of the people we truly are ... And running can provide a context for looking at the world, for seeking explanations to the riddles of life".*

*"Running made me newly aware of my body and my responsibility to look after it. Having a physically improved body showed that I cared – that I had **self-pride** and, more important, self-discipline".*

*"I learned that the rewards in running, as in life, come only in direct proportion to the amount of effort I am prepared to exert, and the extent to which I can summon the required **discipline and application**".*

*"Running in competitions taught me the **humility** to realize my limitations and to accept them with pride, without envy of those who might have physical or intellectual gifts that I lack".*

*"To achieve real success in running, as in any worthwhile activity, there must always be the **fear of failure**: a very real fear that the day will come when we will fail, regardless of how hard we have prepared. It is that very inse-*

*curity that keeps our carefully nurtured **self-confidence** from becoming arrogance. And it is also in our inevitable failures that the **seeds of real personal growth** are sown and eventually blossom".*

*"I have to use running for **relaxation and creativity**, as my form of play. I have found that running is one way of living with everyday mental hassles ... I have found that my thinking during those hours is more creative and insightful than at any other time in the day.... regular play, like running, provides the childlike activity necessary for the creative act to occur, for novel thoughts to appear apparently from nowhere, and for old-established ideas to suddenly take on a new meaning".*

*"Finally, running can teach us about our spiritual component – the aspect that makes us uniquely human. This, I suspect, is the **need to discover and to perfect**, the need to keep moving forward ... So we inherit this **desire to push to the limits** to find out what makes us what we are, and what is behind it all".*

Some brief comments here on the research world because there's some interesting stuff. We could go around in circles and debate research designs, conceptual frameworks, empirical data, statistical methods and so on, but that would be the end of the book and you would be asleep. There are different motivations for running marathons, but we don't really know a whole lot about which motivations are strongest among different types of runners. The research tells us only part of the story.

Building upon previous research that surveyed marathon runners, in 1993 Kevin Masters, Benjamin Ogles and Jeffrey Jolton published a paper that developed a reliable, valid survey instrument in which they isolated the major categories for why people run marathons. Nine main reasons emerged, clustered under four categories: *Psychological Motives* (Psychological coping, self-esteem, and life meaning – which includes things such as sense of meaning, completeness, peace, and purpose to life or having time to be alone with the world), *Physical Health* (general health orientation, weight concern), *Social motives* (affiliation – running as a way of meeting and enjoying other runners' association, and recognition), *Achievement* (competition, and personal goal achievement – which includes questions related to running to beat my best time, trying to push myself beyond my limits, to improve my running speed). Other important factors that have also emerged in other studies include: challenge, addiction, enjoyment, rejuvenation, anxiety dissipation, drive, and other people's influence.

Chances are, we all fit in there somewhere, with some factors more important than others. The research is not comprehensive on this. Masters and Ogles published a paper in 2000 that reported on results from their survey of marathoners in four Midwestern marathons aged either 50 and over (the, gulp, "old" group), or aged 20-28 (the "young" group). Older runners were more motivated by general health reasons, weight concerns, life meaning, and affiliation with other runners, whereas the younger runners were motivated by personal goal achievement. Unfortunately they could only use data from men because the sample of women was too small to be statistically reliable. We know that the majority of marathoners these days are in the age bracket of 30-50 years, but there may not be much difference. As they say, more research is required.

What do marathoners look like in socio-economic terms? The Country Music Marathon and ½ Marathon

in Nashville reports that 33% of its runners have annual incomes of over $100,000 US, with 53% of run-
ners having incomes of over $70,000. Just over 86%
of the marathoners have a college education. The Detroit Free Press Marathon's Race Director, Patricia Ball,
meanwhile, says their average runner has a household
income of about $95,000.

Data from other marathons tell a similar story. A study
conducted by Economic Research Associates on the
New York Marathon's impact notes that 15% of the
runners had an income of over $250,000, while over-
all, runners had an annual average household income of
$130,000. The PF Chang Rock N' Roll Marathon, mean-
while, surveyed its runners and reported that the average annual household income was $81,299. Similarly,
a survey by the Nationwide Better Health Columbus
Marathon in Ohio shows that 33% of its marathoners
have an annual income of over $100,000, with another
32% between $75,000 and $100,000. Forty-one percent have a university education and another 35% have
a college degree.

With profiles like these it's little wonder that there's a
proliferation of gear and gadgets to help marathoners
run better, faster, more comfortably, more knowledgably,
injury-free and looking stylish.

8

PLACE AND SPACE

Base camp for training is my home in rural south-eastern Ontario, Canada. I live on a 56-acre farm two kilometres south of the Village of Yarker, which itself is about a twenty minute drive to Kingston (on the north-eastern tip of Lake Ontario halfway between Montreal and Toronto). A full day's drive from here can get you to New York City or Washington DC, and possibly a speeding ticket.

When I actually get around to doing real-person work I am at Queen's University, where I conduct research on health care, which includes evaluating health programs and services. While my sons spend the weekdays with their Mum, they're with me on the weekends. In summer the boys are with me for longer periods. As the boys have pointed out a few times without any prompting, they have, in their own words *"the best of both worlds."* That's the main thing.

On some days at the farm I hear absolutely nothing; it's

like waking up at 3am. It was eerie at first but I've come to quite like it. I would be hard pushed to ever go back to city living.

First known in the 1800s as Vader Mills, then Simcoe Falls, 'Yarker' had to change its name because another town in Ontario was called Simcoe. The townsfolk voted 'Peking' as the top choice for a new name. 'Yarker', which was the surname of two brothers from nearby Sydenham, was 7th or 8th choice, but managed to get the nod from the Governor as the new name for the town. In its heyday there was a sawmill, a tannery and hub and wheel plant, stores, three trains stopping frequently and a 400-metre indoor running track. By 1913 it had two electric light plants, grocery stores, general stores, blacksmith shops, a hotel, a jewellery store, a hardware and tin shop, a barber shop, a livery, a community hall and a partridge in a pear tree. Soon after, it had its own telephone company. It was a thriving community of over 600 people.

Times have changed. The other day the boys and I returned a video to the only store in the village now – the Lucky Dollar – in the middle of the afternoon, and a beaver was walking down the main street. It's a quaint place with a river running though it and some falls; a very typical rural Ontario village. While a few hundred people still live here, work for most people is generally in nearby Kingston, or Napanee, hometown of Avril Lavigne (but I'm name dropping here, because to the best of my knowledge she does not run marathons).

There are many quiet rural roads around my place and great trails that were once filled with railway tracks. It's possible to go through the trees at the back of my place, get onto the Cataraqui Trail, and hike, run, walk or ride on another trail all the way to Ottawa, which is a 2 ½ hour drive away.

I have a hay field in the middle of what I call my backyard. I looked at it one day and realized it was the shape and size of a running track. I had no option but to hop on the tractor mower and cut two lanes around the outside of the field. And so was born a 400-metre running track. Around the top fields before the forest begins I created several criss-crossing trails. If I run on the far outside trails I have a one kilometre track. Conceivably I could run a marathon naked in the fields if I wanted and no-one but the scattering, screaming wildlife would see me.

My running partner is Fred, my two-year old yellow Lab. He loves to run. I take him on the trails and out the back. He runs barefoot, has more hair, is faster, has two extra legs and is more muscular than me. His tongue hangs out further too. Unlike me, he's smart enough to stop repeatedly running around the track and stops when he feels it's too hot.

I also look after three horses, twelve barn cats, four chickens, a hamster called Gordon and several fish. The horses impose a daily regimen of physical work with mucking the stalls, throwing the hay, feeding, putting them into the fields, getting stood on, and getting crushed against the barn walls. It never feels like work and it's a great way to get some cross-training.

9

Gearing Up

I've been building up the training distances slowly since those embarrassing New Zealand beginnings. The distances have included a couple of 30km runs, and half marathons in Ottawa and Chicago. They were confidence boosters. I've tried to put training runs as the main priority in my days activities. Easier said than done, but definitely easier if you're working from home like me.

'Running gear' to me in the past meant a rugby shirt, shorts of any description, and any shoes that aren't for weddings or business meetings. My friend Karen has been persistent in stressing that I get the right stuff – that it *will* make a difference. If I held out long enough I think she would buy me a new kit. The problem with shorts of any description is that after some longer distances you'll start getting chafing in the inner and upper thighs, and worse (I've heard the stories), and no one deserves torture like that. I've learned that a good pair of loose shorts will make a huge difference, as will a liberal application of Vaseline on the long runs.

In addition to buying real running shorts I've bought real running socks. I'm amazing myself. These are shorter style socks that don't go over my ankles. They keep your ankles cooler than regular socks and the fabric breathes better. I never saw the need before to pay twice the price for half the sock, but it's making sense now.

For now, at least, the top half of me still runs in either T-shirts or rugby jerseys. I've a lightweight running cap and sunglasses both of which are absolutely essential in the Canadian summer. My bright blue running cap has a silver metallic band which is handy for when I divert low flying aircraft in the dark.

If I don't have quality running shoes, I'm told, I stand a good chance of injuring myself. There is an entire industry out there advising me on what shoes to purchase; I risk undermining the North American economy if I don't listen. The best thing to do is to go to a specialist running store and talk about my needs with the sales staff.

I've not done that. Early in the year I bought two pairs of *Asics GT-2110* running shoes, thinking that I would alternate between the two. They're really comfortable, sturdy and fit like a glove. I've tried other brands but have always found *Asics* to be the best suited to my feet.

The old me would just throw clothes on and start running. No watch, no music, and very little in the way of comfort. It makes no sense now that I look back, to not have comfort; it just didn't seem important at the time. Maybe I wanted to toughen up for my later years when children would be calling me Baldy.

There's a range of equipment and accessories available that seduce unsuspecting runners. It won't be long before we can run with portable cappuccino machines. The TV watch is already possible and if I really want, I can watch a movie on an I-pod while I run a marathon.

I spent several weeks reviewing all the accessorising options in the magazines and trade journals (including the global positioning systems such as the Garmins), and talked with experts in the field, several sales reps and runners, and was able to make an informed decision on what best suited my needs.

No I didn't. That would have been the discerning knowledgeable consumer exercising due diligence. My life is not like that. Instead I went into the Runners Choice store in Kingston and asked the folks there.

Two things caught my eye and wallet. First, a Polar RS2000TM *'Running Computer'* that shows me how slow I'm running, and how much slower I get the further I run, as well as showing my heart rate to prove, in those longer runs especially, that I'm still alive. To do this, the running computer is wirelessly connected to a footpod placed on my shoe that transmits running speed and distance, and to a coded transmitter – a strap – that is placed around my chest to detect my heart rate.

So I walked out very soon afterwards a proud owner of the *Running Computer*. There was a time when these things were called a 'watch'. The options are endless. In addition to recording splits and laps, bowel movements, REM, etc, it can also upload my running data to a Polar web application – a 'training diary' – to keep a record of the statistics. There are so many fitness functions and zones to work with that I'll burn calories just sitting there playing with it. Plus it also has a cute little runner image on the watch face, which must be a selling point (not that I would be taken in by such a thing). It even tells the time.

What I'm not wearing, out of preference, is a Garmin GPS, which instead of the direct linkages with my feet and heart, records the distance and speed through an Orwellian connection with satellites too high for us to see. I could eat a four course dinner off the top of some of the Garmins. You'll recognise the Garminian folks at the Start-line as they hold their arm up with their wrist cocked ready for the Maltese falcons to land, but they're also trying to pick up the signals from the satellites before they start their run, and trying not to catch other people's signals in the process. Meanwhile the race has begun, and ... oh well...

Like many others, I love running with music. It's not because running is boring, it's more that running is the best time to listen to music. For some people, it's the only time. Some say they don't listen to music because it's a safety issue with traffic, running in poorly lit or isolated areas, or fearful of not hearing the cougar about to pounce on their back, or the bear looking for her cub just around the corner. Some people have stopped listening to music because of embarrassing moments they've had singing among other runners and not realising it. Everyone has their preference. Obviously safety must rank highest – there's little sense in making your favourite song the last one you hear as the 18-wheeler accidentally veers into the gravel and nudges you into Mr. McGregor's corn field while you're screaming out *Eye of the Tiger*.

So my other toy, well, call it technological necessity, and now almost a life-line, is a *CREATIVE MuVo* N200 MP3 player. It sits easily in the zip pocket of my shorts and has several hours of battery life. I'd feel naked if I wasn't wearing it.

Not surprisingly, it plays music. More importantly, it's *my* music. I've downloaded several CDs, and have a compilation of my favourite songs in a Root selection. I've songs by Fat Boy Slim, U2, Beatles, The Chilis, Joe Cocker, Green Day, Elvis, Travis Tritt, Lynyrd Skynyrd, James, The Verve, Midnight Oil and Frank Sinatra, among many others. It's an eclectic group of musicians, many of whom would shudder if they knew they were back to back with one another, or bouncing around the trails with a complete stranger struggling to find harmony.

After two hours of getting my gear on and plugging in the accessories, I'm ready to run. Most of my running routes are around my home – trails, quiet roads, the backyard, the fridge, unless I'm travelling, in which case I'll get lost in the streets of various cities or fall off treadmills in hotels.

I've decided to have a massage after each marathon. This, to me, is a huge treat – an indulgence. I've had very few massages in my life but the training books seem to agree that it's good for you after a marathon. There is no line item in the budget for a massage, but I'll squeeze it out of somewhere.

Since my trip to New Zealand my eating habits have changed substantially. Food is now a fuel, not something that satisfies a craving. I understand why I'm eating what I do, and why I shouldn't eat the things I do. Of course I could've done that without running anywhere but it's all so inter-related. While I always knew that deep down food is a fuel – *the fuel* – it always seemed like a theoretical proposition or conceptual framework more than anything I'd actually use. My hunch is that the next few weeks will be filled with dietary guilt as I constantly juggle real world realities and previous habits with the most up-to-date evidence on what to eat and drink. This means that I'll have to stop drinking my 12 bottles of beer a day.

I'm kidding. It's usually 15.

I'm going to integrate running with my life, and not let the running consume me. There's a big difference. There will be moments when I'm out with others, or having people over and the diet for running may take a back seat. I may miss a few runs or have late nights – for example, when I date Miss Universe – and not get all the sleep I should be getting. I'm not out to break world records, as much as that would be kind of fun, but trying to see what marathons are all about and how they make a difference in my life.

I'm going to learn a lot. For example, I just read that runners are able to eat 15 eggs a week. Good news if you have four chickens running around the place. Not so good news for me though given that I should watch my cholesterol because there's a history of high cholesterol in my family.

My secret weapon is *The Stick*. It doesn't sound like much but it does wonders for aching calves and other muscle groups. I think it's going to make a big difference in my running over the next few weeks. I bought it at the Chicago Distance Classic half-marathon Expo, where I happened to be purely by chance for some work. Not expecting to buy anything, but rather just walk around the Expo in a daze thinking about everything we'd like to buy, a friend and I stumbled on this *Toothbrush for Muscles* and were given a demonstration. Once we realized it wasn't for hitting one another we quickly liked the idea – which is to roll the stick firmly over your muscles and by so doing, rolling the knots out of your muscles, warming the muscles, and increasing circulation and blood flow. It relieves pain, or gives it to someone else depending on how you use it, helps to reduce tightness and accelerates recovery if you have muscle issues.

I bought The Stick "A". These sticks are typically 2-foot long with 2 rubber handles and 10-15 one-inch plastic rollers that roll as you roll the stick over your muscles. It's one of my favourite conversation pieces at Airport Security. Since it's also used by athletes at the United States Training Centers I figure it can't do me much harm, and possibly a lot of good. Twenty years ago the only stick my orthopaedic surgeon would have predicted me using was a walking stick.

I have several reading companions – the experts – for this Journey. There are more books, I know, but these ones below provide great insights on marathon running. Whether what they say sticks with me or not is another story. The specific books are:

26.2. Marathon Stories by Kathrine Switzer and Roger Robinson (2006)
Marathon. The Ultimate Training Guide by Hal Higdon (2005)
Marathon Training by Joe Henderson (2004)
Marathon. You Can Do It by Jeff Galloway (2001)
Running Start to Finish by John Stanton (1999)

These are great books. I've also started a subscription to *Runners World magazine*. I'm already getting hooked on running and I haven't even run the first marathon.

In the end it doesn't matter how much you read, it's what you do with the information. Kathrine Switzer and Roger Robinson comment that running a marathon involves about 50,000 strides, 50,000 foot strokes on the ground, 25,000 heartbeats, 4,000 litres of blood pumping oxygen to the working muscles at the outer extremities of your body, more than 10 pounds of water exuded through sweat, and 3,000 calories burned.[1] There's a lot going on. If I get bored listening to my music I'll just start counting.

My fuel, and the essential fuel of choice and necessity for everyone, will be carbohydrates. They say the human body typically has enough carbohydrates to get through a distance of 32 kilometres, which is good news for me. The bad news is it still leaves 10 kilometres (6 miles) of what Tim Noakes in The Lore of Running calls the 'physical no-man's-land.' An inviting concept. Tim writes:

"It is at that stage, as the limits to human running endurance are approached, that the marathon ceases to be a physical event. It is there that you, the runner, discover the basis for the ancient proverb: "When you have gone so far that you cannot manage one more step, then you have gone half the distance that you are capable of. It is there that you learn something about yourself and your view of life. Marathon runners have termed it the wall".

Carbohydrates are the energy for my body. They're converted into glycogen in my liver and muscles, and glucose in my blood. When the glucose is all used up my liver converts the glycogen into glucose to make sure there's enough continuously flowing to my muscles. Over long periods of continual exertion my glycogen will get depleted, used up, and I'll end up burning fat instead. I'll switch

---

[1] These are estimates for a 150-pound male running a 3:30 time.

from using my high performance fuels to a new source which will barely help me function the way I want.

Welcome to The Wall, or 'Bonking' as it also called. My gut feeling right now is that I will hit *The Wall* at some point during the next three months. Or rather, it will hit me.

It's a bit like wanting to see a grizzly bear in the wild. Love to experience it, to know what it's like, but uncertain of the consequences. The key thing to know and love and embrace is that a high carbohydrate diet (along with regular training), will help to increase my reserves of glycogen. The more I have the longer I can delay the bonking experience, or possibly not have it at all.

Nancy Clark, a well known sports nutritionist, cites research evidence that biochemical changes that occur when we train affect how much glycogen can be stored in our muscles. Well trained muscles are able to store between 20% and 50% more glycogen than untrained muscles. By completing long slow training runs we get our bodies used to using fuel more efficiently in order to conserve glycogen stores. The more often and longer these long training runs are, the less likely I'll hit the wall.

So my journey begins. Along the way I hope to reap some of those benefits that Kathrine and Roger cited, and learn more about myself. It's an introspective era we're in after all. With so many self-help books now available I wonder how we've gotten so messed up. How different would our parents and their parents have been had they had the wisdom of the self-help books at their fingertips? Or maybe they just got on with it and enjoyed life.

Or maybe they went for a run.

The last and probably most important thing I need is motivation. Fortunately, I've got plenty: my family's medical history; my poor commitment to health and fitness over the past ten years; my renewed desire to feel healthier in everything I do; my desire to be fit and healthy for my boys now and later on in life. To me, the consequences of *not running* are so serious I'd be a fool not to get back into shape. When faced with irrefutable evidence we should do something with it.

Are there any risks to consider over the next few weeks? There sure are. I've my knee to worry about. I have a ton of work to do, and I'll be constantly making choices about when to run and for how long. I'll have to ensure that when I'm traveling to these marathons that work does not fall by the wayside, or else I will in a big way.

I'm doing this with a gut feeling that by turning things upside down and making running a priority every day, everything else will fit into place. If I'm feeling more energized, fitter, healthier, and feeling better about myself, then surely everything else will benefit as a result. Won't it?

The other concern is feeling that maybe I can't do it; that I don't have the ability. But my confidence increases when I read about other people's experiences and motivations. One of the inspirational quotes I've come across is from John Bingham, "The miracle isn't that I finished. The miracle is that I had the courage to start".

Well I've started. Can I ever be adequately prepared? Probably, but is this really *the* best time to be doing this? I don't think I should wait for the 'ideal time' in my life. Who has the ideal time for anything these days? The ideal time to simply *get moving* is now. It should be an interesting few weeks.

10

HERE GOES

I can't find a training program for someone running 3½ marathons in 2 months after a 21-year hiatus. I don't want to say I'm guessing exactly or that I don't have a clue, but after the Athens marathon I will likely adopt the 'play-it-by-ear' approach to my training. I don't even know if I'll be walking after Athens, let alone running.

What I do know is that I have thirty-three days until Athens. I've been running with a general program involving six days a week for a few weeks now. I've followed the typical pattern of most training programs:

- Gradually build up the distance over a few months (i.e., in total distance per week and each week's long runs).

- Do the longest runs on the weekends (i.e., from 10km to 30km)

- Typically 1-2 rest days each week.

- If I plan to run a marathon with hills, make sure I do some hill training.

- Run at an easy pace – the more time I spend running (or walking) the better. Don't think about breaking land speed records.

- Enjoy the moments.

- Listen to my body. Prevent injuries – don't wait for problems to get worse. If I need to rest for a few days, do so.

- Think about improving my form – it makes no sense to train harder with poor form that could lead to injury.

There's no magic but plenty of common sense. The training programs available have evolved from decades of running experience. It's crazy not to pay attention to them.

Between now and Disney I'll do the shorter runs during the week, interspersed with some hills (not many). I'll put all the required distances on a wall calendar, and record my required and actual runs completed in the computer on an Excel Spreadsheet. I'll record my times, where I ran, the time of day and the weather conditions. On occasions I'll probably record my weight, mainly out of curiosity.

It's looking pretty serious now.

I'd like to think I've got a base fitness level from running over the summer. Otherwise I'd be nuts to attempt running a marathon after only 33 days of training. Here's what my planned training program looks like for the next 33 days up until the Athens marathon.

Planned Distance to Run		
Day		**Km**
1	Wednesday	20km
2	Thursday	6km
3	Friday	10km
4	Saturday	Hills
5	Sunday	6km
6	Monday	30km
7	Tuesday	Rest
8	Wednesday	6km
9	Thursday	10km
10	Friday	Hills
11	Saturday	15km
12	Sunday	6km
13	Monday	30km
14	Tuesday	Rest
15	Wednesday	6km
16	Thursday	6km
17	Friday	5km
18	Saturday	10km
19	Sunday	Rest
20	Monday	20km
21	Tuesday	Rest
22	Wednesday	6km
23	Thursday	10km
24	Friday	6km
25	Saturday	6km
26	Sunday	Rest
27	Monday	6km
28	Tuesday	Rest
29	Wednesday	3km
30	Thursday	Rest
31	Friday	3km
32	Saturday	Rest
33	Sunday	42km

As you can see I've moved the long run to Mondays, so I can spend the weekend time with the boys and not disappear on them for 2-4 hours. They're my biggest fans and really supportive. I'd hate to discover they've packed their bags one day and see the car missing when I stagger back from my long run.

There are no major surprises in the table above. Well, except for the fact that I'll actually be doing it. There are a few rest days and shorter distances in the last two weeks – in keeping with the tapering recommended in the training programs, but also re-emphasized with the need to travel to Athens since I won't be using my private LearJet I typically park in the back fields. Presumably, by Day 33, I'm ready to run the marathon, whatever 'ready' means.

And so I'm all set, I think. I wonder if I really know enough to do this right and not injure myself. I wonder if the stress of committing to this program will be too much and will affect other parts of my life. I wonder if my knee will explode. I feel a Del Shannon song coming on. Apart from these thoughts I'm feeling good. If I don't try it I'll never know, and that would grate on my psyche forever.

What about the injuries? I'd like to think I'll know an injury when I feel it, but I'm still new to this running thing. Prevention is the ideal strategy of course. Be defensive – don't get lost in the potholes. Don't run on ice. Don't run into trees. Don't run on the freeways. Listen and look for the signs that my body is in trouble.

Most running injuries are caused by runners pushing their bodies too hard. And if my form is less than ideal, as it probably is, the likelihood of an injury occurring increases even more. The most effective way to avoid a running injury is to not run, but that's not going to make for much of a book is it?

The most common injuries are knee injuries, shin splints, plantar fasciitis, Achilles tendonitis, and Iliotibial Band Syndrome, which I think would be a great name for a rock band. They all relate to overstressing the respective parts of your body. They're all painful when they're more than just niggles. If I run through them, gritting it out running through the pain, I kid no-one but myself. I'll make things worse. Obviously my left knee is a problem. If it decides to fall off the wagon there's little I can do. I could run solely on my right leg but I'd end up running around in circles.

After a while that would get boring.

11

THE ODYSSEY TO ATHENS BEGINS

"The Athens Marathon is said to be one of the toughest, following a course that begins by the sea near the ancient battleground, climbing the base of Mount Pendeli and ending on the plains of Attika, now the center of Athens, at the old marble Stadium, built for the first modern Olympics in 1896." (Internet site)

And so it all begins. One hundred days, roughly. Athens is 33 days away. Cayman Islands is 61 days away, and Disney 96 days. And then I taper, if that's the word at that point.

That's the theory anyway. I read Hal Higdon last night. Good stuff. Hal speaks from the heart, and the experience and wisdom of his years involved with marathons. I read his chapter on nutrition, hoping to get a confidence boost or a shot of reality. I ended up getting hungry. I seem to be eating and drinking the right things, but it looks like more carbohydrates are in order. Using common sense and not worrying about trying to lose weight is important.

To be sure though, and in part to minimize temptation, I excavated the fridge yesterday and removed anything that looked too processed, or should be in a beaker, or sitting over a Bunsen burner.

My diet now consists of multigrain breads, vegetables, fruit, fruit and nuts trail mix, dried fruit (banana and papaya), yogurt, cheese, eggs, turkey and chicken. I drink coffee, green tea, orange juice, vegetable juice, water, and also Powerade after or during runs. I'll drink beer occasionally when jamming with the Band (I play in one), and wine if I'm out anywhere or with someone where drinking wine seems like the absolutely right thing to do, which it often does. If I was an animal I'd be a scatty black bear with a weakness for meat on occasion, and a proclivity to stagger home to the cave every now and then.

I don't plan to deviate too much from that mix of food and drink over the next one hundred days. Hal said the most important advice he could give would be to see a nutritionist, re-emphasizing yet again how important this is in the training. I think I'll do that. It seems that running is not just about running.

THE FIRST SEVEN DAYS:
Planned Distance: 78km

I'm thinking about Athens more and more each day. The books say to visualize completing the marathon – focus on the positive things, and move the negative thoughts and worries from my mind. Hmmm. I should be sitting in the lotus position. It's hard not to think when you run. Thoughts come and go with no set schedule. One second I can be thinking about several vital things that I need to do after the run and the next second I'm wondering if Paris Hilton is real. Some of my best ideas come when I'm running, whether I'm listening to music or not. Paris is not one of them.

In these busy times it's not often that we have anywhere from 30 minutes to 3 hours or more to let our thoughts freely float around and occasionally land. When they land it's a brilliant feeling. There are so many times that I've found solutions to things while running that I now consciously want to run just to let this flow of unpredictable ideas unfold. I'll feel better for it. Many times I find solutions to things without specifically setting out to do so. The clarity that sits around these decisions perhaps partly explains why running is so addictive. Decisions seem quite obvious when previously they were not even in sight.

An encouraging first few days of running. The highlights are a 20km run and a hill run with Fred. There are two hills on nearby Bracken Road that run almost into one another, so I'm almost always either going up or down. Or sideways if Fred is with me on the leash, as he needs to be when I run the roads. He's clearly not a dog that thinks long term with running. The run begins with Fred pulling me, but ends with the roles reversed.

I like the hill runs. If anything I've got to be patient. I want to increase my speed going uphill. I'd run faster downhill too, but I've had several close calls with Fred as defensive tackle. If I speed up I'll need to wear a helmet.

I print the three marathons course maps off the computer this morning and tape them onto the wall in front of my office desk for inspiration. I also print off a picture of runners beginning last year's Athens marathon, which now sits in front of me.

I'm looking forward to the 6km run tomorrow because it's short and flat, and because it's not the following day's run, which is 30km. When Karen and I ran that distance in the summer we felt incredibly proud. This time I'm doing it by myself. I'll pull my big boy panties up for the 30km run but in the meantime I plan to enjoy the 6km run.

The 6km turns out to be a good run, the first I'm writing about now in the book. But even though it's just around the back yard track it's not without incident. A time of 32 minutes, which is probably still too fast for me.

Faithful as ever, Fred runs with me for most of the run, looking along the way for any sticks he can savagely wrestle to the ground. Coming down the back straight and oblivious to Fred running behind me I suddenly feel a sharp piercing pain in my left calf. I drop to the ground like an Italian soccer star, except I have a reason, but I'm confused as to what's going on.

Fred comes to a screeching halt, as does the eight foot stick, no, to be fair, the small tree which he is carrying in his mouth. How he manages to spear me with the point of the tree remains a mystery. After interrogating Fred about this pioneering lumberjackian acupuncture I get up and continue running. For the rest of the run I keep looking over my shoulder at the smirk on Fred's face, wondering when the next attack might occur.

In the evening I go over to see my good friends and

neighbours – Liz and Rob Vinkle – for Thanksgiving Dinner with their friends and family and a 32lb turkey, which is dead for the occasion. Rob is telling everyone about my running and the book, and the response is encouraging. I'm trying to keep a low profile about the running but it's good to talk more about it, as the more people that know about the marathons the more real it all becomes, and the harder it is to pull out. In the back of my mind throughout the night, and mixed in with wine, turkey and pie, is the hard cold fact that my Thanksgiving Day will include a 30km run. In just a few hours.

I get home quite late, say important things like 'blah blah blah' to Fred, and hoist my body into bed. I get up soon afterwards and take my clothes off. I remind myself of the early morning run. 'What am I thinking? That was a crazy, stupid thing to do' I say, as I try to recount the amount of wine consumed. I'm shaking my head in horror, burning calories at least, until the time I get up, which seems like five minutes later.

It might have been. I can't remember looking at the clock when I got home. I've planned to do an early morning run – sevenish, or at worst, just fashionably late soon after. But it's now 10:13am, and I'm putting it off – writing this, and mentally oscillating between running or not. Aside from a late night and all the excuses I can think of around such a thing, my mind is playing tricks, telling me maybe I have a serious left leg calf injury because of Fred's jousting, and perhaps I shouldn't run. Will I make it worse?

But the sun is starting to break through the heavy morning fog. Dang. It looks like conditions could be near perfect. The Fall colours on the trees are spectacular. I'm laden with guilt and don't have any really good excuses not to run. I'm going.

I munch on a pre-run chocolate power bar, thinking this will make all the difference on the run. I ate these before my other two 30km runs with Karen. They worked well. Mind you, when we ran it was at the crack of dawn in mid-summer before the heat of the day, I'd had nothing else to eat, and I'd not had a thanksgiving dinner bash the night before. This is a different run entirely. I can't wait to finish it.

**

Wow! What an absolute buzz. I did it. No one is more surprised than me. No pulls, strains, Charlie horses, vomits, collisions with trees or anything. The most noticeable effects of the distance were my thighs turning into anvils at the 25km point and my breathing being more labored in the 28-30km range. But at least *I was* breathing. That's part of the point of running these longer distances – my body and mind are getting conditioned. It was feeling so good at 10km that I got big-feeling thinking maybe I'd do 35km. That thought stayed with me for about 2 km. I realised I should just be grateful for 30km and enjoy the day. Endorphins kicking in, perhaps.

It's a hard feeling to beat. I've just done a double loop along the back roads to Yarker and then to Colebrook. About five cars passed me in the whole time. Spectacular colours, my favourite music, perfect temperature ... feeling alive ... I wonder how much better I might feel if the night before hadn't been strategically placed at this juncture in the training program.

I never felt the nagging calf muscle I'd sensed earlier this morning. I don't know why I didn't. Aside from the usual aches and pains, the only suffering is the cheese grater chafing on my groin. Which is why they invented Vaseline I suppose. Next time.

I also used Jeff Galloway's run-walk approach, with 10 minutes running and 1 minute walking. I stuck to that faithfully except for when I was scheduled to stop right beside the rather large teeth of a rather large dog.

There are several hills in this double loop run, although the hills get longer and steeper the second time around. I need to do the hills because the Athens course has them. My time for the 30km is 3:08, which I'm happy about.

It's amazing how many thoughts go through your head when you're running. One that often comes up for me is the image of Eric Liddell in the 1981 movie *Chariots of Fire*. He's running tall and straight in the 1924 Paris Olympics 400 metres final. At this one particular moment he looks up, smiles wide, expands his chest and seemingly kicks into a higher gear. He loves running. It's a truly inspirational moment in a very inspirational movie that's etched firmly in my mind. I think of trying this on these country roads but fear I'll fall flat on my face.

Well obviously it wasn't Eric Liddell in the movie because he's dead at the moment, but rather the actor Ian Charleson, who did this beautifully, and without falling. He says at one point in the movie, *"Then where does the power come from, to see the race to its end? From within."* I would like to finish the Athens marathon like Eric Liddell. Or like Ian Charleson, for that matter.

After today's run I'm more optimistic than before, but there's still lots of work to be done. I eat some black bear food when I get back from the run and take two Ibuprofen, trying to be proactive with any swelling of my knee. I ice my legs all over. I use The Stick. And then it's back to being a normal person again. I'll sleep well tonight.

**

After a deep sleep I wake up in the morning and check to see if all my limbs and muscles are still working before I get out of bed. Horizontal yoga. Everything seems to move so I take the first step of the day. Wow. I can walk. The final check, and it's a good one, is seeing if I have the strength and fluidity to walk downstairs to the kitchen. If my knees are going to cave in this is the moment.

Without a harness or karabiner I make it downstairs. My legs are tight and stiff but that's to be expected. Every other part of me feels like it's just another day. Phew.

My travel agent – Lorne – calls to tell me I'm booked into the Hera Hotel in Athens and it looks good. A view of the Acropolis from my room apparently. Lorne adds I should be careful because the Athenian air is very polluted due to the inversion layer effects of the surrounding hills, which block the pollution from destroying other parts of the Mediterrean. I didn't recall seeing anyone wear masks at the start of the Athens marathon last year and I'm not used to running with one myself.

This is quite ironic because Athens is named after Athena, the goddess of wisdom, wit and morality, and, no kidding, clean air. A goddess ahead of her time. How bad would the pollution be if she wasn't present? I ponder this briefly and think of my local air filled with manure, horses, cattle, rotting trees, dead animals, and swamps.

Training in country air may not prepare me for Athena's home.

Summary

Planned distance = 78km;
Actual distance run = 78.7km

12

THE 1896 ATHENS MARATHON

Michel Breal convinced the 1896 Olympic organizers to run the marathon footrace. He also offered a silver trophy for the winner. The race was referred from that point on as 'The Marathon', and was made the final event of the Olympics. Another supporter of the race, the Greek Ionnis Lambros, a wealthy collector of antiquities, donated an antique vase to the winner.

It wasn't as if long distance running was a new thing. In his book *Olympic Marathon* Charlie Lovett notes that in the 1700s Foster Powell ran 402 miles around England at the age of sixty. Between 1870 and 1890, in fact, six-day races were popular in England and the United States, with some runners covering distances over 600 miles. These were mainly run on tracks, with runners taking rest breaks. This 'marathon' was going to be different – 25 miles non-stop along open roads.

In preparation for the Olympics the Greeks held trials. Grigorou won the first marathon trials in February 1896, in a time of 3:45. He was the only one that finished. The Greeks decided to have another two trials before naming their Olympic team. Whether or not that was because three runners allegedly died while training for the marathon is unknown. The winning times for the next two trials were 3:18 and 3:11.

On Friday 10th of April, 17 runners began the Olympic Marathon. Without sounding too much like a joke, there was an Australian, an American, a Hungarian and a Frenchman. Of these, only the Hungarian, Gyula Kellner, had run the distance before. The Australian – Edwin 'Teddy' Flack – had already won gold in the 800 and 1500 metres. The rest of the marathoners were Greeks, all of whom had run the distance before.

So on a cool, but sunny, afternoon off they went, with an entourage of officials and doctors on bicycles and horsedrawn wagons. Even though the eventual winner was well back in the pack and off the lead, he stopped for a glass of wine at about halfway and said he was confident he'd not only finish, but that he'd win the race. I've been known to think like that after a wine or two myself.

The early leader, Frenchman Lermusiaux, was paying for his fast initial pace and slowed considerably by the halfway mark. Soon after he was hit by another Frenchman riding a bicycle and had to be carried off, unable to complete the distance. The Australian Flack now took the lead. In the true spirit of cockiness he sent someone off on his bicycle to inform the stadium that he was soon to arrive the winner. But he was tiring quickly. Meanwhile Spiridon Louis, a Greek water carrier, was catching up and passing others. At about the 20 mile mark he passed Flack, who soon afterwards collapsed and was carried away. Not long after, at Mile 23, Spiridon's girlfriend Eleni was waiting for him with some orange slices. If ever you wanted an energy boost that would do it, and I'm sure the oranges helped also.

Whatever Eleni did, or said, it worked. Spiridon Louis ran harder as he entered the downhill portion of the course into Athens itself.

The crowd at the stadium had already been silenced with the news from Flack, but it went into ecstatic celebrations when they heard the latest news that Louis looked like winning the race. When he entered the stadium the two crown princes – Konstantinos and Georgio – ran with him to the finish line, and carried him to the Royal Box. He was a national hero.

He was led away amid the roars and cheers into a tunnel near the end of the straightaway at the northeast of the stadium. There he asked for some coffee, and ended up having two cups. The Queen and other royals arrived to congratulate him. David Martin and Roger Glynn write in their book *The Olympic Marathon* that the Queen is said to have held his calloused hand and realised he must have been a common labourer. She gave him the rings off her fingers and apparently said "The honor you have given to Greece is worth far more than these simple rings."

Louis had finished the 24.8 miles in a time of 2:58. Two other Greeks came second and third. But the Hungarian Kellner complained that the third placed runner had cheated, covering some of the distance in a carriage. The Greek runner admitted his guilt and Kellner was awarded third place. A few days later Louis and the other Olympic medalists were given their medals at a special awards ceremony – silver medals, as they did not have gold medals at these first Olympics. He also received an olive branch and a diploma (as did other winners), the 25-centimeter trophy that Breal had donated, and the vase given by Lambros. He later gave the vase to a museum. The whereabouts of the trophy was unknown until 1989, when it surfaced in Amaroussion, Louis's home village.

Charlie Lovett writes that there has been so much written about Spiridon Louis that it's hard to know fact from fiction. Lovett writes that Spiridon has been described as a peasant, well-off farmer, soldier, poor shepherd, and a postal carrier. He's also been a water carrier. But we do know he was 24 years old when he won (well, some say 23 actually), and such was his significance that there is now a saying in Greek that goes *"egine Louis"*, which means 'to become like Louis' or 'take off like Louis'.

It was the Olympics, of course, and committed to the amateur status of athletes, which is why a professional runner, Italian Carlo Airoldi, was disqualified from entering. He might have been a favourite, as he had already run several 50km races. It wasn't to be, however, as the amateur status was upheld. It must have been a real kicker for Carlo, who apparently had walked almost 1,000 miles from Italy to participate in the event.

Everyone, even foreigners, wanted a Greek to win, in part because they had not been very successful in the other events.

France, Hungary, Denmark and Norway held similar marathon events in 1896 following the success of the Olympic marathon. The first Olympic marathon had struck a chord in the hearts and minds of many in Athens, including a group of competitors from Boston, who returned to the United States excited at the prospect of such a race west of the Atlantic. The Boston Marathon, now the oldest annual marathon, found its place in the history of running with its inaugural race a year later in April 1897. The original Boston race was won by John McDermott in a time of 2:55 over a course distance of 24.5 miles.

In 1898 Germany and Italy held marathon events, and Sweden followed suit in 1899. Marathon running had begun. The world has not been the same since. By the 1920s, relatively obscure countries such as Egypt, Cuba and India had athletes running marathons at the Olympics.

13

ONWARD
GOES THE ODYSSEY

DAYS 8 – 14
Planned Distance: 73km

I'm thinking more and more about the air that I breathe. Today I'm in Toronto for work. I thought of running outside but changed my mind. Running in the rain and amidst traffic, noise, pan handlers, suits, lights, exhaust fumes, and roads to cross doesn't seem especially rewarding to my soul or my body. Instead I opt for a treadmill on the top floor of the 27-story Delta Chelsea hotel, which looks out onto the city.

I straddled the treadmill and thought of Hal. I remembered his comments about the Kenyans training with slow runs and how he felt awkward if he ran past them in Boston before the race day. Graced with neither the quality of Hal or the Kenyans, I lurched over the treadmill determined to go slow. At first it went well. Then I realized I hadn't turned it on. In contrast, the gentleman beside me was running the 100-metres final as his treadmill smoked its way across the room. If it hadn't been bolted to the floor he would've disappeared through the floor-to-ceiling windows in front of us and sped even faster to the pavement twenty-seven stories below.

Running slow is hard. I'm not a fast runner but going slower than what you'd normally run is tricky. I was also due to meet a friend in the Lobby, so the slower I ran the 6km the more likely I was going to be late. My MP3 ran out of power part the way through so I spent the remaining time I'd allotted converting the miles on the machine into kilometres with my usual high level mathematical calculations. Or was it the kilometres into miles?

In the shower I was feeling good – good that I'd got the run in and was still able to meet my friend. I remembered back a few years ago in Argentina when I had fallen out of the shower. That involved intricate Fred Astaire footwork, a bruise the size of Fat Albert on my elbow, a ripped shower curtain and a sense of helplessness watching myself crash in slow motion to the floor. With this memory quite fresh, I took an excessive amount of time getting out of the shower, to the point where I was almost dried naturally by the time the manoeuvring was complete. Runners can get injured anywhere, anytime, and I didn't want to take any chances.

Tonight I checked my email. I received a message from Gregg, an old friend working in New Zealand Tourism, now living in Australia. As Gregg had lived and travelled extensively in Europe for years I'd asked him for any advice on Athens. He replied *"Don't breath the air? Seriously from friends that ran it pre the games they said it was excellent but polluted"*.

Maybe Pheidippides didn't die from exhaustion after all, but rather the cumulative effects of air pollution enveloping Athens.

**

I didn't think running on the treadmill was a great indicator of how my body really felt after the 30km run, so the next day I get onto the roads and trails as soon as I get home from Toronto and do a 10km run.

It's now bow-hunting season in these parts. Men and women in camouflage gear hide in the woods waiting to skewer the next animal that walks by. Makes you think twice about running along the trails. The season has been on for about a week now and I've been wearing bright colours, consciously trying to not run, sound, or look like a deer. Or a bear. Or anything actually, other than someone training to run marathons. I talk to my friend and neighbour Gord about running during bow-hunting season. In an understated philosophical tone he tells me not to worry as bow hunters have to be within about a 50-foot range, in which case they should be able to see me clearly. He reassures me that if I'm hit it won't be an accident, just murder.

On this particular run though I'm having trouble convincing myself that I'll be safe. And when I see *Mr. Apocalypse Now*, apparently out on a day pass from the Montana Mercenary Camp, lurking in the bushes I realise that running on the roads is quite enjoyable really, and the treadmill also looks quite inviting.

Apart from wondering if I have a big bulls-eye on my back the run itself is good. A strong cold wind at my back outwards probably helps my confidence. But coming back on the return 5km I discover how strong the wind really is, although the horizontal rain takes my mind off it. Gone are the summer days. This is my first run with my bright blue jacket on, which is about the only bright blue thing around today.

Still, for all that, I arrive home without an arrow in my back, so I should be grateful. It also seems that I run faster in miserable conditions, and I don't think it's just because I want to get home faster. I wonder if it's some sort of coping mechanism where I just want to dig in. In any case, I finish well, and reassure myself that the weather can't get worse than this before Athens.

It snows in the evening.

**

The next day I run the hills with the same arctic winds as yesterday. At least the overnight snow has gone. Now I'm wearing tracksuit bottoms, feeling that this a common sense thing to do.

I drive over to the Bracken Road hills again, where the Fall colours had been so spectacular the week before. The dead porcupine on the road is still there, only looking much more dead than he did last week.

I feel pathetic later when Karen tells me her 9-year old daughter Emma ran in her 2 km cross-country event this afternoon wearing shorts.

A crisis emerges today. My MP3's right-ear piece is continually falling out of my ear. I can move the earpieces around or move my ears to different sides of my head. I choose the former. I juggle my earpiece for most of the run to the extent that someone could easily think I'm having a seizure. It would be more effective to stop, disassemble the MP3, and wait for a new part to be sent from rural Bangladesh.

My beautiful mind concludes that my left and right ears have different dimensions. I don't know why; some faulty construction perhaps. But I do know I can't run a marathon continually manipulating an earpiece. I could run without one, of course, but I've fallen in love with music while I'm running. The solution is to buy a new pair.

Of earphones that is, and see what happens. Either that or undergo surgery to make them fit into my right ear.

Fred comes with me but doesn't run much; he's still getting over an infection. The considerable lump growing on the side of his head looks as if he'd run into a brick wall or was beaned by the barn cats with a sledge hammer. The vets removed the lump which turned out to be a hematoma, and not an absess as first thought (I'll spare you the gory details). He came home with two holes in his shaved head, and a huge plastic cone to wear around his neck to keep him from gnawing on his wounds.

The first night he turned into a statue when I put his cone on him. Not even a cookie sitting on the floor could make him move. I put the cookie in the cone thinking this would help but he just watched it irritatingly slide out and crash onto the floor. He was almost crying. So was I. That night I slept on the kitchen floor with him, waking up every now and then as Fred either banged into the cupboards, and froze, or tried to get the cookie but instead slammed the cone into the floor, and froze. A restless night for me, but it must have been worse for Fred.

That same night my four new chickens arrived. They were scheduled to come at the end of the month – about 3 weeks from now. But they were delivered to the Feedstore in the morning. I was totally unprepared, which means I'll spend much of the weekend trying to build their new house. In the meantime, they're in a stall in the barn with the horses and barn cats. Fred hasn't seen them yet.

The good news from today is that I can feel my muscles building up. From today and the experience of other hill days, I'm one hundred percent convinced of their importance in training, especially when I'm going to run a hilly course like Athens.

The bad news from today is that I bought a micro-cassette recorder to do interviews with people while at the marathons and dropped it almost immediately into dishwater. I could hear it drowning as I frantically thrashed around with my hands amongst the dishes and sharp knives. I found it, without any cuts, and dried it off as much as possible before setting it aside in the kitchen for a few days to dry out naturally.

**

It's Saturday today and it's just my oldest son, Callum, with me, as Jack's away at a friend's place. It doesn't seem right to leave Callum watching Fred for too long, even though he's quite happy and wanting to watch the kid's Saturday morning TV programs. Callum's happy to do that as well. And so, in a somewhat guilt ridden decisive moment in the morning, while thinking of not running at all in the day, I decide that as Callum is happily watching TV I'll do a quick 6km run on the backyard track.

But I want to do more than that, as I feel a slow 6km won't be enough, even though at least *I am* running. In a fit of boldness on a cool cloudy day, I decide to compromise – a fast 10km (it's relative, of course) which will give me a harder work-out, more distance, and still be within a time frame that doesn't make me feel I'm neglecting Callum and Fred.

So I run what I think is fast and push myself while trying not to put undue pressure on my legs, especially my knee, which hasn't been giving me any trouble at all over the past couple of weeks. I'd like to keep it that way.

It feels great. In the end, 10km in 45 minutes. My earpiece only falls out twice. Can I keep this pace up for 42km though?

Not a chance. But at least I know what that pace feels like, and that's worth it in itself. And I don't feel my knee throbbing as if I'd been kneecapped by the IRA. As a precaution I ice it anyway, and take two Ibuprofen pills to help reduce any swelling. I also use The Stick, like I usually do.

This was a risky run. Foolish really. But also beneficial in many respects. Tomorrow, Sunday, is a light 6km run before my scheduled 30km on Monday.

These days I'm thinking more and more of race day strategy in Athens. The balancing act of hope and desire goes something like this:

1) Don't try to do too much in this first marathon because I have the Cayman and Disney races to come in fairly short turnaround time.

2) Aim to simply finish the race and feel good about that. A bonus if there are no injuries.

3) What if I think I can run it in less than 4 hours without jeopardizing 1) and 2)?

4) If I find myself hovering around a potential sub
   4-hour marathon in the later stages of the race
   should I push harder – possibly risking injury
   for the race, an injury that will affect training
   and other races?

I should be grateful I can think like this in the first place.
I should probably just err on the side of caution. But it
may be a different story on race day if I get swept up in
the moment.

**

Well, I was right. I wake up this morning with a knee
the size of a pineapple. *'That was really stupid,'* I think.
Throughout the day I wonder why I should even risk
doing any speed work. It's apparently a good idea but
maybe not for someone starting out.

Hal sheds some light on this for me as I ice my knee,
which thankfully starts to shrink over the day.

The obvious starting point is that speed is relative. No-
one confuses me for a cheetah. Some plants grow faster
than I can run. Hal advises against first-time marathoners
doing speed work. Although speed work may increase
the risk of injury for beginners and also experienced runners (if not done correctly), if you want to improve performance and run faster marathon times you will likely need
to do speed work at some point.

I think I've come incredibly close to blowing the three
marathons. I had better learn my lesson from this.
Today I do a light run. The best thing about today's run
– in the backyard again – is that Callum runs with me. I

remember reading how, in 1970, a 16-year old girl from Oregon ran a women's world record marathon time (3:02). So I'm imagining Callum a few years from now running a marathon. He's hearing more and more about what I'm doing, so he decided to run with me. He's already more of a runner than I'll ever be – he has that natural runner's stride, which several people have commented on. He doesn't get this stride from his parents so it's a bit of a mystery. In any case, he runs the first 2km of the 6km with me. We talk as we run, both feeling really good about it, and running strong. He then collapses as if he's just been shot leaping out of the trenches; it would be an Oscar winning performance if I filmed it, but in fairness I think he's exhausted.

Callum or no Callum, I'd decided to do this run very, very slow. It ends up being a 35 minute run with no pain, which is the main thing. Tomorrow I'm scheduled for 30km. I'm burning calories just thinking about the prospect because my knee has re-emerged as something to think about, the weather could be lousy, and it's such a long time to be running. Success tomorrow will be completing the distance injury-free.

14

THE SPEEDSTERS

My world record-breaking 10km pace the other day got me thinking about the other marathon speedsters.

The current men's world record holder is Ethiopian Haile Gebrselassie, who on the 30th September 2007, ran the Berlin marathon in 2:04:26. I'm happy with a time of 2:04 for half the distance. The women's world record holder is Paula Radcliffe of the United Kingdom. She won the London marathon in 2003 in the record time of 2:15:25. There are very few men in the world, now or even through history, who can beat her time. I certainly can't.

Will we see further improvements in the world record times? The research suggests that we may be reaching the limits of human performance. It's unlikely we'll see a substantial lowering of the 2:04 time in the next decade or so, but then we really don't know for sure. If we were to characterize the future sub-2:00 hour record holder, it's a good bet that it's an African male with an almost incomprehensible name but with the perfect physiology – light, long legged, amazing heart capacity for pumping oxygen-rich blood to the muscles, the 'right stuff' psychologically, appropriate training build-up, and race day conditions that provide the perfect temperature, competition, and a fast course. On all counts, don't be looking for my name.

A good, well perhaps different but still effective, example of elite training is the amazing Emil Zatopek, the legendary Czech runner who won the 1952 Olympic marathon (and 2 other gold medals in the same Olympics). Emil reportedly trained on mountain trails near his home while carrying his wife on his back. That's dedication for you, and I'm not sure from whom exactly. If you're looking to mix up your training program, or reenergize your relationship, consider the Zatopek gambit. If nothing else it will make for an interesting dinner conversation.

I scanned the national record holding marathon times around the world, thinking that if I really train hard, decrease my potato chip intake, stretch more regularly and solve my ear bud problem, I could become a record holder. The world record may be out of my reach but there might be a place where my speed could be good enough for the record books somewhere.

Only four countries have a fastest marathon time of *over* 3 hours; Laos (3:06), Liberia (3:08), Tonga (3:15) and Niue (3:30). I would get lost in Laos, so that's out. Having guerrilla insurgents shooting at me in Liberia might just be the motivation I need for a PB; let's not rule that out yet. Tonga is quite possible since it's on my way home to New Zealand, but then I may as well try Niue since it's just off to the left from Tonga, a parachute jump really. It may even be possible, which scares me that I'm actually thinking about it. The chance of breaking any other national record increases dramatically if I decide to change my sex.

15

STILL ONWARD

But back to reality. It's my day to run the 30km. Like my 30km last week I don't much feel like doing this one either. So after taking Fred back to the vet to remove the tube in his head, and rushing through research work, I'll head out.

I promise myself several things before this run:

1) Go sloooooooow,
2) Listen to my body – extra carefully,
3) No euphoric superman speed bursts, and
4) If it feels alright, no one minute walks every ten minutes (a major strategic departure from the previous 30km, but I want to know the difference).

The other thing I promise is to try for 35km and not 30km. Sound familiar? But I have to wonder: what gets into my mind that I would want to go for 35km instead of 30km?

**

The Athenian gods are looking after me. Well, someone is and it may as well be them. The weather is a complete turnaround from the previous wintery days; sunny with a coolish breeze – almost perfect. I've already decided this is going to be my longest long run of this training odyssey, so there will be considerable mental and emotional reward at the end of it, if I can do it. But maybe I am courting total disaster.

Throughout the run I think long and defensive. Yet at the same time I want to test myself – specifically with the distance, but to also include as many hills as I can find. I know where they are of course; I just have to run to them. I quite like hills, perhaps because I grew up with them around me in Dunedin, New Zealand, which has the steepest street in the world as well as several others for which you need climbing equipment and oxygen masks.

Growing up on these hills as a kid, a close rival to the life-changing seconds of a bungee jump was hurtling down the street uncontrollably on a trolley with dubious brakes, or none at all. Especially if your friend promises he's fixed the problems from the previous crash. If the speed wobbles or our faulty mechanical work hadn't already thrown us off into Mrs Birtle's hedge, or into a passing car at the bottom of the street, we'd emerge as heroes. It was a badge of honour, worthy of a medal, to fall off and carry your badly beaten body back up the hill. Even if you had soiled your pants in the process. Running 30kms seems tame in comparison.

On this run, more than any other, I am deep listening to my body. Right from the beginning of the run I hear my left knee, which is no longer a pineapple but just an apple that had fallen off the tree from a fair height and been kicked around by 5-year olds for a while. I stop listening to my knee at the 6km mark when my right groin starts coughing up. It goes on and on, giving my knee very little opportunity to get its complaints through. At 7km my stomach reminds me of the nuts and dried fruit I'd eaten earlier. Shortly after, the 800 cups of tea I had consumed throughout the morning reminds me of another bodily function. The wheels, it seems, are coming off the 35km wagon.

At 8km I peel off the road for a 30-minute pee break. Well, alright, a slight exaggeration, but things definitely felt much better.

For the first half of the run it seems that a train wreck is inevitable. I am seriously considering abandoning it completely. Self-doubt keeps popping into my mind. No, actually it pretty much stays there and doesn't do much popping at all. But I at least have some free space in my bladder now, so I drink some Powerade. That seems to make all the difference.

At 12km I feel like I could run forever. At 14km I am ready to stop. My mind has bounced back and forward like a possessed metronome. The range of emotions I can cover in such a short time is remarkable. In a one kilometre stretch I have solved the global warming crisis, developed a 12-step plan for Britney Spears, complained to myself about my big toe, pondered the future of the English soccer team and machinated over when a secret stops being a secret.

My entire run is consistent on one thing; total uncertainty – doubt – no-doubt; push – hold back; possible injury – just-a-niggly. I am Jeckyl running with Hyde. No, Hyde running with Jeckyl.

No one sees these things. To the passerby, or the motorist who swerves incredibly to the far ditch in case I spontaneously deviate twenty feet into the road, I must look like someone running without a care in the world. The internal angst is not readily apparent.

But I do it – and, despite the doubting mental gymnastics, end up doing 35km with plenty of hills, no walking, and no serious emerging injuries. I'm not sure if I could've run further or not, but at 35km it feels wise to stop. If it had been the Athens marathon, you could've dragged my face over burning coals for the last 7km so long as I finished. The biggest concern, I find out later, is chaffing of my right groin, the details of which aren't really necessary or interesting here but you can imagine, if you really want to imagine, my right groin. You'd think I'd learned from my earlier runs wouldn't you? My nipples are quite tender also. Yet another reminder of things to prepare for – another benefit of the long training runs.

It's an amazing feeling of accomplishment, even if it's just a training run. Maybe that's the point. It's *not just a training run*. It's a smaller goal towards the larger reward. A confidence booster. And if I think of each training run like that I'll do better. The long training runs teach me patience, resilience, perseverance, and the importance of keeping faith in myself.

This run also taught me a valuable lesson about good form. I've been trying to work on my form over the past few weeks. Today it clearly made a difference over some of my rougher patches, of which there were plenty. In the latter stages my body was bending over like a willow tree, so I straightened myself out more; my body almost immediately felt better and my breathing was easier. I could feel my centre of gravity shift and the improved feeling in my hips. It felt good.

It's a constant surprise to me how quickly time goes by when you're running. For this run I was on my feet for 3 hours and 27 minutes, doing nothing but running. And it was never dull or boring; there was always something to think about or look at. My senses, all of them, came alive. I had astonishing moments with unrivalled clarity of thought.

A good chunk of my time was spent thinking about how the countryside is so smelly. 'Stink' may be the word. Especially when I inhale a constantly changing combination of cow and horse manure, skunks, rotting things that I can only speculate on, and possibly myself. I jumped over three live garter snakes, six dead snakes, five unknown rotting indescribable animals, and saw many other dead characters such as skunk, porcupine, chipmunks, squirrels, and that one animal that when smushed always looks like it's never been discovered. I'm assuming Athens will be quite different.

I'll look back on this run, the second furthest I've ever gone, and be proud that I stuck to it and didn't give in. But I came very close.

Fred is really pleased to see me return. I'm feeling quite sorry for him. Although he's still wearing the cone around his head at least he's had the tubes taken out. If the holes don't heal I'll have a yellow Lab that whistles when he moves.

**

It's a rest day today. I love rest days, especially after long runs. I drive to Ottawa for a business meeting, first impressing myself that I could still walk the morning after – just some stiff muscles and my left knee a bit tight, but not badly swollen. By the end of the day I am itching to get running again.

At a business lunch with three other middle-aged men it suddenly occurs to me that I'm in the age group where operations and joint replacements are conversation pieces. While I could chip in about my knee, and could honestly say that my knee has improved *because* of running, the bulk of the conversation, the whole lunch, in fact, is about deteriorating physical health. Quite depressing. Even the food wants to leave the table. I don't mention my running at all, as two of the guys are all over each other trying to win the *Most Debilitated Middle-aged Male Award*. A bizarre form of one-upmanship. For me to say I was training and feeling great would sound arrogant and would ruin their lunch. Our table must sound incredibly boring to anyone sitting nearby. I keep myself busy by trying to stop my eyes from rolling to the back of my head.

I'm glad to be back in my car heading home. I'm heading in the right direction.

Summary

Planned distance = 73km;
Actual distance run = 72km

16

OF MICE
AND MEN

DAYS 15 – 21
Planned Distance: 47km

It's getting cooler. Today was a nutty day that continuously changed due to different things on my work
schedule. For one thing, I'm sick of sitting in front of
the computer. I end up running in the early evening –
after Karen and Emma drop off some feed and shavings
for the horses, and drinking two glasses of wine sitting
around the woodstove. It feels very cosy. The last thing
I want to do is run. But I do run. Part of me is saying
'have another rest day, you need it' but this is weak and
pathetic, and simply not true. It could've gone either way
but when Karen and Emma leave I quickly throw my gear
on and head out to the back fields for a 6km run.

The run starts fast – I just feel like running, or maybe
the wine feels like running. It feels comfortable, which is
reassuring after the 35km the other day. At one point I
am easily running sub 5-minute 1kms, and I know that's
silly. Here I go again. I ease off, much more conscious
this time of a potential show-stopping injury. That would
be unforgiveable.

The run ends in complete darkness. I can't see anything by the end of it. For the last kilometre I run out to the road where at least if I crash into something, like a car, I'll see it coming. Even though there are no lights on the road it seems safer than pitch black fields. When the one light I do have, that tiny blinking green light on my foot-pod, gives out, I'm plunged into total darkness. The fire is still burning when I get back inside. I silently congratulate myself for getting out there and 'doing it'.

I'm starting to feel optimistic about Athens. According to the marathon pace charts in John Stanton's book, if I run a 5:40 pace per kilometre I will break the 4-hour time (my 35km time was at an average 5:55 per km pace). A sub 4-hour marathon pace would be fantastic, but only if it doesn't affect my ongoing training for the other marathons.

**

A couple of days later I do some more hill training; the same Bracken road hills as other times. The hills have the same slopes as before and nothing else has changed, except the porcupine has finally withered away. It is, by far, the worst day for running yet, with heavy rain and a cold, cold wind. I spend the morning continually looking out the window, trying to crystal ball when it will be best to run. In the end I decide there is no such thing as a best time, it is just one of those really wet days. At least I'll have shelter among the trees.

Apparently not. If this is a sheltered run I'd hate to see what an unsheltered run looks like. Even the trees are looking for shelter. The only time I get respite from the rain is when the wind blows it over the trees. I take Fred with me for the exercise, almost having to harness him to prevent the winds from blowing him to Kansas with Dorothy. I'm running on the spot at times. Character building I'll call it. Good preparation for Athens. Who knows?

There is something about adversity that tightens your focus and resolve. Years ago at King's High School in Dunedin we played rugby in similar conditions against the visiting Waitaki Boys High team. Being country boys, they were all about two feet taller than us, a foot wider, and shaving daily. Half the field was a foot deep in mud. The other half was completely underwater.

Playing at fullback I tackled their winger, about twenty-two metres from our goal line. With me clutching him tight to the ground we slid in the water towards our goal line, during which time we exchanged contact information, talked about girlfriends past, present and future, and were within seconds of forgetting we were in a game of rugby when our waterslide ended. We quickly got up when we saw all the other players swimming over to us because we were scared we'd be trapped underwater with two rugby teams lying on top of us. The rugby ball was so full of water it would've been easier to kick Fred over the goals.

I've always enjoyed these conditions. Memories like this come flooding back when I'm on today's run. I would've been dryer floating in the Atlantic Ocean. But I am warmed by the feeling that I have pushed myself and by so doing have notched up another training run according to my schedule – one more step to Athens. I don't get a medal for this, but the sense of self-worth is irreplaceable. I'm also warmed by the thought that I'll return home to place myself in front of the hot wood burning stove for the afternoon and evening.

An hour later it snows. Incredibly, the rest of the day is even more miserable than what I'd been running in.

**

Over the next two days I train in the back fields. The snow has disappeared over night. Fred is my running companion once more. I'm running towards the forest with Fred about thirty feet ahead of me. We both hear what sounds like three snorts coming from the trees. Trees don't snort. Not the one's I know. Showing his royal lineage and finely evolved animal instincts Fred screeches to a halt, pretends not to hear anything and then runs behind me. Using equally evolved instincts I walk backwards, careful not to trip on Fred who is doing the same thing, and keeping my eyes on the spot where the snorts are coming from.

A bear? Surely not. Maybe. After all, what would a deer be doing standing in the trees snorting? Having a break from the rigours of country living? Sinus problems? Why wouldn't Fred run in and chase it? Fred isn't offering any sage advice. With the race just days away I'm not about to go in and look. No, actually I wouldn't have gone in even if there wasn't a race. We keep walking slowly backwards, our hands resting on our holsters just in case. Later, Gord my neighbour tells me that rutting deer make these sorts of sounds when they want to fight for a given territory.

Later in the day the boys and I take Fred around some of the trails in the fields. We find some interesting fresh scats, some of which have been neatly placed on top of older coyote scats. Pooping on another animals' poop has never been one of my favourite pastimes but it seems to be quite popular around these parts. Not being well versed on scats I consult my animal track book. After what seems an eternity of looking at black and white poop sketches, I conclude I'm no further ahead. Sometimes when I run in the back fields now, I have an image of a demented psychopathic beast lurking behind the trees and bushes, dropping the odd scat here and there, and cocking his head left and right trying to make sense of the two-legged animal running around and around and around the same place.

I see the same look sometimes when I tell people I'm running the three marathons. You're what? Really? Well good for you.

Crazy man.

**

It's Sunday, and one of those days when a run just doesn't seem to fit into life even for a minute. Although it was only 6km I simply couldn't find the time. It rained again for the whole day. I half expected to see animals waving to us as their Ark floated by the house. My friends Susan and Logie from Toronto came to visit for most of the day. Great to see them; a fun visit. When they left I'd promised the boys a trip to Toys-R-Us.

To complicate things further, the night before I had rolled over in bed and heard what sounded like the door being taken off its hinges. Seconds later I realized that the noise came from my right shoulder blade. Don't ask me why. And why now?

So I move slowly, like in the movies when the bad guys

are told to put their weapons down. I can feel it when I breathe deeply. I get up and walk around the house quietly so as to not wake-up the boys. Am I becoming just a little paranoid with every little thing that happens to my body? Maybe my body always does these sorts of things but I never noticed because it never seemed important before? I console myself in the fact that I've booked a massage in a few days time.

All this is to say that I didn't run at all, and have been living with the guilt ever since. I was going to, really, right up until driving back from Toys-R-Us at the end of the day. The rain was still hammering down, darkness was upon us, and time was running out to cook dinner and muck the horse stalls. I'm still chasing the bigger goal, so missing the 6km run today is a small thing, I think. Tomorrow is my 20km run, the last long run before the marathon, which is only two weeks from today.

..

This day has started out to be a ridiculously, embarrassingly long day that started almost the day before. I'm not kidding. I get up at 12:15 am. That's right, 12:15 am. Fortunately, it has nothing to do with my shoulder blade. Piercing animal screeches are coming from downstairs and Fred is sprinting frantically around the kitchen.

What now?

An out-of-practice burglar perhaps? I stand at the top of the stairs listening. As natural laws dictate, the screeching stops as soon as I pay more attention to it. Maybe it's a new species of uber-mouse; the noise is too loud for the regular field variety. Possibly it's the snorting thing from the forest stalking me. If he could speak, Fred would be yelling "There's a screeching noise, there's a screeching noise, there's a screeching noise". Training advice says to get good night's sleep. Not tonight, Bucky. I'm wired. I pull my big boy panties up and go downstairs.

At the foot of the stairs there's a cupboard on which Gordon, the hamster, spends his life. I can't see him very well from the top of the stairs because its 12:15 and if I'm going to surprise the a) burglar b) snort-thing c) new species of rodent or d) all of the above, putting the light on is not going to help.

But Gordon is obviously restless. So, despite the possibility of imminent death, I put the light on.

It turns out I'm not being robbed or bushwhacked by some Yarkerian Sasquatch. It's not been a good night for Gordon. He's crashed his running wheel into his impressively self-made wood shavings igloo. I reach in and put his wheel back upright. I'm surprised to find Gordon is attached to the wheel – his fur entangled in the mechanism that turns the wheel, or to use the technical phrase, the spinny-thing. When I put the wheel upright Gordon slides along the cage floor hanging upside down and screeching.

He's in shock. Fair enough, I would be too. He's such a big fluffy ball of fur I can't tell which part of his body is actually tangled. It's scissors time. If it's his leg it's bad news. If I'm wrong he's about to lose a leg. He's not happy to say the least, so I take decisive action. Fred keeps running around and jumping up and down, staying cool, calm and collected in this emergency.

I'm almost sure it's not his leg. Pretty sure. Kind of sure.

No, I'm definitely probably sure it's not his leg. Sort of. What are the odds, really?

Then I realise I'm still half asleep. Is this a good time to be using scissors? I squeeze the scissors slowly, figuring if it's his leg he'll lunge at my hand and chew it off. That will wake me up. He doesn't, but then he's probably in need of morphine or a sedative by now anyway. So, gulp, I cut.

He's free! Oh my God, he's free! Happy Dance. He hobbles to the west wing of the cage six inches away. Still in shock.

And so is Gordon. His cage looks like a battlefield from World War I. His food dish is turned over and his water bowl is buried under a load of shavings. His upper deck is completely dislodged and lies against the side of the cage. His ladder is upturned and also wedged against the side of the cage. Neighbours down the road probably heard the carnage.

Fortunately Fred is now applying his coping skills, relentlessly hitting my legs with the half-eaten soccer ball he's been dismembering over the past two days. As Gordon moves happily into post-traumatic stress disorder Fred decides the best thing to do is roll over and be patted on his tummy. So at 12:30am I make coffee and get to work at the computer. Good preparation for the morning 20km.

What a total grunt of a run. I would've preferred my 30km run two weeks ago over this one. Cold, rainy, windy. By the time I start running – which ends up being in the afternoon at 3pm – it's clear that I've been up for far too long. I should've, by rights, been going to bed by now. Too much coffee and too many chocolate-coated coffee beans.

I tell myself confidently that this is only 20km. What arrogance. There is only one moment when I feel confident and in control. Tying up your shoelaces shouldn't be that moment. But I have to admit that running the last kilometre, which is around the backyard track, feels like I'm sprinting to Olympic fame. I'm enjoying it. It may simply be the sheer adrenalin rush knowing I'm so close to finally finishing. My time for the 20km is 1:53, which I'm really pleased with given the horrors of the early hours. The whole time I felt like I was running in lead shoes. I am totally exhausted, no doubt the wind and cold taking it out of me in ways I hadn't fully realized until I stopped running.

I can barely keep my eyes open as I write this. There's a huge reward mentally each day when I accomplish what I set out to do – even more so when conditions are less than optimal, which is more and more frequent these days. I'll sleep well tonight. And I hope Gordon takes it easy, off the wheel.

**

The next day is a new day, a happy day, a rest day. I'm sitting in a hotel room in Toronto, soon to meet a friend. I'm reflecting on yesterday's run. I feel fine today and itching to run. I remind myself again how far I've come. At the beginning of the year in New Zealand the tide was coming in faster than I was running along the beach. Now I'm talking of 20km as a 'shorter run'. I can't help but smile and feel proud because *I do know* 20km is still a long way. But now my thoughts, with less than two weeks till Athens, centre on avoiding injuries and maintaining a positive attitude. I'm anticipating the mental anguish associated with this tapering phase. And, hopefully, will enjoy it all!

What I really like reading about in the books now is the part where they say at this point – the tapering phase – that doing more running will not improve my performance on the race day. In fact, I'll increase the chance of injury by trying to do more. Running less now almost seems like a reward. It's all getting very exciting. Dare I say it? Well alright, I will. I'm getting quietly optimistic.

I check my phone messages. The nutritionist has called back. Turns out I know the nutritionist. Teresa and I used to work together on a research project several years ago. Looks like we may finally end up talking about nutrition over lunch sometime.

Tomorrow I'm back to running. 6kms. On the treadmill.

Summary

Planned Distance = 47km;
Actual distance run = 45.9km

17

IMMERSION

I'm getting pumped up more and more as the days get closer to Athens. I'm like a sponge reading up on the history of the race. It's fascinating stuff. By the time of the 1896 Olympics running long distances was already popular in France. An 1885 race, for example, was run between Paris and Versailles (38km). The 1896 race held in Paris after the Athens Olympics had 191 competitors.

Marathon running literally 'took off' between 1896 and the next Olympics, held in Paris in 1900. That marathon was known as the *Hot* marathon, with temperatures reportedly between 35 and 39 degrees Celsius (95F and 102F). Sixteen runners from seven countries competed, including seven Frenchmen, but there were no Greek entrants. Several runners dropped out during the race. A Frenchman – Touquet-Denis – at around 12km went the wrong way, stopped for a drink – beer – had two – then decided to leave the race. Fellow countryman Michel Theato won the race, a distance of just over 25 miles, in a time of 2:59.

Over the years marathon running increased in popularity, with both professionals and amateurs running. The 1904 St Louis Olympic marathon is known for its extreme difficulty – hardly any water available, seven hills, unpaved roads, dust being blown into the competitors by an endless stream of automobiles, and a suffocating 32 degree Celsius heat. The eventual winner was Thomas Hicks of the US, in a time of 3:28 for the 40km course.

The Olympic marathon went back to Athens in 1906, and it was there that Canada secured a gold medal through Irishman William 'Billy' Sherring. I mention him not because he's Canadian, although that is reason enough, but because Canada didn't have enough money to pay for an official team. Billy had to raise his own money for the fare to Athens. The story has it that he got the inside scoop on a horse at 12-1 odds. He wagered $40 Cdn and won, securing enough money to finance his Olympic dream. It's thought that he worked on the ship that he travelled on to Europe. He arrived in Athens a few weeks early to condition himself to the environment and train on the course. He even took on a part-time job as a railway station porter.

One of the sport's most dramatic moments occurred at the 1908 London Olympics. It was the quintessential marathon moment – the leader, Dorando Pietri from Capri, Italy, came into the stadium disorientated – he went right when he should've gone left, then when he did turn left, he fell. He fell another four times on his way to crossing the line, each time being urged on by race officials and the roaring crowd. There are famous photos of Dorando being helped along, and a photo showing him being assisted after crossing the line by Sir Arthur Conan Doyle and others. Dorando finished just thirty-two seconds ahead of American John Hayes and one minute and twelve seconds ahead of South African Charles Hefferon. The American team lodged a formal complaint that Dorando had been assisted. The appeal was upheld and he was officially disqualified. The Queen, however, was so impressed by his tenacity and spirit that she awarded him a special trophy.

Marathons by now were spreading across the globe. In 1908, prior to the London Olympics, inaugural marathons had been held in South Africa, Canada and Great Britain. There was a 'mania' write Switzer and Robinson, immediately after the 1908 Olympics; the drama and sheer physical 'danger' as it appeared, served to only heighten the marathon's mystique further. As if in a Hollywood plot, and perhaps it should be, Pietri and Hayes faced off a few months later in New York, billed on a poster in English and Italian as "The Famous Olympic Race to Be Rerun. America vs. Italy."

Dorando Pietri won.

The London Olympic Marathon is also famous because this is where the 26.2 distance was established. The course was meant to be exactly 26 miles, and was to start on 'The Long Walk' in the grounds of Windsor Castle. On the day before the race – to be started by King Edward VII – the distance was extended because the King had a cold and it was felt that it would be best that he did not go out. So instead, he started the marathon from the Great Courtyard of the Castle, which was 385 yards up the hill. By doing this the competitors could still finish in front of the Royal Box where his wife the Queen would be waiting in the Olympic Arena (White City Stadium). Thus the distance was 26 miles 385 yards (42.195 km).

It remains the official marathon distance to this day, because in 1921, at the fifth IAAF Congress in Geneva, the IAAF agreed that the distance, finally, be standardized. As David Martin and Roger Glynn note though, there was no rationale given for the decision to go with 42.195 kilometres. Was it, as some authors might suggest, because of the British influence and/or the enormous publicity surrounding that particular marathon?

And so the Olympic marathons continued through the century. The Olympic marathon has become 'the' marathon race to win, as are many Olympic events. There have been some amazing close races and drama. A Portuguese marathoner died in the 1912 Stockholm Olympic marathon. Abebe Bikila from Ethiopia stunned the world in Rome 1960, by winning gold running in bare feet, and then repeating the win four years later in Tokyo. Frank Shorter changed the face of running in the United States with his 1972 Munich gold. Japanese marathoners, building on their country's history of long distance messengers, emerged as top international competitors, and the role of drugs in sports became an enduring story from the 1976 Montreal Olympics. Most importantly, in 1984 women were finally able to run in an Olympic marathon. These days it seems astounding that women were not on equal standing with men. There's much more of course, but that would require another book. If Olympic marathon running history is your thing, then read David Martin and Roger Glynn's book 'The Olympic Marathon' published in 2000. It's an absorbing read with substantive levels of detail.

18

SLOWING DOWN AND GEARING UP

DAYS 22 – 28
Planned Distance: 34km

Meanwhile, I'm just a week away from clambering around the Acropolis. On this day, Day 22, running hopelessly collides with my work in Toronto. I get to run but have to squeeze it out of nowhere. I run for 20 minutes, at best – well likely less actually, as I only run 3km.

A big part of me doesn't want to run due to my work pressures. I convince myself it wouldn't matter since I'm tapering anyway. The smaller part of me genuinely wants to run. I know I'll feel really guilty if I don't run. I end up *running* between and during business calls, in order to run on a treadmill at the Hotel. It feels desperate. It is desperate.

I'm pretty sure no-one on the telephone conference call hears me fall over in the changing room. I become Mr. Bean; changing clothes and juggling the phone like it's a bag of hot coals just out of the woodstove. My trousers fall loose and I trip into the lockers.

So I've already burned enough calories for the day just getting my gear on. Relieved that I haven't injured myself and pleased to see I have all my essential gear on (i.e., shorts), I enter the Fitness Centre exhausted. In front of me, like a futuristic herd of metallic animals, are fifty un-used treadmills. In the far distance I can see through my binoculars another person, or maybe it is a manikin. I'm thinking of sending semaphores to them asking if the world ended while I was destroying the changing room.

But no time for that. I've a few minutes free for a few kilo-metres before I'm off to my next meeting. I throw myself onto the nearest treadmill and race away, staying still. As did the ear bud in my right ear, without any tape, for which I'm grateful.

The run is good, but rushed. As short as it is, it still leaves me late for my next meeting. If my pre-run antics were Mr. Bean, my post-run change is Mr. Bean with his hair on fire. My God do I move. I can run for over three hours and feel good afterwards, but I'm totally exhausted here running for just seventeen minutes.

Did I really need to run today? Physically, I'd say no. But for my own mental and emotional well-being – yes – it seemed important to make myself do it, however short the run. Although it created angst, by the end of the day, I'm glad I did it.

**

The next day I'm back home. The countdown is on. Athens race day is taking over more and more of my mental space. I end up running a short run at the end of the day again; cool but sunny.

The following day I run 10km from my home and down Yarker Road and back – a few hills in this run, but nothing requiring Sherpas. It goes well. I'm seriously thinking, maybe, just possibly, perhaps, kind of, who knows, I might have an outside chance of breaking 4 hours in Athens. I check John Stanton's marathon pace chart when I get back.

I also have a massage today. I don't typically have a massage. Ever. But I feel so good afterwards. Even when the therapist walks all over my back, like she did a couple of years ago. I felt spoiled then. She was tiny and light though. She could've done a Russian Cossack dance with her twin sister and I wouldn't have noticed. She didn't fall off either.

I'd just come from a hairdresser around the corner while staying in Vancouver for a couple of days. I've never had a haircut like it before and doubt I ever will again. The hairdresser, fractionally smaller than your standard garden gnome, and perhaps inspired by the challenge of creatively reconstructing the 16 hairs on my head, embarked on an artistic journey of epic proportions. Presumably his student assistant was learning the ways of her Japanese Master.

At first I didn't understand why they were playing a movie for me, the only customer, but as the first hour went by I started to work it out.

With only $20 on me, and an hour already on the meter I was thinking how foolish I'd been not to ask how much the haircut would cost. It was a bit late now to ask, so I settled back and watched the movie. At one point I forgot why I was there. As I contemplated asking for popcorn he stood up on a wooden box to reach the top of my head. I was sipping my tea and getting lost in the movie plot when suddenly I felt a pull on my frock, saw a flutter of movement in the mirror and watched in horror as the Gnome fell off his wooden box, flew through the air with his scissors waving around and crashed into a counter filled with hairdressing equipment. Not a pretty sight.

Right at the best part of the movie too. An awkward moment. No-one knew where to look, or what to say. In complete silence, he picked up the box, hopped back on, and resumed cutting. I continued drinking my tea but decided to pass on the shave.

It cost just $15 for the show, drink, movie and the haircut. I looked at him and his assistant incredulously, wondering if the fall had dulled his business senses. I gave a great tip, because it really was a great cut, and disappeared into the bleak afternoon with a great memory. The only regret was not seeing the end of the movie.

All of which has nothing to do with my massage today, except that your thoughts on new experiences are in part based on previous experiences. Jas is not likely to walk on me and I doubt he'll fall over. He has me sign a bunch of forms that absolve anyone of any responsibility for what happens next. A small room, lights low, a bed to lie on, the sound of waves gently rolling into shore, and that guy who's always playing the flute. By rights I should be going to sleep.

Jas is happy to talk – no polite chit-chat – just straight into the details about what he is doing and feeling. He starts with my neck and works downwards with a general massage. Good thing too, because he discovers sailors knots and camel lumps and other stuff with polysyllabic names all over my body. Working at a computer for several hours in a day plays havoc with your neck and back. He finds problems I didn't know I had, which is a bit disconcerting given what I'm about to try. I came in feeling fit and leave feeling out of shape. Or perhaps, back in shape, after he's finished manipulating my body.

Overall, Jas feels I'm in fairly good shape for the marathon. He says he has seen a lot worse from other marathon runners. Or maybe he was being kind, recognizing that critical analysis at this point could put me out on the ledge.

He doesn't do any deep tissue work – it's not good to do this so close to the run apparently. But he still finds plenty to work on – in particular my gluteus maximus (left side), my gluteus medius (right side), and another trigger point at the top of my right calf, where the calf muscles meet with the hamstrings. He applies point pressure on each of these spots and is asking me as he does this if the pain is decreasing. It really is. I tell him about some discomfort in my right hip. He says this is likely because of my gluteus medius being the way it is, and the pain spreading across my backside. He gives me some stretching exercises to work on at home, in bed. Cool.

**

The next day I'm taking Fred out on the trails in the backyard, for a 6km run. I'm conscious of injuring myself and then not being able to run in Athens. It's a good run, because again, my times seem lower yet I don't feel I'm expending a greater effort in getting these times. I'm able to run well within myself.

Saturday quickly follows – another 6km run, which now feels like a very small distance. It's raining yet again; it's been relentless for the past two weeks. I focus on good form and try to breathe correctly.

I'm still running with my music and really hope that this is allowed in Athens. I can't tell from the Athens marathon website whether it is or not.

**

The plan for Sunday is to run 6km. But ... it's Jack's birthday (October 29th) and the weather is still disgusting. I decide to make it my rest day. Call it tapering. The decision feels good. I spend most of the morning with the boys and Gord, who helps me pick-up two cords of wood in Yarker. Rain, cold wind and us loading and then unloading a sixteen foot trailer full of wood. This isn't a Rest Day at all. This is cross-training.

I'm becoming paranoid about injuries now. Visions of slipping on the wood (which I did), being donked on the head by a poorly directed toss of wood into the trailer, a horse flying through the air in the strong winds and landing on me, me tripping over Fred, or the boys, Fred tripping over me, and so it goes on...

But ... no injuries yet. Meanwhile, I'm now reading a lot about tapering. Everyone agrees tapering is essential, but there's no precise agreement on how many days, or weeks, we should taper (2-4 weeks?). Or, for that matter, how much less our distances should be when we are running less.

One thing is certain. I don't know. What stays with me is the comment that it doesn't matter how much running I do in my last week or so, it will not improve my race. If anything it will only increase my chance of getting injured.

So I'm guestimating what looks right based on Joe, John, Jeff and Hal. The basic message is to cut out the long runs, and do the short distances with two-three rest days in the last week. Don't over-train, don't overindulge in foods, and don't drink to excess. Eat carbohydrates, visualize the race, clean my teeth, brush my hair, clean behind my ears, and so on.

Also, on my 'things-to-do' list are: pack as if I'm going to Greece for a week, make sure someone can feed the horses, cats, hamster, fish and chickens, remember to drop Fred off at the kennel, clean the fridge, finish up my work as best I can, don't worry about the several hours difference in time zones, and remember, for the 100th time, my passport and running shoes. And make sure I get plenty of sleep. Daylight saving kicked in today as well; we've fallen back an hour. Thank God I don't have much on my mind otherwise I wouldn't be able to focus on the race.

It's getting exciting. In one week I will be running the marathon from Marathon. *The* Marathon. Just being there will be a thrill in itself. Actually running it will be incredible. I hope the Kenyans are ready for me.

**

Karen and I meet up for a 6km run with her four dogs and Fred. It's a bit nutty at times but still fun running with the dogs. The smallest one – Lilly – is about the size of my running shoe. I enjoy this run, in part because I don't crush Lilly, and because we talk the whole way. Karen and I, that is.

I've been running the long distances with a 'fuel belt' that has room for 8 plastic drinks containers; in a small pouch on the belt there's room for an Energy Bar if I fold it in half. I'm probably good for walking in the desert for three days. It's highly unlikely I'll run out of drinks on the run, especially as there will be water stations throughout. The belt is heavy with all this fuel, but psychologically it's my security blanket, so I've decided to keep wearing it.

I think one of the riskiest things I'm doing is the red-eye flight to Europe from Canada. As a precaution I call Air Canada today to see if I can get an aisle seat. I could've walked to Athens in the time it takes to reach a real person. I cry pathetically about running the marathon and needing to be able to stretch out my legs. It works. An aisle seat. Buoyed by this success I ask about First Class. We both have a good laugh and wish each other luck in life.

The next day arrives with incredible speed; it's my last day at home before heading to Athens via one night in Toronto for work. It's a manic day. I think of squeezing in a 3km run but there's not a hope in wherever that place is.

Thanks to the tapering advice, I don't get overly worried about it. Nevertheless, I may still run tomorrow morning in Toronto before I fly out later in the afternoon. I can't help myself.

But before I leave home I take The Grim Reaper and Zorro trick-or-treating on Halloween night. They do well as they usually do. I'd thought of dressing up as a marathon runner, which would have scared a lot of people.

Like my hairdresser, for example. When Linda heard I was running the marathon a look of horror came over her face. She started talking about someone she knew whose daughter had died after starting up running. This is the third time in five days that someone has mentioned death when I say 'marathon running.' It's a bit unnerving, but a reminder of the feat and the range of perceptions that exist about marathon running.

Karen and I have constructed an elaborate plan to avoid leaving my car parked at the airport, me being dinged a few hundred dollars for the privilege, and her having to do the same the day before I get back. The details are impressive but not necessary here, except to say that for two people who have a history of losing cars at airports, this is a very proud moment. In any case, the plan is to meet up in Toronto the next morning after I've driven down the night before.

I drive to Toronto with a feeling that I've done everything I need to do, which doesn't happen very often. I turn my attention to race strategy. Logically I should simply focus on achieving the big goal, which is to finish the marathon and not get injured doing so. But I'm thinking it might be possible to do it in less than four hours. I could risk an injury, which may either prevent me from finishing or compromise the training for the Caymans and Disney. If I try and break four hours, should I aim for a negative split, positive split, or an even pace?

If I run a faster first 21km, can I be sure I won't tire myself out for the later 21km? If I run a slower first 21km, can I be sure I can go faster in the second 21km? I'm very aware of the fact that I have no recent experience running marathons, the hills come into play in the last half, and I have no idea how I will feel in the final 35km to 42km section. Perhaps my best bet is to plan an even pace throughout, checking my times constantly with my *running computer*. And what about the weather? How will the wind, cold, or heat affect me? Will my nagging hip thing, which I think is connected to the gluteus maximus, minus, medius ... cripple me midway through the run? Will I be too pig-headed and continue running anyway? If I feel good at the end will I be kicking myself if it turns out I just missed breaking the 4-hour mark? The fact that I'm even thinking like this almost makes me laugh. Somehow, over the past few months, I've acquired a new body of knowledge and a new language.

That night I look at the oxygen power tables in Hal Higdon's book (p258-259). They provide predictive running times based on your times at other distances. There are plenty of these on the Internet as well. It looks like I can run just under 4 hours. According to John Stanton's book, if I run a 5:40 pace I could finish in at 3:59:06. Not much of a margin for error there, but it's looking possible. I hope the gods are with me.

Summary

Planned Distance = 34km;
Actual distance run = 31km

19

ATHENS BOUND

Departure Day. I wake up in the hotel feeling a pain in my right hip area. Not just a niggle, but an ache. Perhaps from the driving? It's causing discomfort even when I bend over. I don't know how to remedy the problem, but I'm guessing sitting on a red-eye flight to Europe isn't the solution.

I go for a light run in the morning and feel the pain. But if there's good news in this it's that I know I can probably run and bear it if I have to. It's Wednesday and the run is on Sunday. Of course I'll run, but I don't want this marathon to compromise the others or be a complete showstopper.

I'm wondering what I would've done differently over the past few weeks? I'm guilty of not doing enough stretching exercises, and not working enough on my core body strength (whoops, none at all actually). But in fairness to me, it has been really hard fitting everything in at times.

I've made compromises and choices throughout. I knew this would happen when I started.

I purchase a Greek phrase book at the Toronto Airport. I don't typically do this, certainly not with the hope of having a conversation with someone in their native tongue. While there is admiration by locals that you've attempted to speak their language, if you've done a decent job with your translation they will reply in the local language. At that point there's a really good chance you're completely lost and have to resort back to English, Marcel Marceau impersonations, charades, or possibly sign language. They then smile, and either say something back to you in perfect English, or the whole line of communication is completely lost. Instead, I travel with a smile, a few key words like *thank-you, good morning, good night* and *hello*, and stumble through the rest the best I can. There have been purely magical moments with this as the basis of communication.

Greek is almost beyond comprehension. With other languages like Spanish, French, Italian and even German, there's a fighting chance I might have an idea about what is generally being said or read. Greek on the other hand, is, well, Greek to me. If I want to write 'I love you' it would look like this "Γρ∀(∀Bφ, and I would have to say, and forgive me if you are Greek, "sa-gha-po". It doesn't romantically roll off the tongue does it?

But not to panic. The phrasebook is useful. My favourites are *'The fat priest ate thick lentil soup'*, the more generically useable *'easy tiger'*, and the 'well-you-never-know' phrase *Australian Rules Football*. I'll sleep well over the next few nights knowing that, in a crisis, I'm prepared. Especially if someone wearing a shirt with a kangaroo on it stops me and asks angrily what the big guy who looks like Friar Tuck is eating at the sidewalk cafe.

I also brought along with me Homer's classic *The Odyssey*. I've resolved to read this as part of my Greek immersion. On a long flight it's great to get into a book with depth and meaning and come away having learned something.

But I don't have a good track record with reading on a plane. Several years ago I bought a book at the Vancouver Airport out of sheer desperation as I mentally prepared for a long haul trip to New Zealand. It was a 500-page biographical account of the Kennedy Family. There I was on the plane feeling happy, proud and impressed that I was reading the book. A truly amazing family.

But by the time I'd read to the bottom of the first page my concentration began to wane and dinner, with real cutlery, appeared. I remember the book quite clearly to this day, if not its content, and think maybe one day I will get back into it and read the other 499 pages. Perhaps on a long flight somewhere.

But for now, I have Homer. If I could possibly curl up in any position in the seat I'd get started. If I don't finish it on the flights there will still be plenty of time before and after the race. And if I'm slow enough, maybe even during the race.

The first leg of my trip is a short commuter flight to Montreal. We arrive at the Trudeau Airport in time for my connecting European flight. Bad news. There is no entertainment center on the back of the seats. It looks like we'll have a movie on a three-inch screen about one hundred metres away in economy class. They should provide binoculars along with the throw away headphones. The announced movies are the opposite of those scheduled in our entertainment guide. If correct, we're travelling from Europe to Canada. I won't be happy if after seven hours of flying we arrive back at Trudeau Airport.

The good news on this flight to Frankfurt (from which I then connect to Athens) is that I have lots of leg room and no-one sitting beside me. With a seven hour time difference and me on this red-eye flight my plan is to stay awake the whole time and then crash into a deep sleep once I arrive at my hotel in Athens. I arrive Thursday afternoon, with the race scheduled for Sunday. According to the training books, the most important sleep is two nights before the race; in my case, Friday night.

A Middle Eastern lady the size of my eight year old son Jack and almost completely covered in her traditional burqa, attempts to place her bag, which is three times her size, in the overhead luggage compartment a few seats in front of me. Besides simply not being able to reach the height of the compartment, she's disappearing under the sheer weight of the bag. No-one is helping her. I walk down the aisle and lift it off her head from behind without asking if she wants any help, partly because I couldn't see where her head was by now anyway. I place her luggage in the compartment for her. Clearly embarrassed by this, and with the few millimetres of her skin exposed turning red, she offers a nod of thanks and sits down as if nothing has happened.

'Chicken or beef, Sir'? is the question. I say 'chicken', excited by the fact I'm getting more than just crackers on this flight. It comes with rice, bread and vegetables, and an expansive set of plastic cutlery to finish off the ambience. The rice seems hard but it's because I'm actually eating a piece of the fork that's broken off.

I'm drinking lots of fluids, as part of the tapering plan, but also because its common sense when flying. By mid-flight I've worn a passage to the toilets at the back of the plane, partly explaining why the cost of air tickets keeps rising. I've probably clocked 3km on this flight alone.

We arrive in Frankfurt Airport's Terminal A. I'm still awake but only just. The Middle Eastern lady comes back to me and asks if I could help her with her bag. It's a special moment between us and we both have beaming smiles.

I must now find Terminal B. It turns out they've put it somewhere near the border of Greece. I'm glad I've been training over the past few weeks. It may even be quicker to get another flight from Terminal A to Terminal B.

I finally arrive at Terminal B, another bit of cross-training, and immediately face a crisis. Frau-Airline-Seat-Person requires my baggage ticket before she will give me a seat. I pull out everything in my bag and show her where the sticker was placed, at some point, on my ticket. Not good enough, but worth trying. 'Keep looking' she says. More and more people converge on the gate now. The runners among them are easily spotted, looking lean and healthy, and wearing running shoes, tracksuits and shirts with logos of races around the world.

Unlike me, as I'm mimicking a frantic airport security guard searching for the time bomb. Much to my surprise, an hour or so of forensic searching uncovers the ticket. 'Oh thanks', she says, now with a pleasant smile, and bingo I have my seat, which I thought I always had, but maybe I didn't.

On the flight to Athens I sit beside an older guy – I'm guessing sixties, and about 280-300lb – someone that's big enough to be more comfortable sitting in my seat as well, so long as I'm sitting somewhere else. It's Jack of course, for that is his name, and he's off to run the Athens marathon as well. Really? Well, yes. Why not?

Jack has run Boston twenty-five times and has run Athens on other occasions. He says he's known as a Clydesdale in the marathon world. The Middle Eastern woman would have fit handily in one of his pockets.

I'm quite stunned; impressed with his number of marathons to begin with, and also because he simply doesn't look like what I would typically think a marathon runner would look like. My whole understanding of marathons and those that run them is changing by the day.

We have a great time talking all the way to Athens. One year at the Athens marathon Jack and his friends ran with wild dogs over the first 13km. Another time he picked up a two year-old girl that had run out onto the course and took her back to her mother. Jack finished one race saluting to a senior military officer as he ran the last few metres in the Stadium. The officer saluted him back, at which point a couple of thousand cadets threw their hats into the air. The weather is quite variable, Jack says. It was over 80 degrees Fahrenheit one year, but another year there was water up to his ankles over the first 2km. And the hills, he says, there are plenty of hills.

I really admire how Jack does it, and why – it's a very social thing. He's not out to smash records – it's about the experience, the fun, the triumphs and the people. It's very much about the people. And in Athens, it's also about the history. Jack has come with a tour group, along with Jeff Galloway who is essentially the Host and Guide for the tour group.

I'm wide awake now as we land at Athens International Airport – Eleftherios Venizelos, built 27 kilometres outside of Athens in time for the 2004 Olympics. It's hot. I hop into the Metro Line 3 train at the airport and head into the city. My hope is that the train will take me to just metres from my hotel.

As we rumble through the countryside I begin to see more and more signs dotted over the landscape in Greek and think, 'Wow. I'm really here!'

20

A Lot of Hype

As we get closer to the city I'm thinking about Jack's Clydesdale size and my own body's ability to cope with a marathon.

Dr Jake Emmett in Charleston, Illinois, studies the physiological effects of marathon running. He wrote on this subject in *Marathon and Beyond*. Even runners who finish in four hours or more, he says, have a 10-fold increase in their metabolism, which requires their cardiorespiratory, endocrine and neuromuscular systems to function at a much higher level for a very long time – an "inordinate amount of time" is what he said actually.

Death is obviously the biggest problem of all, although fortunately it doesn't happen to many runners. But it does happen. The research literature has studied the nature and extent of deaths in marathons. Having reviewed this literature Dr. Emmett says that sudden death is much more likely to occur in runners who have a family history of heart problems, elevated cholesterol, and have had warning signs like angina, nausea, and epigastric discomfort. The experts all agree that if we have any of these signs we should see our family doctor before beginning any marathon training. He also mentions that the research shows that sudden death is more likely to occur while jogging than in a marathon.

Besides injuries, the big risks we need to consider are hyperthermia, hyponatremia and hypothermia. Each of these can turn marathons (and training) into a serious medical condition. I don't need to be an emergency physician but I need to know something and use common sense.

I'll get hyperthermia when my body overheats. Our hearts work to pump our oxygen rich warm blood through our bodies and eventually to our skin, where sweat, if necessary, helps to cool our temperature. But that may not be enough in some cases, like when running long distances. When there's high humidity, for example, our bodies won't be able to release heat quickly enough. And if we're dehydrated, our body's ability to transfer heat from our muscles to our skin is impaired. Dr. Emmett says that when our body temperature reaches 105-106 degrees Fahrenheit muscle weakness and disorientation can develop. A loss of consciousness can occur if the temperature reaches close to 107 degrees Fahrenheit. Not good.

On the other end of the scale is hypothermia – the reduction in body temperature. This is unlikely to happen in the middle of summer, but always possible in colder, wetter conditions. The best advice is to dress in layers, with the outer layer waterproof and wind resistant. The significance of the layers, especially over longer distances, is that weather conditions can change. We need to be able to adjust layers according to whether it's warm or not, or if we have wet layers that require changing. It's also possible to get hypothermia after a race as our body heat continues to escape even though we've finished the activity.

Liquids, especially water, play an obvious and important role here. The latest research says to drink when we need it; take smaller sips continuously and as comfortably as we can, as opposed to large quantities at set times. It's as if we're creating a constant flow of fluids that works through our body. Dr. Emmett says we need to drink in moderation before and during our run.

The flipside of this, however, is too much water, resulting in hyponatremia. If I drink too much water – being concerned about dehydration – I risk diluting the amount of sodium in my body. Low sodium levels in my blood can cause swelling (or edema) in my brain. It's dicey up there at the best of times, but in the very extreme situations this could cause death. Again, not good.

The research shows that this is more common in women, slower runners (over four hours – i.e., most marathoners), and in those who take over-the-counter nonsteroidal anti-inflammatories. Before you throw away the running shoes though, the good news is that hyponatremia is, according to Dr. Emmett, "extremely rare" (0.3% of all marathoners), and likely to become more so, as runners become better educated on the importance of fluid intake.

And then there's hypoglycemia. If we don't consume enough carbohydrates during a marathon we can suffer from liver glycogen depletion in about two hours, which will lead to hypoglycemia. In other words we will have a low blood-sugar level. Symptoms can include nervousness, sweating, intense hunger, trembling, weakness, palpitations, and trouble speaking, and, not surprisingly, a decline in running performance. So adequate carbohydrate intake over longer time periods is important to ensure we don't head down the horrible road to hypoglycemia.

There is a lot to consider. We can't ignore the impact that marathons have on our bodies, which is all the more reason we need to take training seriously and get to know more about what we are doing to our bodies. That's partly what makes it all so interesting – that marathon running is multi-faceted; we learn so much about ourselves.

And that's why it's so rewarding when we complete a marathon; it's no overnight accomplishment, and we have entrusted ourselves to complete a feat of endurance while minimizing the risks of doing so.

21

GROWTH

By the end of the 1950s there were marathon events pretty much all over the world. The number of competitors running, however, was still relatively small compared to what we see these days. In the United States in 1960, there were less than six marathons, but by the end of the decade the number had risen to forty-four.

The numbers rose to seventy-three in 1970, then to one hundred and one in 1971, and one hundred and twenty-four in 1972. By the end of the 1970s marathon running had been transformed, not unlike the current movement. It was part of a much larger social movement which saw, among other things, an increasingly affluent society with more leisure time and a growing desire for fitness and health. A book on marathon running by the editors of the American Consumer's Guide publication in 1979 wrote that "People who run marathons are the healthiest people in the world". Of the crossing of the Verrazano Bridge as part of the 1978 New York marathon the authors wrote it was one of the most amazing sights of 1978: "marathon mania is sweeping the country. No aspect of our culture is immune".

David Martin and Roger Glynn wrote in *The Marathon Footrace* published in 1979 that "Running paraphernalia literally exploded in quantity and innovativeness as entrepreneurs sought to capture, and as runners were delighted to provide, the dollars that were being poured out in enjoyment of a newfound sport. To run a marathon became a profound ambition of many people. The marathon footrace became an end for which the means were fully incorporated into daily activities".

Tim Noakes, in his book *The Lore of Running,* noted the huge increase in participation in marathons after 1976. He attributes the 'boom' to twelve inter-related factors: the publication of Ken Cooper's *Aerobics* (1968), the Mexico City Olympics (1968), the first New York City Marathon (1970), the 'birth' of Nike running shoes (1971), Frank Shorter winning gold for the United States in the 1972 Olympic marathon, the marathoners' heart immunity theory (1972), the Montreal Olympics (1976), the first 5-Borough New York City marathon (1976), publication of Jim Fixx's book *The Complete Book of Running* (1977), publication of George Sheehan's book *Running and Being* (1978), the first London Marathon (1981), and the Los Angeles Olympics (1984).

Similarly, in a 1997 article in *Marathon and Beyond* Michael Sandrock commented that the modern era of marathon running started with Frank Shorter winning the 1972 Olympic marathon. Before then, he said, "marathon running was associated more with the 19th century than the 20th... Shorter's win started an inexorable mass movement into the marathon". The biggest change in the 1970s, he says, was that marathons were "no longer considered a circus sideshow, done by skinny eccentrics for God-knows-what reason".

The USA *Running Wire* reported in March 2000 that in 1990 there were twenty-six marathons in the United States that had 1,000 finishers or more. By 1999 that figure had grown to forty-five. The actual number of finishers rose from 260,000 in 1990 to 435,000 in 1999; a 67% percent growth rate over the 1990s.

Significantly, there has been a surge in the number of women completing marathons. Women accounted for just 19% of finishers in 1990, but by 1999 the share had risen to 35%.

The new boom is bigger than that of the late 1970s. In a 2002 editorial in *Marathon and Beyond*, Rich Benyo estimated that in 2002, the number of marathoners in the United States (close to half a million) was about five times the number running them in what he referred to as the First Running Revolution (1976-1984).

Tim Noakes considers the more recent boom to have occurred since the mid to late 1990s. He writes that older runners are now running to complete, not compete: "The new revolution reflects the maturing approach to the value of running. The sole focus is no longer on each runner's finishing time. Now it seems that there is equal merit in just finishing – a welcome change".

Pamela Cooper meanwhile, observes from a sociological perspective in her 1998 book *The American Marathon* that "The American marathon footrace has evolved into a cultural performance, a chance for people to tell a story about themselves". She talks of the marathon's "theoretical openness" as the runners receive encouragement and support from the spectators, who themselves get "new respect for human physical potential and pride in national, ethnic or social community. Most of all, the spectators share in the story told by each marathon runner".

The histories of individual marathon events exemplify the broader growth being observed. The famous "Grandma's Marathon" along Lake Superior has grown from 150 runners and a budget of $649.51 in 1977, to 9,888 runners, a budget of $2.5 million and seven year-round staff. The number of volunteers has risen from 30 to a staggering 4,500. Ryan Lamppa, a researcher for Running USA, a national non-profit organization that promotes distance running, believes that Grandma's could expand by a few thousand more runners, especially with this new boom in marathons where, he says, people are running for good health and not simply for competition. Quality, however, is first and foremost in the mind of Scott Keenan, the race organizer, which is why the race has allowed on average only about 275 new slots each year over the past decade.

The London Marathon began in 1981, when 7,747 runners took to the streets. Over 22,000 had applied to run the event but the numbers were restricted by the police. Timothy Collings and Stuart Sykes in their book *The Story of the Greatest Race on Earth* write that Norwegian Inge Simonsen and American Dick Beardsley tied for first place as they ran hand-in-hand over the line, reflecting the spirit of sportsmanship, camaraderie and comradeship. Seven hours after the starting cannon two others – Marie Dominique de Groot from France and David Gaiman from the UK – came in last, again both holding hands as they crossed the finish line.

Today, as we'll see shortly, the London Marathon is an Event into itself; with over 35,000 finishers each year, and a staggering 60,000 others who miss out on getting an entry. Since its inception over 711,000 runners have finished the course. (The table below shows the standing for the largest marathons in the world in 2007).

And now, in 2007, the total estimated number of finishers in the United States alone was over 400,000. We've seen a growth rate of over 25% in the past seven years. If we were able to collect data similar to that which we have readily available for the US from other countries around the world we'd likely see similar increases.

DATE	RACE	# MEN	% MEN	# WOMEN	% WOMEN	TOTAL
THE LARGEST MARATHONS IN 2007 (#FINISHERS)						
NOV	New York	26,042	67.5%	12,515	32.5%	38,557
APR	London	24,815	69.5%	10,852	30.5%	35,667
SEP	Berlin	26,032	80.0%	6,498	20.0%	32,530
APR	Paris	22,507	83.7%	4,303	16.3%	26,880
OCT	Chicago	16,945	58.8%	11,870	41.2%	28,815
DEC	Honolulu	10,731	51.9%	9,961	48.1%	20,692
OCT	Washington	12,621	61.0%	8,058	39.0%	20,679
APR	Boston	12,364	60.8%	7,974	39.2%	20,338
FEB	Tokyo	approx 20,000				
MAR	Los Angeles	12,207	63.6%	7,809	36.4%	20,016
APR	Hamburg	13,274	80.5%	3,208	19.5%	16,482
JUN	San Diego	7,729	48.4%	8,228	51.6%	15,958
JUN	Stockholm	9,574	77.4%	2,796	22.6%	12,370
MAR	Roma	10,195	84.8%	1,832	15.2%	12,027
JAN	Orlando	5,780	52.8%	5,156	47.2%	10,936
NOV	Tsukuba	8,718	85.7%	1,451	14.3%	10,169

Source: Association of International Marathons and Distance Races

It's no exaggeration to say you can run a marathon anytime anywhere in the world, assuming you can afford it. But even on a shoestring budget, accessing a number of marathons regularly is still possible. Unless, of course, you happen to be living somewhere like Perth, Australia, where you are pretty much smack dab in the middle of nowhere, or just to the left of it.

Not being in the smack dab of nowhere, but actually somewhere, I can pretty much go anywhere, budget permitting. For most runners the question is two-fold; where do I want to go to run a marathon and where can I run a marathon? After that there's a drop-down menu of decisions we need to make. The time of year is important. Do I want a January marathon in the wintery reaches of North America, or in the Caribbean? Is the run going to be part of a vacation; or am I running it specifically for the marathon and nothing else? Do I want to spend valuable vacation time traveling to marathons? Then there's the terrain. Flat? Hilly? Mountainous? Do I want an urban marathon or one in the country? Do I want to run with thousands of runners, two hundred runners, or maybe just a few dozen? Do I want to run on pavement or trails? Do I want a course that will give me a qualifying time for Boston? Is it a point-to-point marathon or does it loop back to the start line? Do I prefer to run in the heat, or in conditions more temperate? Do I like the look of the medal? Do I care? Have I ever run this marathon before? Will friends also be running in the marathon?

Is there a perfect marathon? What does it look like? That's part of the fun in this nouveau marathon world. Right now I'm committed to three marathons, but after this is over an exciting world of possibilities opens up.

22

I'M HERE,
WHERE AM I?

Well, that's starting to sound a lot like daydreaming. I know that when these three marathons are over it will be exciting looking for other races to run. It's a bit of a big feeling though, isn't it, since I haven't even successfully run any of the current three on my list yet.

Right now I'm rollicking into Athens, which starts several miles out from its core. Like other major European cities, Athens prides itself on being the 'historical capital of Europe.' With a known history dating back some 3,500 to 6,000 years, depending on which book you read, it probably has more right to this than any other European city. It's got history before history. As one guide book puts it *'Athens was the womb of western civilization.'*

Today that womb has expanded – 3.7 million people compressed into a small amount of real estate. From what I can tell so far, there is little option but to live in medium or high-rise apartment buildings, and drive crazily in small cars along narrow streets. On the wider boulevards Athenians can drive faster, and they do.

I've reached the inner womb now, and stumble up and out of the Akropoli Metro station. If I've read my maps correctly, I'm just metres from the *Hera Hotel*. Like a Morlock I squint and arc my head around in the daylight and discover I've entered another world.

Except for the horns of cars in the background and the odd Moped whipping between my legs it's eerily quiet for being in the centre of a city. Or a womb. I'm surrounded by five to eight storey buildings all squeezed into one another like an accordion; apparently the *God of Spacious Living* never made it to Athens. The streets are about as wide as my hall at home and there's laundry out on many of the miniscule balconies. People across the street from one another may even share the same washing line. This is urban Europe. I sense antiquity. I sense I have no idea which way to go.

I walk in what I think is the rough direction, which turns out to be a very rough wrong direction. I'm already lost. How can that be? I ask an older Athenian woman for directions. We smile a lot. At least I can say *'Hera Hotel'* as I stand there looking pathetic. I move from pathetic to ridiculous as I imitate Riverdance, charading 'Where's-the-Hotel?'.

But much to my surprise, it works. After much laughing, perhaps a precursor to sudden heart failure, my new friend directs me to the hotel, which turns out to be one hundred metres from where we're standing. I've not slept for over 24 hours now, so it's a great feeling to finally arrive at my hotel; it wouldn't matter to me if it was just a cardboard box.

Fortunately Lorne my Travel Agent has a knack for making reservations that are not in cardboard boxes. The Hera Hotel is a three minute walk from the *Gates to the*

Acropolis. Equally, and perhaps more importantly, it's within easy walking distance to the Stadium where we will be picked up by bus to go to the start line in *Marathonas*, and where we will finish. We didn't know this when we booked the hotel, so I'm feeling pretty happy and quite lucky. At the time I was more concerned with getting a room close to the Acropolis.

And why not? Everyone wants to see the Acropolis. In its barest, simplified form it's a huge chunk of flat-top limestone standing all alone. If that's not reason enough to want to see it then you might be enticed to go knowing that it's been the centrepiece of Athens, and Europe, according to Greek mythology and throughout history. It was formed by the gods, has withstood battles and wars, been the haven of different religions, and home and inspiration to some of the greatest thinkers in western civilization. Back in the 5th century BC, the Athenian leader Pericles began the building of the temples and various structures that are still standing on the hill today.

I'll visit the Acropolis at some point in my stay, but already, over the tops of the buildings I can see it's a fairly steep climb to the top. With my paranoia now setting in I decide its best to leave my visit until after the race in case I do some damage to myself.

The hotel, although small, has a sense of grandeur. I feel out of place, but happy to be in place. It's stylish, with a beautiful circular indoor courtyard and a rooftop restaurant. My room is small, but I'm not entertaining any shipping magnates or doing any last minute indoor training so it should be fine. I've paid a bit extra for a view of the Acropolis. Seemed like a good idea at the time. I can see it, from my window, if I stand on the chair and look up to the right, but it's a disappointment really. The 0.0002%

of it I am seeing – that bit of bare rock just jutting out above high-rise apartment buildings to be precise – has scaffolding around it. Still, it is the Acropolis, and I pinch myself. It's hard to believe I'm really here. I have one of those *one-step-and-you're-off-the-edge* European balconies, which looks directly out onto the street. The view to the left is of older medium-rise apartment buildings blurring into the horizon. To the right the street turns and heads up to the Acropolis. I'm in the middle of the middle of the middle of Athens. Certainly not the middle of nowhere.

I lie on my bed and try to get my locational bearings on the map. I notice the Hard Rock Café is close by. I'm in shock. Aside from the obvious but sad connection between rocks and the Acropolis, it seems a Greek tragedy that such businesses are located here. Another tragedy is that my razor has been smashed somehow en route. I now need a razor. I take my first steps into the world of Athens.

For some reason I wander out of the hotel thinking I'll immediately find a store selling razors. Had I known I could've been easily killed in the process, twice, I might have decided to grow a beard instead.

It seems that a green 'cross' light for pedestrians is a poor, perhaps totally incorrect, proxy for suggesting when to cross the roads safely. Perhaps Athenian drivers are colour blind? Fortunately I'm not alone. After soiling my pants making my first crossing, I wait at the next one even though the lights say I can cross. A good call. I watch the couple in front of me defy death by vaulting cars to get to the other side. Running a marathon already seems easy in comparison. Eventually, limiting my street crossings, I manage to find razors, and some *Depends*. Just in case.

Someone speaking Greek asks me for directions when I walk back to the hotel. I'm pleased – no – amazed, they think I look as if I know where I am. I can't help them, of course, but my confidence gets a big boost, even if the language is completely beyond me.

Back at the hotel I strip off, unpack, and have a hot bath. Like the streets, cars, balconies and my escape from death, the bath is small and narrow. I fold myself into it, my knees somewhere over the top of my head. I check to make sure I'm not sitting in the sink by mistake but I see it's over there by my crushed razor.

I've no complaints really. The Hotel is comfortable, the location great, and I'm in one piece – actually I'm almost a ball right now – as I sit in the bath thinking about the race. I can barely keep my eyes open, not having slept at all on the flights, and I'm looking forward to stretching out for many hours as soon as I can get untangled and pull myself out of the tub. Tomorrow I'll stand at the curb for several hours and pay homage to the *God of Traffic*, visit the stadium, register, get my 'commemorative bag' at the Expo, and talk to some runners. Homer's Odyssey sits close by on the night table by the bed. The cover looks good.

**

It's with great relief that I don't wake up until 10am the next morning, but then realise its only 3am back in Ontario. I feel rested though, and anxious to register – I think it's about a five-minute walk away. I can still feel my hip but there's little I can do about it. I review my map again and discover I don't know where I'm going. Registration is in a building nowhere near where I'm staying, or near the Stadium. After a quick breakfast in the hotel's court-yard I get instructions on how to use public transport to get to the registration centre. Registration, it turns out, is a long way away from the hotel. An hour at least, using public transport, assuming I can find it and get on the right route. My time is limited in Athens and using most of it being lost doesn't make much sense. I order a taxi.

Within minutes a taxi driver greets me at the hotel and off we go.

But not for long. We stop about five metres from the hotel. He doesn't know where the place is either. Fortunately another taxi driver does. There's no point in me getting involved in the conversation so I sit in the back of the cab and watch the traffic fly by.

My driver takes off, thinking perhaps I'm about to have a baby any minute, and the hospital is across town. By comparison, walking across the street in Athens is as safe as lying in bed. When the G-force drops and my jowls stop flapping I try to make polite conversation. When did you retire from Formula One racing? Where do you keep the passenger helmets? He speaks as much English as I do Greek, so we sit quietly and enjoy what seems to be our aimless drive around Athens.

We eventually arrive at the Hellinikon Olympic Sports Complex, which we see from the road, and I'm pleased to see the race hasn't been run yet. Registration is out at the old Athens airport. It's a huge, vast complex, but we have no idea how to get to the building itself, and there is a 12ft high wire fence around it. We peel off the road and turn into an obscure dead end. We're still half a kilometre from the building itself, but at least we've reached part of the wire fence. It's definitely not the entrance, but an older Swedish couple are there too, and look like they know what they're doing.

They're about to climb over the fence. My taxi driver calls out, either asking them for instructions or giving guidance on how to avoid getting tangled and caught on the wire. A rapid assessment of the situation in three languages and we're all able to agree that, although small, we still can't lift the car over the fence. We also agree that we've found the Registration site (and Expo). The taxi driver invites the Swedes into the car, 'no charge' he says, and we continue our Expedition.

Bruno has run twenty-eight Stockholm marathons. I'm impressed. I don't think I've run any route twenty-eight times let alone twenty-eight marathons. He and his wife are here because this is THE place where marathons started. They're in their sixties, maybe seventies, but they're lean, healthy looking, bursting with energy, and likely proud owners of hearts that are the equivalent to a twenty-five year old's. We strategise on the best route to take to get to the building without having to climb the fence. Weighing up the various options open to us we decide to 'drive-around-till-we-can-find-a-way-to-get-in.'

It works.

We're greeted by a tight security check-point at what seems to be the main entranceway. Maybe the G-8 countries are meeting there as well. Perhaps Brad and Angelina are registering their children, or adopting some more. Whatever the case, we're stopped at three different checkpoints through the parking lot before finally getting to the building's entrance. If nothing else, perhaps the driver thinks we are more important than we really are. It was a 10-Euro taxi fare, but the entertainment has been worth twice as much. The Swedish couple insist on tipping the driver, or maybe paying for the entertainment, I'm not sure. We're just pleased to finally arrive at the Registration and Expo.

The Hellinikon Olympic Sports Complex is the size of several enormous aircraft hangars glued together, only much, much bigger at the ends and the sides. If the weather is bad on Sunday we'll be able to run the marathon with a couple of loops inside the complex.

Once inside I think I see in the distance what might be the Expo, but it's a mirage. Truth is, with or without binoculars there is barely an Expo to be seen. At the main entrance there are listings on the wall of all registered runners and instructions for obtaining the goody bag, race bib and so on.

Also at the front entrance is a large 'Climate Partner' billboard that reminds us of the CO_2 emissions we have contributed to by travelling to Athens to run the race. That's a downer. I'm feeling guilty now, and thinking I should have swum across the Atlantic. The Climate Partner initiative aims to reduce the ecological footprint of the event, a strange phrase to use in light of the fact that it's a marathon where each of the 3,100 of us will be stamping down anywhere between 30,000 to 50,000 footprints on Sunday morning. We're encouraged to offset our emissions at the corner of the Hall. 'Hall' obviously has a different meaning in Greek, as I could easily fit about 500 Halls in this complex and still have room leftover for a game of rugby.

Over in the distance are a few tables, one of which is giving away energy bars and another is selling official Greek stamps that can have a photo of you running the race. Cool. I purchase these on the assumption that I'll look good enough running in the photo. I'm rolling the dice on that. At another table I can fill out a tourism survey, and at another I can subscribe to the Greek running magazine 'Runner', which looks quite good, except for the fact it's all in Greek. In all, there are about six booths, most of which are not manned by anyone. 'Spartan' would be the word.

A nice touch, though, is the big screen TV's showing the men's and women's 2004 Olympic marathon races. It amazes me how fast, and yet effortless, the elite runners are able to run. I feel healthier just watching. The TV's are beside a refreshment area where we can buy drinks and sandwiches. More importantly, it's a place where runners, family and friends can sit down and talk.

I muster up some courage to ask for a drink at this portable cafe. For some completely unknown reason my mouth starts babbling out a tired smattering of limited High School French as I ask for a cup of coffee. A short, older man, in his seventies I'm guessing, with receding white hair and wearing a stylish burgundy waistcoat looks at me with amusement, barely containing the laughter inside. I'm pretty sure I've not said something right.

I see that the coffee will be prepared over a small gas burner like the one I've used camping. It's about the size of single cup, with the water coming from a large metal cylinder that looks like the housing of an unexploded bomb from World War Two. It doesn't look like I'll be getting a Starbucks coffee. Mr Burgundy Man doesn't speak much, if any, English, or if he does it's on a break right now. In my desire to avoid awkward moments, and with time moving on, I ask instead for water, pointing to the fridge like a two-year old who knows there are cookies in the jar that's on the counter just out of reach. Mr. Burgundy Man has an endearing warm smile and we close the transaction both feeling the better for it. I didn't really want water though; I had my heart set on a coffee.

Like many of the runners I talk to, I was eagerly anticipating the Expo for the memorabilia, clothing, running gear, books, souvenirs, the atmosphere ... this is the home of marathon running after all. I'd checked in the Goody Bag for goodies as soon as I registered. There weren't many goodies in the Goody Bag, especially compared to what I've heard about from other races. A few pamphlets, critical race day information, like the start time and when and where to be picked up, a souvenir towel with the race logo on it, a couple of souvenir pins and race number and bib.

My Expo experience could have been completed in about ten minutes; three minutes if I didn't have to walk so far around the hangar. It makes me think about the symbolism and meaning behind the actual run itself. Maybe that's the point.

Had I known what the Expo would be like ahead of time, I could've rustled up something more substantial for everyone back in my hotel room. Despite it being a very efficient registration process the whole Expo experience hasn't, on this first encounter, been anything like what I'd hoped for. Like the other runners I've spoken to, I'm disappointed.

Organisers could make millions of dollars here by commercially developing the marathon as a product, with various lines of apparel, souvenirs, cups, trophies, photographs, sightseeing tours along the course ... the possibilities are endless. But they clearly don't want to do that. Perhaps we lose sight of participation and celebration of the actual event if we are inundated with material commercial artefacts that are created to do that in a different way, and at a price?

There is little point staying at the Expo unless I want to

watch the entire 2004 Olympic Race on the TV. I've already done three laps of the tables in case I'd missed anything on my first pass by. I walk out of the Complex in search of the public train system that will take me back to the centre of the city. As I have much more time on my hands now, I am willing to get lost.

I walk across the parking lot with two American women, Leona and Kathy. It's a biting cold wind and I feel a little conspicuous wearing my summer shorts while the rest of Athens is poised for hibernation. Leona was a competitive mountain biker who had a serious injury three years ago when she rode into a rock. She suffered a broken back, needed a new shoulder and underwent two years of recovery doing nothing. She decided to get back into activities again and focused on running the marathon. 'Thank god for helmets', she said. Kathy's birthday is on the day of the race, and she's looking to finish and finish well. As we walk over to the train, Athens 5-0 Security intercept us to tell Kathy and Leona to stop taking photographs. We can't understand why, especially having now seen the Expo, but they are clearly serious.

Fortunately the train platform isn't too far away, but still far enough in the sub-zero temperature. The train platform becomes the unofficial Expo site as runners from around the world huddle to keep warm as we wait to be taken back into downtown Athens. I stand shivering and talking to several Americans. Kelly and Chris are two other good friends sharing the Athens marathon experience. Kelly ran the Boston marathon a few months earlier, but six weeks ago seriously injured the cartilage around her knee. Her Doctor has done everything he can and she herself has done as much as possible to ensure there is minimal if any damage to her knee during the race. Kelly's planning 'to finish' and that will be a success regardless of the time she records. Chris is another mountain biker, and not so long ago competed in a 9,000 ft climb through the wilderness. Running is not her thing but says "she'll see how it goes."

We're all here because this is Athens, where it began. But it's more than that – being here is about promises and commitments to ourselves and others. It's to celebrate achievements. It's about sharing experiences with friends, and with strangers – strangers who quickly become friends.

Right now we're all getting friendly cramming into the train and keeping warm. The fact that the train is taking us somewhere we want to go is a bonus. There is a sense of excitement, uncertainty, adventure and sheer cold as we share stories about our own personal marathon paths.

There is something comforting about being with a bunch of people who, like you, aren't one hundred percent certain where they are going. About forty minutes later we get off the train at the right spot, we think, and each go our separate ways. We have exchanged information on the hotels where we're staying, and wished each other luck finding our way back. We've bonded with complete strangers and have already struck a warm familiarity with one another.

I strike it lucky and recognize the road where I was almost killed the previous day. I've an afternoon to explore now, and I'm looking forward to it. I decide to wander aimlessly around Plaka, which is a densely packed area of narrow cobblestone medieval streets filed with tourists at the foot of the Acropolis. Not so long ago Plaka was full of brothels and seedy nightclubs. You don't see any of that today, at least I don't.

I'm one of those day-time tourists for one thing, and my mission now is to find a place for lunch. I'm ambling around Anafiotika, which, to some people, is considered the most beautiful part of Plaka. Directly at the base of the Acropolis, the tiny Anafiotika district was reconstructed in the 1800s by stone masons from Anafi, who had been brought to Athens to build the King's palace. They missed home so much that they decided to recreate it by building what I'm walking through today. It's filled with tacky and not so tacky craft and souvenir stores, restaurants and cafes, enough T-shirts to cloth several African countries, and cats, dogs, tourists and locals alike.

The streets and pathways are narrow and irregular, and there is seldom a sidewalk. Just to keep me on my toes, Mopeds, motorbikes and the occasional car or truck amble through. It's a fantastic atmosphere. It's an ideal spot for lunch.

On a corner at the intersection of five streets is *Milton's* – a new age modern restaurant that seems out of place, but it's the perfect place to sit and watch the Anafiotika world go by. Superb food. With a street front courtyard and three sides of the restaurant all glass I could easily spend the whole afternoon here.

Halfway through lunch a black cat arrives at my table and sits on the chair opposite me. We look at each other and give a courteous smile. Other tables look on as we begin our blind date. Washing behind the ears, and in the parts we never mention – the cat that is – I could tell that this was part of a daily routine. She is seriously tempted by my chicken penne if her facial expression and nose twitching is anything to go by. A few minutes later a large table of American tourists, or rather a table of large Americans, talk about the cat and I making a wonderful couple.

I agree, adding that there is still a lot to learn about one another. The cat jumps off shortly after.

After a wonderful carbohydrate-loaded salad and pasta lunch I get back into serious marathon training and wander all over Plaka. While buying a t-shirt I ask the store owner if she knows of a grocery store nearby. She draws a map, and then, thinking I'll end up in the middle of the Mediterranean Sea, takes me outside and walks with me in the general direction of where her instructions and maps suggest. The least I can do is make an effort to head in the right direction.

The least I could do turns out to be the best I could do. Mopeds and cars – the size of which you could buy at Toys-R-Us – navigate slowly among the tourists. A truck putters by that is almost as big as my fridge except not as tall. Presumably someone is inside it, but it is too low to lean over and look inside. Designed perhaps by the same person who designed my bath.

I wander through Plaka for a couple of hours. It seems that *time* has simply missed Plaka. I'm walking through streets filled with the age of previous centuries.

It's a total surprise when suddenly a beautiful, high end hotel appears in front of me. There's no sign on the street frontage which seems suspicious, so I walk in to look around. A bellboy/ host/ Interpol agent/CIA man in a dark suit approaches me before I get too far, so I deke him and make a play for the reception desk. Up to 170 Euros a night, I'm told. I ask for a brochure because I still don't see any name. It's the Electra Hotel, which strangely is where some of the Americans I'd met on the train had said they were staying.

I leave the hotel under the watchful eye of the Security

Man in Black. I resume my increasingly irrelevant mission to find a grocery store. I stumble quite by accident into a small convenience store and buy some 'Energade,' which looks and feels like Powerade, my drink of choice. I'll fill my plastic bottles with this for the race. I'm about to leave when the waitress from Milton's walks in. I don't know anyone in Athens, but here we meet again. More alarming is the fact that she has the cat, my blind date, in her arms. Without a second thought she puts the cat down in front of me. I don't know why this sort of thing happens.

I eventually emerge onto a street I recognize and head back to the hotel. What had started as a cool day has warmed up. I'm feeling pumped now to go for a short 2-3km run over to the Panathinaikon Olympic Stadium. Besides simply wanting to see it, I need to know exactly where it is and how to get there for the bus pick-up on Race Day.

What a run. Short, but full of drama. Probably one the most surreal runs I've ever had. A run of contrasts, like the city itself. The relentless noise and pollution of the heavy traffic juxtaposed with the beautiful National Gardens, originally planted in 1839 by the first Queen. I doubt she actually did it all by herself, if any, really, but she had over 15,000 plants brought in from Genoa for the Gardens, many of which are still there, despite the air pollution. The gardens were opened to the public in 1923. I'd go there often if I was the public and lived in Athens because of the endless paths that wind past statues, fountains, duck ponds, open areas and promenades.

The National Gardens are over the road from the Temple of Olympic Zeus and Hadrian's Arch. We all know that large scale construction projects have delays, but the Temple may hold the record. It was first commissioned in 515 BC by Pisistratos to honour Zeus, but moreso apparently to keep his subjects busy. Idle hands and so on. Because no one liked him and it was kind of fashionable back then, Pisistratos was overthrown, after which no-one wanted to work on the project because it symbolized his tyranical rule. Fair enough. Centuries later the Roman Emperor Hadrian saw an opportunity for immortality and fame and had the Temple completed within seven years. Only sixteen of the original one hundred and four columns remain, but they are huge; it must surely have been an amazing site when it was finally completed, after almost 700 years of development.

Historians tell us that the Athenians then thanked Hadrian for the completion of the Temple by erecting an arch nearby in AD 131. It's an impressive structure not far from the Acropolis, and right beside Syngrou, a major arterial routeway for traffic. Don't be fooled by the traffic lights and pedestrian signs that say you can cross. If you have failing eyesight or a lack of confidence in your ability to see with any acuity, or cannot burst into a sprint at a seconds notice, ask someone to piggy-back you across this road.

I'm still running though, and heading towards the Panathinaikon Stadium. My mind is partly on the sights I feel very privileged to see, partly on the roads around me, because death is such a final thing, and partly navigating by guess work to get to the Stadium. The biting cold wind has become more prominent again as the sun goes down.

I stand out among the Athenian commuters in my sky blue jacket, running shorts and sky blue cap. Dork, they might be thinking. I kind of feel like one. I finally arrive at the Stadium. There are a few other dorks milling around.

The Panathinaikon Stadium was first built in 330 BC for the first Panathenaic Games. Originally the stadium was made of wood, but Herodes Atticus decided it would be more appropriate constructed of marble. It's a deceivingly huge petal shaped marble stadium which can seat 60,000 spectators. Like much of Athens, over its history it became ruins, and most of the original marble was used for other construction projects over time. When they weren't at war, establishing the cradle of modern western thought, or rejoicing and celebrating the gods, the Athenians kept busy making big rock things.

The Stadium was rebuilt for the first modern Olympics in 1896 and cleaned and restored for the 2004 Olympics. And once again it was the site of the marathon finish.

As I am trying to visualise my completion of the race, a woman in her forties approaches me asking where she can register. She speaks little English – I'm getting used to this now – and the best I could do is point 'a long way away' with my flailing arms, and for her to get a taxi. We smile. Had I tried to explain the security precautions we both would've missed the race.

By now the sun has completely gone and the day is rapidly cooling down. Heady with my glimpse of the stadium and thinking I know where I am, I soon find myself going in the opposite direction through the Gardens, arriving at the Greek Parliament Buildings.

Built in 1842 for King Otto, the first King of Greece, it again is an impressive structure with yet more marble – they are not short of it here. It's been neglected and restored over time – there's a theme emerging – and has also served as a homeless shelter refuge. Today it's where the politicians do their thing, and where tourists assemble to take photos of the Evzones – guards who watch over the Tomb of the Unknown Soldier that rests in front of the buildings. The kilt-wearing soldiers have a ceremonial changing of the guard every hour. I'll catch it next time, perhaps.

I keep moving. A much livelier looking place is calling out to me from over the road – it's the Hotel Grande Bretagne – which the guide books describe as a great place to walk around and feel rich and famous.

Well they don't actually, but they could. It first opened in 1874, so it's had its fair share of history. Crowned kings and princes, Heads of State, Prime Ministers and Ministers, business tycoons, famous writers and artists, actors and actresses, and cold New Zealand marathon runners have now all shared the opulence of this luxurious hotel. If you're looking to spend as much money as possible in Athens in a short amount of time, staying here would be a good place to start.

About 82 million Euros were invested not so long ago to reconstruct the Hotel from top to bottom. There are 290 rooms and 31 suites newly refurbished and redecorated in keeping with the old Grande Bretagne's traditional style. There's also a Presidential Suite and a Royal Suite; I'd like to know the difference between the two, even though I won't be using them today. Still, the hotel's spa looks awfully tempting for someone anticipating that his body is about to take a beating.

I'm fashionably attired in my blue running gear and knobbly knees. I can pass as a wealthy businessman returning from a spell of fresh air to combat the stench of affluence, much of which is sitting in the Piano Bar drinking Manhattans, wine and Scotch. Quite rightly, I'm asked if I'm in the right place as I pause at the bar's entrance.

I ask for the menu and glance casually over the railing looking for Aristotle Onassis. But he's not there because he's dead, so I try to soak up as much ambience as possible before being politely asked to leave.

It turns out to be a Shipping Industry event. I walk around as if Aristotle Onassis *will* actually stand up and wave me over for a drink. He's still dead though, and no-one else is exactly leaping up and down to see me. I catch a glimpse of a glass of New Zealand Cloudy Bay for 9 Euros and realise I have to come back another time. This could be a place to celebrate, hopefully, after my run on Sunday.

It's dark when I finally meander back to the hotel for a plate of vegetables and pasta in the rooftop restaurant. There's a better view of the Acropolis up here. I'm mentally oscillating about my race day strategy. I really want to take my camera on the run, so I devise a way to wrap it around me. It might work, but I'll have to test it first. At this particular moment, with a glass of wine in hand, and more carbo loading, I'm also thinking I should just be pleased with finishing and not worry about trying to break the four-hour margin. But I could change my mind.

At nine o'clock I go to bed, conscious of the fact that it's only 2pm at home in Canada. The marathon books say it's the night before the night before that you should really try to get a good night's sleep. I rationalize that this is the reason I pass again on reading Homer's Odyssey which is staring quietly at me. Tomorrow. Yes, tomorrow I will get into it.

**

I'm relieved when Saturday morning officially arrives.

My night's sleep was a disaster. There was no sleep. I'm lying actually. The one time I did sleep was just before the alarm went off. That was at 5am, which sounds early, I know, but I was trying to simulate race day. I was so tired by then that I couldn't get up. Eventually I got some sleep - about two hours worth. There is little I can do about this but rest my body the best way I can. At least I was horizontal.

I must look tired and useless at breakfast because the waiter shows me the intricacies of the toaster and how to pour milk into my coffee. Thinking that today, surely, I may be missing something at the Expo, I get a taxi out to the Hellinikon Olympic Sports Complex once more. This time, it costs 13 Euros. Maybe the extra 3 Euros is because the driver knows where he's going. Just one checkpoint to get through today.

I enter the complex with high hopes only to discover I'm not missing anything after all. I wander around anyway.

Over in the northern region of the Expo the sponsor, Alpha Bank, is hosting a video-based 'run': you run on the spot on a special platform, and your pace is instantly transmitted to a large video screen on the wall, showing an animated 100-meter sprint. I can't resist, because there's nothing else to do. I'm up against four other runners also looking for something to do at the Expo. The start gun goes off and we are sprinting on the spot as fast as we can. I'm looking at the screen but have no idea which runner I am. It's a close race though. Several seconds later it's over. Someone has won but none of us know who. I'm asked to stay on the platform.

I'm the winner! I've won my first international race. I could do a lap of honour around the hangar, or, more appropriately, run on the spot for 50 seconds. I do neither. Instead of a medal, I receive a vinyl Alpha Bank business carry-bag thingy, which I now have to carry around with me, promoting the bank. I'll use it to store the free muesli bars I keep being given. If the generosity continues I will have enough bars to open a curb-side stall at the Acropolis.

At midday I join the runners' pilgrimage to the unofficial Expo at the train station platform. We all huddle together waiting for the train as the bitterly cold wind slices through us once more. We're getting good at this. Everyone is absolutely thrilled to be in Athens, despite the winter winds I've brought with me, but 'what's with the Expo?' we all ask.

I meet Dave Major from England on the platform. Dave is there with his wife Linda and several running friends. He's in his early forties, of medium build and wrapped sensibly in a winter jacket.

Dave tells me matter-of-factly that this Athens run will be special because it's his 200th marathon. My eyes would have popped out had it not been so cold.

Two hundred?

Plenty to celebrate then. And Linda has just recently completed her 100th marathon in Munich Germany. They and their friends here are all from the 100 Marathon club in the United Kingdom. John just ran The Triple – a marathon on Saturday in England, one on Sunday in Wales and the third in Ireland on Monday. Who are these people? I'm impressed and amazed. I could easily spend a day or so asking questions, but the train doesn't take that long. Dave and I talk all the way back into downtown Athens and talk some more while dodging traffic as we walk towards the Acropolis where they're going sightseeing.

Dave is not a slave to running. He says it's very much a social thing and that running enables him to eat and drink what he wants. There are the obvious health benefits and the travelling is great, but what makes the marathon running special are the people, he says – the club members and friends, and the many people that they meet at the races. Most weekends they seem to be running a marathon somewhere. There is no one 'best' marathon for Dave, but he mentions three that stand out for different reasons: the New York marathon (which he has run three times); the Porta marathon in Portugal; and Death Valley. Those who complete the Death Valley marathon get a rubber turkey instead of a medal. Dave says they are as proud of the turkey as they would be of the medal. He's running above the Arctic Circle in Finland later in the year.

I do the math. Assuming I run 10 marathons each year, I will hit 200 in twenty years. Who knows what Dave will have tucked under his belt by then! He says, 'Yes, he's addicted to running, but there's nothing wrong with that.' He's got a point.

It is fascinating talking to Dave; I'd never realised people ran so many marathons. My understanding of this marathon social movement must have at least doubled in the fifty minutes that I've been talking to Dave.

I realize again that I am walking in the same place where Aristotle, Plato and others once walked. They had to really, because the extremely clean and efficient transit system had yet to be built. But this is not just home to western thought, it is the home of the Olympics and the marathon, and the Greek salad. History is so compressed in one place that the past and present cohabitate, and those that live and visit here are merely flecks in time. I see what look like really, really old rocks, and they are, but I can't describe why or how they actually look old. I ask some of the other runners to describe what an old rock looks like and the best they can come up with is that old rocks look 'really old.' I see holes in the ground and piles of rocks alongside them. I don't know if these are archaeological finds or the sewer being repaired.

I spend most of the afternoon in my hotel room taking it easy and getting my running gear sorted out for the morning. Later in the day I go back to the Hellinikon Olympic Sports Complex, not because I'm obsessed with buildings the size of small African countries, but because it's the Official Opening Ceremony. Fifteen Euros, another taxi driver who knows where he's going and, no checkpoints later, I'm pleased to find hundreds of people now at the Expo.

There may be more non-runners than runners. These include a school choir, children who will walk with flags representing all the countries running, all the children's parents, friends of the children's parents, children of the friends of the children's parents, a brass band, and important official looking people looking official and important. But how important can they really be if there are now no security checkpoints?

There are some very nice touches at this Opening Ceremony. I sit close up front as the speeches begin because I want to see what the important people look like.

The pasta party is to follow immediately after the

speeches. The speeches are tied together with the theme of everyone congratulating everyone else and wishing everyone the best of luck with everything and everything else. The pasta dishes are ready and waiting behind us though, so the speeches seem to take even longer than normal.

Few people are really listening anyway. Most of the speeches are in Greek, mixed with a bit of English interpretation. The most interesting speech is from the delegate representing Nagano, Japan – one of Athens' twinned cities – who speaks to what is now a mass of starving marathoners. I don't grasp the subtleties of his Japanese language, or its translation into Greek, but I think he is congratulating everyone and wishing everyone the best of luck with everything and everything else.

There are four highlights of the speeches. One is the presentation to a family of the naming of a 10km race after someone who had devoted a life to promoting running in Athens. There is the choir singing and the band playing, and, best of all, the march to the front of the ceremony by the children with the flags of the sixty-seven different countries represented.

Some people have already gotten going on the Pasta Party while the speeches were on, but I line up afterwards. Plenty to eat and drink and the quality is first rate. We sit at tables or on the floor, or walk around and talk. But it's getting late, we're miles from anywhere, there's that arctic wind in the dark outside, and we've got to get up early in the morning and run 26.2 miles. It will take quite a while to get to a warm bed. A warm anything, for that matter.

The good news today is that I hear that MP3's and drink

belts are allowed on the run. In some marathons they're not.

The sad news is that I read in the marathon material that Spiro Louis, although now much revered, actually died a poor and lonely man. It's becoming clearer to me that marathon running is not just about the people who run them, because they can. It's about the many of us that think that maybe we can't run marathons. And so to run a marathon is about testing yourself. It's about making yourself accountable to yourself. And to others – which is part of the reason you should tell as many people as possible that you are training to run a marathon. You may seal your fate this way, as a promise is nothing unless you keep it. And when you promise a marathon to yourself and others, you set yourself up for success or failure – it's a powerful motivator.

The Pasta Party starts to wind down as we runners head over to the train platform. I'm getting used to this. It's pitch black as we wait crowded in a small space for the train. The wind is still there, cutting through those on the outer perimeter of our circle. Everyone is in great spirits despite the adversity. Perhaps because of it.

The train arrives and frozen runners from sixty-seven countries storm inside, not caring whether it's the right train to take or not. If there were seats you can't see them now. There is no need to hold on to anything as the train moves because we are more tightly packed than a can of sardines. At least sardines get to lie down. The shorter runners' feet are not touching the floor as we all press together. Some of the shorter runners, like Anna, for example, about to run her first marathon, can barely see over everyone else. There may be Athenians in the train but they are lost in the sea of foreigners, including a sixteen person American Peace Corp currently working in Sophia, Bulgaria, who have come to run the marathon.

Meanwhile, an older couple, Michael and Christine, have *just* arrived from Atlanta, Georgia and gone straight to the Expo. Now freezing in the darkness of Athens, they will look for their hotel, unpack, and get ready to be at the buses at 5am. I'm glad I'm not them, and shudder to think what their next twenty-four hours will feel like.

You don't hear any complaints on the train. That's not because we are tough, finely tuned, seasoned athletes, it's because it's too cold. After about forty minutes of standing on the train with speculations rife as to whether this is the right train or not, there are rumours we could all be receiving Certificates of Accomplishment for successfully enduring the ride and getting back to the cradle of civilization.

The instep of my left foot is painfully throbbing, probably because of the length of time I've been standing in one spot on this train. Or maybe it's an injury sustained in my triumphant 100 metre race earlier.

As we finally disembark my thoughts speed to the prospect of a hot bath in my hotel room. The two previous nights I'd gotten second degree burns from the hot water, and tonight such heat would seem perfect.

It's one of life's mysteries that sometimes the more you want something, the less likely it is that you'll get it. Maybe it's the machinations of the Greek Hot Water God, but the water temperature is somewhere between not-quite-warm and cold. This is cruel. Perhaps, at precisely that same moment, runners from sixty-seven countries are simultaneously filling their baths, only to be victims of the same drama I'm facing. Desperately seeking warmth, maybe they are all now boiling water at the same time, to fill the bath, as I'm doing.

Several kettles of boiling water later, I'm finally in my bath. The bottom of my left foot is really sore and the throbbing is now replaced by a constant pain; it feels like a muscle has been pulled. What irony. Coming all this way to run in the foot race only to be scuppered at the last minute by a foot injury received on the way back from the Opening Ceremony.

My body cries for heat while my left foot needs something cold. I hobble out naked to the fridge and grab a cold can of Mythos Hellenic Lager Beer. Back in the bath I rest my foot above the water-line on the can of Mythos. Hardly precision medical care but it's all I can think to do. It's a long way past 'bed time' but my internal clock is completely wackadoo. I'm sensing a restless, possibly sleepless night, because of the time difference, the pain in my foot, and concerns that I'll sleep through the alarm. On top of that, I've had little sleep over the past few days. No angst then.

At least everything is laid out for the morning. I've flipped again and have decided not to run with my camera. I had bought a small camera case earlier in the day, and tried running with it but it bounced around a lot and the last thing I need on the race is a frustration like that. I compromise, deciding to take the camera to the warm up area so I can take photos there, and also at the end when we pick our gear up.

The last thing I do before lying awake for several hours is go over my race strategy.

**

I wake up well before the alarm that I'd set for 5am. Hallelulah. I don't want to miss this day. I'd finally turned out the light the night before at 1am. I didn't sleep much – another recurring theme for this visit to Athens.

As I fumble around preparing for the marathon I'm thinking of the early morning 30km runs Karen and I did in the summer. They went well and we felt great afterwards. All I ran on then was an energy bar and a cup of coffee. Seemed to work well, so why change now?

Well, I'm in Athens and its 4am right now, for one thing. And I'm hungry right now. Probably because I burned up so many calories tossing and turning through the night.

The hotel kindly prepared a breakfast plate last night – a ham and cheese sandwich, and something that looks like a lemon cake. I've never eaten these foods before running, but the alternative of not eating anything isn't desirable so I'll take my chances. I eat two nut bars as well, and take a chocolate power bar along for the bus ride to the start line at Marathon. I drink some instant coffee as soon as possible to get the bowels all sorted out before I leave for the race. It works. The details are not important, are they?

My left foot feels fine. I'm surprised. No, I'm incredibly relieved. I'd jump up and down with joy, but that would risk injury. I don't get it. I'll tuck away a Mythos beer for future races. My hip pain is barely noticeable. The signs are good.

I'm dressed, packed and ready to go. If I'm tired I don't know it. All my thoughts and actions are now coalescing around this singular event that is about to happen. It's been months on my mind and much of what I've done over the past few weeks has been for this moment. It's a good start to the day. Off I go.

In the hallway I meet a fellow runner, from northern Greece, We wait for the elevator together. We've not met before, but we shake hands like we are cousins who haven't seen each other for a few years but have fond memories, and very sincerely we wish each other the best of luck. The bonding begins. It's that kind of day. It's great. It feels like we're in a movie. These are special moments.

My Greek friend waits in the warm lobby for his friends and I head off to the Panathinaikon Olympic Stadium. It's still dark outside. And cold. That slicing arctic wind has not left the city. I turn the corner and it slices me in half again. Maybe this is to make me feel at home. Ten minutes later I'm crossing the road at the Stadium and step around 5,000 buses that are lined up waiting to take runners to the start line in Marathonas. Runners are climbing into the warmth of the buses. As much as I want the warmth, I want to savour the moment as well. I go to edge of the stadium and take pictures – it's too dark to create any award-winning images but it feels like the thing to do.

Coenraad from South Africa thinks so as well. He offers to take my photo and I reciprocate. We get on the bus together and talk about our running and our strategies for the day, and anything else that comes to mind. There's a lot of nervous energy bouncing around.

Coenraad is in his early thirties, has short blonde hair and looks like a runner. He's currently working in Rotterdam. Sooner than later we start talking about rugby. Today's a bit different as Coenraad and I are very much focused on running, and getting warm on the bus. This is Coenraad's first marathon, although he's run seven half marathons. He started his training because he was getting overweight and sitting on the couch too much. He's hoping to come in under 4 hours. He feels good, but as he says, 'you never know.'

We're in the middle of a massive convoy that's taking all the runners along the route we'll be running. We're starting to see it now as the day emerges from the darkness. We see the twists in the road and the numerous hills we'll be running. They look okay from the bus but I'm sure it will be different after a couple of hours of running.

Depending on your viewpoint the bus ride is either too long or not long enough. No-one really wants to get off when we arrive at the start-line. That's because we can see runners from the earlier buses sprinting for shelter from the wind. At least earlier in Athens there was some shelter and possibly an urban heat island effect, but out here the start-line is desolate and barren. There's nothing here, really, except the start-line and a few buildings. We're on the plains of somewhere and the village of Marathon is over 'there'.

We peel out of the bus like we are having our first sky-diving experience. Once outside, the bitterly cold wind asserts its control again on our actions. It's chaos. Most runners are looking, no, diving for shelter of some sort, and a low level school nearby offers some relief. Other runners dig foxholes in the soccer fields. Some runners walk around like it's a beautiful summer's day, but they're either brain dead or sleep-walking. If I was in Canada I'd call it a cold winter's day.

Sensing hypothermia, frozen and unhappy runners, and maybe even lawsuits, the organizers, who are clad in winter jackets and long trousers, are dispensing see-through garbage bags to everyone. We put them on. These are our wind breakers. Style is out. Warmth is in. And I need to keep it in. I'm dressed in my garbage bag, blue running jacket and jeans, but I know I'll have to give these up soon; they'll be taken to the finish line in the trucks where runners are currently handing over their personal belongings. Some people are wearing gloves. I'm wearing a pair of black socks on my hands. An electronic temperature sign reads 4 degrees. My experience of living in Canadian winters since 1984 suggests that with the wind chill it's at least 10 degrees *below* zero, and likely colder.

I walk around trying to take in as much of the atmosphere as I can, pose for photos in front of the New Zealand flag and take photos of Coenraad in front of his flag. I feel like wearing the flags. The flags were a nice touch at the Opening ceremony and they look good here again at the start of the race. Credit to the organizers for this attention to detail. Coenraad and I shake frozen hands, exchange addresses and wish each other well. We may see each other in the race, who knows.

I find a low wall near the back of the pack at the start-line and crouch down out of the wind, checking to see if there is still blood circulating around my legs. Some people are running – warming up I suppose. Others are standing, waiting, waiting for the race to begin. The Kenyans are likely here now, right up front most likely, possibly having run to the start-line from Athens while the rest of us took the bus. At least they'll be warm.

It's closing in on 8:30 and we're asked to get ready, to

line up for the start at 9am. I look around once more to soak in 'Marathon' but there's really nothing to see – no dramatic landscapes, no massive memorials commemorating 'The Marathon' heck, no 'Marathonas' either, except the scattered low level buildings on the other side of the dried up creek bed and wasteland, where some runners stand relieving themselves for one last time.

We huddle close together. I do a final check. MP3 set up, footpod on, garbage bag off, socks on. I'm ready as I'll ever be. I'm near the back for now so the Kenyans don't suspect anything. They're probably quite warm up front being sheltered by the 3,000 runners behind them.

The gun goes off and so do the Kenyans. The rest of us in our giant huddle creep slowly to the start-line like the Orcs in battle but without the chanting. About three minutes later, just as the blood begins to move more freely around my body, I reach the start-line.

I push my running computer as I cross the start-line to begin my elaborate pacing strategy. I really want to beat four hours now, and figure my best chance is to keep an even pace throughout the run, even if I feel good and could go faster in the first half. My idea is run within myself, as they say.

Nothing happens when I push the button on my running computer. I'm running now, trying not to run into other runners as I keep looking at my watch. I push again. Then again. Then again. Then again. Nothing. Nothing except something unreadable that is only half there.

My watch has been perfect through all my training, and now here, of all places, of all times, it seizes up. I've no idea why, but for the next few minutes I'm pushing the button frantically as if I'm playing a video game. I'm in shock. Disbelief.

After a few minutes I come to terms with the fact that my running computer is not working. I'll be running this race without any sense of time, except when I can ask other runners along the way. How will I pace myself for finishing in less than four hours?

I still keep looking at my watch, though, hoping for a miracle. There isn't one. The cold had kept my mind off the run and now the watch is keeping my mind off the cold.

Meanwhile, I'm actually running. This is it. No time to day-dream. Over the first few kilometres tons of clothing layers are tossed along the roadside by runners. They'll be picked up and used in some way by locals. Some lucky person will have a smart but slightly dirty pair of black socks with a tiny hole in the heel of one of them.

At least the wind is behind us; that should shave a few seconds off the time. The course is flat for the first few kilometres, but we all know the hills are coming.

At the 3km mark the 5-hour pace push bike goes past me. Really?

This is the most depressing sight for me up until now. I speed up but I'm not feeling that great, and the thought that I'm behind a five-hour pace is not sitting well either.

We turn off the main road and head along the road that runs by the tomb of the 192 soldiers who died in the 450 BC Battle of Marathon. If the battle was on a day like today and the Persians were tired, their joints stiff from a few rough nights on the boats, and they had no garbage bags to use, it's little wonder they were routed by the locals. There's not much to see here really, other than the mound, which you get a better view of if you're a bird. I'm not, so I make do with what I see from the roadside.

By the 8km mark I'm starting to finally get in a groove. Mentally I'm much more settled. Once I let go of the fact that the watch isn't coming back, I relax more and start to enjoy things. But there's still 34km left to go.

There's the odd smattering of spectators but generally it's quiet over the relatively flat route. There's a few buildings scattered around but we're basically running in that no-man's-land between rural and urban.

I catch up with four Canadians and we chat for a bit. I'm wearing a Canadian flag (and a New Zealand flag) on the back of my shirt, and so are they. There are pats on our backs and high fives all around, smiles and laughter; everyone's in high spirits.

But I've not seen the five-hour bike again so I'm not feeling too confident. Not much I can do except keep running. My music is great though, and is making a huge difference to me.

At 10km I'm feeling like I just ran 30km. Everything feels heavy and my breathing is laboured. I can't explain it. It's going to be a Yo-Yo run. Within another kilometre I'm feeling good again.

Then ... good news. I don't know where the five-hour bike is, but I've now caught up with the four-hour bike. I've got a new lease on life. I run past, feeling confident. It's a rural stretch of road now for the next couple of kilometres.

We get our first real hill at around 14km, Mati, with an elevation gain of about 100 metres. The hill proves to be no trouble. At the crest of the hill the four-hour bike suddenly appears alongside me. But not for long because he then free-wheels it down the hill and disappears around the corner in a sudden burst of speed.

He's playing with my mind. My primary form of calibration with a sub-4 hour time has just sped by. It's agony but I'm oscillating with the unknown. If I knew I had no chance of a sub 4-hour I wouldn't feel the way I do.

A kilometre later I see the bike ahead of me. As if my life depends on it, I speed up to catch him. Any notion of a steady running pace is out the window. I catch him and run alongside for a while. I ask if his pace flag denotes actual gun time, when the race started, or if it refers to a later time, like me. It's occurred to me that if he's gun time, then it's okay if I'm two or three minutes behind him.

It's a moot point because he doesn't speak English. I can't possibly convey this in any type of charades right now. We smile anyway. He nods but I can't tell if it's a Yes nod or a No nod. Suddenly, as if he's just been bitten in the butt, he speeds away again. Gone.

Other runners are slowing down now. After a while I start to recognise the same faces and we smile and make small talk as we run. But there's much less talk now compared to a few kilometres ago. Everyone around me is quite absorbed and the hills seem to be taking it out of people. I'm guessing, but it looks like a lot of runners started too fast and are now feeling the effects of their faster pace. There's a young couple, perhaps in their early twenties, both of them are short and stocky. I can't work it out completely but it looks as if they're trying some form of Jeff Galloway's run-walk approach, except that when they run they are sprinting. I don't think that's Jeff's intent. It's made worse when the guy trips and falls face-first into the curb. He quickly gets up and starts sprinting again. Just a little blood, not too much.

We're heading more inland now. We've had views of the Mediterranean Sea on our left, which has been good, but as we turn almost on a right angle, from miles twelve to twenty we're gradually gaining elevation. There is much more undulation now.

I'm constantly re-evaluating how I feel and what might be possible with *the Bike* somewhere ahead of me. I think of the different training runs, the fact that this will be over soon no matter how I feel, and that it's absolutely fantastic that I'm here. I feel privileged to be running in such a historic race. I'm getting close to the halfway mark and I'm still going. My finishing time is becoming increasingly unimportant.

At about 21km we start to climb again – and I'm not feeling that great. But I've no major injuries either. Every step is a step closer to finishing. We've passed through small towns and villages like Nea Makri, Agios Andreas, Mati and Pikermi, in which a smattering of people are out waving to us or watching in disbelief. The children are the most fun and they have wonderful smiles. I clap as I pass the spectators. We're now heading into the cityscape proper as we run into the City of Pallini. At 22km I'm really hungry, and decide to take a nutrition bar from a water station. I've never eaten on any training run before. I slowly get halfway through it but can't eat anymore. I spend the next 10 minutes trying not to gag as I attempt to get the fragments of bar digested.

According to another runner I talk to we've been running for about 2-hours and 20 minutes. The Kenyans have probably finished by now and have their legs up resting back at the hotel. I calculate that it may even be possible to finish this race, hop on a jet and fly to New York, in time to still run that marathon on the same day.

At the 22km mark I pass a Greek soldier from the Battle of Marathon. Not a real one, as they're all dead, but a runner who is dressed like one in full armour, complete with spear and shield.

The wind has picked up and we're now running into it, which can't be much fun if you're running with a shield.

I can feel myself slowing a bit now. At about 27 kilometres I come up alongside a fellow New Zealander, with a silver fern on her shirt. Being so far from home we instantly make the connection and start talking as we run. Robyne's feeling a bit dizzy but insists on continuing, and not walking at all. We keep talking about almost anything and everything for about a kilometre or so. You get to know other runners quite well after a while. Robyne's husband is somewhere up ahead apparently, hoping to run a sub 3 ½ hour race.

At a water station Robyne urges me to continue and not wait for her. I ignore her to begin with, but then feel maybe it's best that I continue on for both our sakes. I hope I see Robyne at the finish.

At about 30 km I head up the longest, steepest hill of all, Agia Paraskevi; the good news is that it's mostly a downhill gradient from here to the finish. I run up it probably too hard and then wonder on the downhill if I should've been easier on myself.

Probably. But then I haven't given up yet on seeing the 4-hour bike.

I'm running at a steady pace on the flats once more and everything seems to be functioning as it should. I'm getting tired but that's to be expected.

At 33km an amazing feeling comes over me. Endorphins kicking in, I suspect. I feel fantastic, like I could run fast and forever. Foolishly I start to run tall, increase my stride length, and pick up my speed. I find the 4-bike and continue to race ahead. I'm feeling unstoppable. The sub 4-hour run feels very doable right now. Everything is in synch. I have no feelings of fatigue whatsoever. It's incredible.

We're in the city proper now and the road is lined with spectators cheering us on. I'm caught up in the moment, slapping hands and doing high fives with the spectators. With less than 10km to go I'm feeling like an Olympian.

And then it hits me. Or I hit it. It's a collision. Within seconds nothing is in synch. I'm feeling completely fatigued. My thighs are now giant redwood tree trunks. My feet are cold except for tingling in two toes, and there's a 'Danger Will Rogers' flashing light going off in every internal organ in my body. As if on cue, there's now a series of slow songs playing on my MP3. What seemed a minute ago like a short sprint to the finish now appears like another marathon in front of me. It's not good.

Other runners are passing me now, and, depressingly, so is a man on a 4-hour bike. Moments later I lose sight of him completely.

The struggle continues. I'm barely able to get one foot

in front of the other now without some imminent disaster threatening to occur somewhere else. So much for a sub 4-hour run; I'm wondering if I'll finish at all. I'm refocusing all my thoughts and energy on simply finishing without injuries that could compromise my other marathons. It's hard to believe, but I start running even slower than I had been. A vine growing on a nearby building moves past me.

My mind fills with hundreds of relevant and irrelevant thoughts. What will the finish line look like? Am I close? Why didn't I like broad beans as a child? Is my heart going to shut down? Did the Lone Ranger really have to wear a mask? Did he know Zorro? My toes hurt. Do they? All the while the road is filling up with more and more spectators urging us on. I'm still waving and applauding the spectators, but it's not easy. I'm pretty much in auto-pilot now, or slow motion action replay, hoping to see the stadium soon. I've lost track of how far I still have to run.

From behind me I hear a "How ya doing Malcolm?" It's Robyne, who has had a second wind and has caught up with me. She's looking good; much better than me for sure. It's just what I need.

We soon see signage telling us there's just 2km to go. "Let's go, Malcolm," Robyne says, and we kick into a higher gear for these last remaining kilometres, deciding to run it in together. I didn't know I had a higher gear but with Robyne running with me now I find something from somewhere. It's as if a magician has passed by, noticed how pathetic I looked, and chanted a spell to make my feet and legs move faster. They are dead weights right now. I'm not sure how it's possible but I *speed-up*, using that word very loosely.

We're into the last stretch of the race now, as we run by the American Embassy, the Megaro Mousikis (Music Hall), the Hilton Hotel, and the National Gallery. I don't actually notice them as I'm too busy putting one foot in front of the other and talking to Robyne. My peripheral vision has shut down for the day. I'm doing everything I can to keep moving. Who knows what kind of disaster may have occurred without the support from Robyne.

My confidence is coming back as we talk our way to the finish line. Exhaustion and excitement all in one. And then, suddenly, there it is, we see the Stadium. Adrenalin kicks in. Agonizingly, we run past it for one hundred metres, then turn back sharply again, a 180 degrees turn, which is about 179 degrees more than my body wants to turn. We head back and run into the Stadium for the last 120 metres.

Wow.

This is it. If there's any pain I can't feel it. I want to be running these last metres forever, but at the same time I can't wait to finish. I look up at the Stadium and see hundreds of runners, friends and families sitting there, or lying dead maybe, as we later runners continue to stream in.

I try to look as fresh and energetic as possible. I'd like to think my knees are rising high, my stride smooth and relaxed, my face calm and casual looking. But it's more likely my feet are barely lifting off the soft running surface we're now on and my body is entering its final wobbling phase while I grind and grimace to a halt in just a few metres. Robyne and I are side by side as we look at the clock and cross over the line. My official time is 4:01.

You're kidding!?

We hug each other and perhaps are holding each other up. We congratulate and thank one another for the help we each gave. Robyne goes to find her husband, and I continue through the chute – receive my medal and a certificate, and return the timing chip from my shoe, which thankfully is taken off by someone else as it's too far away for me to reach. I then pick up some food and drinks. I continue around the bottom of the Stadium to get my clothing at the entrance pick-up point and begin my recovery and celebration. I'm not sure, but I may be the fastest ever left-handed New Zealander in the 45-49 age group living in Canada that's ever run the Athens marathon.

On my way around the Stadium I hear my name called out. It's Dave and Linda and their friends who I'd met at the train station a couple of days ago. It's great to see them again. We talk about the run for a bit. They're just as excited about my run as I am. They'll be off celebrating Dave's successful 200th marathon tonight. Amazing. Right now I can't even imagine two of these things let alone two hundred. I'll see much more of Dave and Linda and their friends, Jim and John, in the months ahead, but that's another story.

It's beginning to sink in that I've done it. It wasn't pretty but it wasn't a disaster either. I'm feeling the cold even though it's still sunny, so it's good to get my jacket and jeans on. I walk around to take in the atmosphere and snap some photos.

My legs are no longer tree trunks. They are rocks. Questioning my own mental acuity at this point I decide to walk up the marble steps to the top of the Stadium to take photos. The height of the steps is greater than usual – really, they are, go and see – and it's a struggle going anywhere. Falling backwards is at even odds right now. I'm completely exhausted, but I know if I sit down for too long I may seize up. The problem with going up the steps is I'll have to come down.

At the top I sit down and gaze at my medal. A good looking one that features ancient Greek runners and a blue and white ribbon; the Greek colours. I check my running computer and see it's still frozen. I eat a nutrition bar, but don't enjoy it at all. I can hardly eat it. But the banana tastes much better. Well it would've, only they'd run out when I went through the chute earlier. But I see other runners eating them and they look really happy. I've reached saturation point with the Energade drink, but know I should have some anyway.

Other runners are doing the same thing as me. We're all offering to take photos of one another. For the next hour I'm sitting and hobbling around the Stadium watching the remaining runners come in. It's a wonderful feeling to be consumed by the thought that I've done what I've set out to do. And being here at the finish line sharing the emotions and experiences of the runners as they come in feels like a privilege to me.

I'm getting cold now so I figure it's time to head back to the hotel. It's a long, slow walk – past the National Gardens, the Temple of Olympic Zeus and Hadrian's Arch – but it's a very proud one. People all around are wearing their medals while non-runners – real people – are smiling and congratulating those with medals. My body wants to lie down, or, rather, keel over and become an ancient artefact, but the rest of me wants to walk around all day.

All my remaining energy is used up carrying around a big smile on my face.

I've done it. I've really done it.

Right now the words can't describe the feeling but it's an immense sense of satisfaction and accomplishment. It's mine to keep forever, regardless of whatever else happens in life. Powerful. And for many people now, including me, life changing.

2006 Athens Marathon Results				
Place	**Name**	**Country**	**½ split**	**Finish**
1st	**Henry Tarus**	**Kenya**	**1.08.05**	**2.17.45**
2nd	**Lomol Lopio Paul**	**Kenya**	**1.08.05**	**2.18.07**
3rd	**Habtamu Bekele**	**Ethiopia**	**1.08.07**	**2.20.04**
4th	**Mark Saine**	**Kenya**	**1.08.06**	**2.20.18**
1208th	**Malcolm Anderson**	**New Zealand**	**1.55.08**	**4.01.29**

Note: there were 2,626 finishers.

Running partner after a long run.

Panathinaikon Stadium on left and Temple of Olympian Zeus Centre. Blue Sky above.

Start line Athens Marathon from 26 miles away

ATHENS
·
CLASSIC
·
MARATHON

ALPHA BANK

Length of stride likely to cause problems later in race.

Coenraad Groenewald frozen on the spot. Race day.

Anything to keep warm. Athens Marathon start line.

Dave Major wondering if coat is warm enough. Athens race day.

Marathon race about to begin.

Greek soldier battling the winds, Athens Marathon.

Pheidippides on a warmer day, many years ago.

Acropolis from the entrance to the Panathinaikon Stadium.

The Afterbath

Not long after I get back to my hotel room – seconds actually – I slowly peel off my layers of clothing and gently lower myself onto the bed. A forklift would be handy. Oh ... does that ever feel good! I do a post-mortem of sorts. A quick count confirms all my body parts are still there, but much is not what it used to be.

The end of the second toe of my right foot is throbbing as if a Sumo wrestler has just jumped on it from a balcony. My left knee looks like one of Snow White's dwarves is hiding inside it, Grumpy, most likely. It's beyond throbbing. I'm not sure what that's called. Other than that, there don't appear to be any major injuries. There's no blood either.

I lie on the bed for a bit, simply because I can and it requires no effort, and then ready myself for another bath in my sink. The books recommend a cold bath to soothe the muscles after a run like this, so I follow this advice as best I can. I take a couple of Ibruprofen for the swelling in my knee, and who knows whatever else that's inflamed right now. I grab my new friend, the Mythos Beer, and cans of Coca-Cola, to wrap them up in a towel and place around my knee.

In a wonderful feat of human engineering and dexterity I lower myself into the tub for my cold bath. On the floor beside me is a ham and cheese sandwich and a bar of chocolate I bought at a store on the way back from the stadium. I eat, have a celebratory drink of Orange Fanta, and let the bath do its magic. Everything feels terrific, even the pain.

After a while I move into 'spoil me' mode, and fill the bath with warmer water. My throbbing feet sit out of the water at the end of the tub resting on two cold cans of pop because that's the only place they can go. They're either out like that or my swollen knee is curled wobbling around my head like jelly in order to get my feet in the water, which is physically impossible right now.

Uh-oh. Instant cramp in my left thigh. It's no surprise with me folded into the bath like this. Fortunately the walls are solid, so my left foot does not appear as a new coat rack in the guest room next door as I kick out. It's an awesome front kick all the same. The hotel is well made.

The kick probably hurts but I can't feel it because the cramp is still killing me. I now focus on how to slither my way out of the bath without hurting myself anymore. It's time to get out anyway; I've finished the chocolate. More importantly, I have a massage to go to.

It may be exactly what I need. That's what I tell myself anyway, as I blow my budget on an indulgence I feel almost embarrassed to admit to others that I've had. I'm in trouble if any of my friends read this book. Then again, perhaps a massage should not be seen as an indulgence at all when you've run 42.2 kilometres?

After several hours of putting my clothes on I avoid the stairs, hobble into the elevator and go to meet my taxi for a short and deserved ride back to the Grande Bretagne, looking to be spoilt. I even iron a white shirt for the experience.

I'm a few minutes early so I mingle with people who have lots of money and lots of time to spend it. I have neither. But I'm hoping my 120 Euros for the 55-minute massage will be worth it. Don't do the math – it's a ridiculous amount of money. The Spa is in the richly ornate basement. It's as if I've just come out of the Time Tunnel into the decadence of a Roman Empire at its peak. It's hard to put a price on ambience sometimes.

I'm welcomed by one host and two hostesses, all three dressed like goddesses. I'm handed over to Goddess Three who escorts me to the men's changing room. Five minutes later and without falling I reappear in the waiting room wearing GB Sandals, fresh and fancy throwaway baby blue underwear, and a white robe that is about 5 sizes too small. I'm in a short-sleeve mini-skirt but at least when I breathe in it still wraps around the front.

I'm met by Helga of the SS School of Massage Therapy. She escorts me to our therapy room. Helga is short and thin, but her vice-like grip would have King Kong on his knees begging for mercy. I receive my instructions – well, orders really – to relax. Fearful of the consequences if I don't, I retreat into a blissful world. Mentally at least. It's hard to imagine my body being anything but relaxed after what I've just been through. The massage is effective and efficient, bordering on ruthless, and not a muscle is left unmanipulated.

The massage finishes far too quickly. I'm ordered to sit up. Twice apparently, because I didn't understand the first time. Helga ushers me into another waiting area, leaves and returns with a pot of tea and milk and honey. I could easily drink three pots just to get started but figure that won't look good. Helga returns shortly after to give me a handshake that almost rips my arm off, perhaps to see if my body is still working. She thanks me deeply for the mutually satisfying experience we've shared. I leave the Spa knowing nothing about her, or she about me.

But it was a great massage all the same.

In search of that celebratory Cloudy Bay wine I attempt to infiltrate the Piano Bar once more. No luck this time either, as it's full. But they recommend I try the Bar and Restaurant on the eighth floor.

Why not?

I'm glad I do. It's spectacular. The outside wall is completely glass, and not too far away is the Acropolis – not just a hint of its scaffolding like I have in my hotel room, but all of it to see, and brilliantly lit up. I don't think there can be a better night-time view anywhere in Athens, possibly in all of Europe. I'm feeling so special right now I order that glass of New Zealand Cloudy Bay Sauvignon Blanc.

And dinner? What the heck. How often can I ever do this?

Not too often, judging by the price, but this is a special moment.

I have an uncontrollable urge to eat a huge steak. The first one that appears, by glass two, is so rare it walks off the plate and introduces itself. I ask for another. It's the sort of restaurant where things like this simply don't happen, so I'm hoping the chef doesn't lose his job. I see it's the topic of conversation among the waiters and kitchen staff. The second steak is spot on. So is the third wine, but by now I'm getting really sleepy. I'm totally mesmerized by the view I have but punctuate my gaze every now and then by looking at several people in the restaurant who proudly wear their marathon finishers' medals.

Everything is catching up with me now. I'm tired, my body is ready to shut down and I'm filled with feelings about everything possible. What I really miss right now is someone to share my experiences with. Oh well.

Soon after, I'm back in my hotel room. It's about 10:30pm. Barely able to take my clothes off, I see Homer by the bed looking at me again, so I slink under the covers. Within seconds I fall asleep. It's been a great day.

**

I wake up from a very, very, deep, deep sleep. I lie there motionless, not certain if I feel rested. But clearly, I am awake. I check the clock to find it's12:15am.

12:15am?!

Which means it's 5:15pm in Canada.

Less than two hours sleep. This is not good. I try to go back to sleep but it's hopeless. I turn the TV on and watch one of my favourite actors, Denzel Washington, coach a high school football team to an undefeated season. I'm still wide awake, if not actually pumped from the movie.

There's nothing on after Denzel except CNN.

So I lie there immersing myself in the world's problems and the rehashing of other problems and the world's problems of yesteryear and the potential problems we may face in the world's future, and the problems of reporting on such problems and the problems with not knowing much or knowing too much about such problems then, now and in the years ahead, and fortunately we have CNN to clarify everything for us, and there's always commercial breaks somewhere anyway to make us forget about the problems until more problems pop up while we take a break as they're sneaky like that.

Yet I still don't fall asleep. I'm also hungry, on top of being tired. I think about eating my arm and finally fall asleep at 5am, only to wake up again at 7am. At least I've been horizontal all this time.

Now I'm almost giggly. It's Monday, I've just run a marathon and can still walk. Ahead of me is a complete day off. No running. No internal pressure, angst or thoughts about the upcoming race, no sense of *having* to do anything.

My original plan was to walk around the Acropolis, but with the way my body feels – stiff, sore and heavy – I feel it's best to wait another day for that expedition; Wednesday morning to be precise, before I fly home.

So instead, after a significantly large breakfast I walk, slowly, around Plaka once more, taking photos, buying gifts and eating and drinking whenever I get the urge. I'm still basking in my own glory. Everything I do feels good. I hobble around the national gardens like a ninety-year old street person, not worried if I get lost but really pleased when I emerge by accident directly opposite the Stadium once more. Although emptied of the marathoners it's still a spectacular sight. At lunchtime I return to the hotel and book a three-island tour for the following day. I'm in Greece, so I should try and see some of it.

I see I can also book a half-day trip to Cape Sounion for later today. Apparently it's one of the most impressive ancient ruins this side of Delphi. More importantly it is the Sanctuary of Poseidon, with well-preserved ancient columns sitting on a dramatic cliff facing out over the Aegean Sea. It's a temple constructed in about the 5th Century BC to honour the God of the Sea. I can't resist.

And neither could the famous English poet Lord Byron either. He was captivated by the Temple, and Greece more generally, so much so that in 1810 he etched his name into one of the columns. Byron even refers to the temple in his *Don Juan*. Apparently he and countless others are still on the columns today, but tourists no longer get to see them as the main area is roped off. Ironically, for fear of more graffiti.

It's an hour and a half drive along the coast road to the Cape. I have the back seats of the bus to myself, so I'm able to keep my legs up. It's quite relaxing.

We're going past numerous villages and communities, the beaches of Glyfada, Vouliagmeni and Varzika, and incredibly expensive houses dotted along the way. It costs about 400,000 Euros to have a house built along this coastline. That's not even waterfront property, and the houses are so close that your neighbour can reach through your window from his own kitchen and eat your salad. It will cost another 400,000 if you want to have things like interior walls and floors in your house. A new law also forbids any building that is 300 metres or closer to the shore. The authorities are adamant that they want the sea to be accessible to all Greeks. Fair enough.

When we arrive at the Cape, our guide Hellena attempts to provide a guided walk around the Temple. It doesn't go well. She's visibly upset when, after just 5 minutes, we lose some of our group. No worries really though as they've just gone looking for a washroom. Hellena is a bit on edge today.

Sixteen columns still remain. Some of the columns have fallen and lie on the ground in broken chunks, but even these give you a sense of the enormity of the Temple's engineering. They're huge. I can't help but marvel at the ability of people back then to build such structures. Imposing in our age, they must have been immensely symbolic edifices of power and significance in their time. Poseidon would've been pleased.

About 500 metres below is the Sanctuary of Athena. It's basically a bunch of ancient rubble, but in its time it was a Temple to the Goddess. Several of these were built around what is now Greece. The Sanctuary of Sounion, first mentioned in Homer's *Odyssey*, was where Menelaos stopped during his return from Troy to bury Phrontes Onetorides. If I'd been up on my Homer I would have known this.

The Cape is also a prehistoric site, with proof of human habitation well before the Greeks decided to create myths, souvlaki, ouzo, Mythos beer, and marathons. I'm caught up in the moment and feel compelled to buy a souvenir. I walk around the souvenir store for about twenty minutes until the second hand smoke finally overwhelms me. There's so much to choose from that in the end I choose not to buy anything. Some souvenirs pre-date the Temple. Someone else will need the trinkets, ashtrays, figurines of Goddesses and the Pope much more than I do.

Instead I settle for much needed fresh air and a cup of coffee out on the patio overlooking the Aegean Sea. It's a beautiful tranquil night as the orange sun sets on the horizon. Quite spectacular. By the time we return to Athens it's dark. Hellena tells us it's speculative really, that Byron actually etched his name – maybe someone else wrote his name there instead. We're shattered. It takes the romance out of the story. But history is like that – do we ever really, really, know who wrote what – or did what – when we look back?

It's a good story all the same, which is why it remains in the travel books on Greece; a bit like Pheidippides perhaps. Ultimately we'll believe what we want to believe. I believe it's been a busy day doing as little as possible, perhaps because I'm functioning on two hours of sleep right now. I've got the back seats again – my muscles are still aching and my feet hot and throbbing. Still feels great.

Rolling back along Syngrou I recognise the downtown area and mentally prepare myself for crossing the roads. Hellena gets off with me. I'm comforted knowing she'll make the crossing with me. It's dark, which, along with the two stone columns masquerading as legs that I'm carrying, makes the sprint that much more challenging. Unless we're wearing two full beam headlights and sitting on four wheels there's little chance that drivers are going to stop for us.

Hellena is laughing as we proceed to play real Frogger, running for our lives among cars and motorbikes as the 'Cross' sign beams defiantly. At best, the sign is a general guideline. I don't know why Hellena is laughing. When we make it to the other side I ask if it's always like this – putting your life on the line each time you cross the road? "Yes," she says, in a very casual disconcerting way, "there are many accidents." It just makes the medal I received yesterday for running 42.2 km on the roads into Athens even more special.

The bed looks awfully inviting when I return to my room. Homer is there sitting patiently once more. I bet it's a great book. But it's time to sleep. It's been time to sleep for about four days now.

**

Three hours later and I'm wide awake again. We'll call it what it probably is: morning. On goes the television. I watch the beautiful but complex high school girl win the hearts of everyone as she cheerleads her team to victory and finds the boy of her dreams. It's a heart rending roller coaster of a movie that toys with my emotions throughout. I'm betting they'll break up after a month. It's the sort of thing you watch, it seems, when in Athens, when you are not engrossed in CNN's account of the world's problems. I flip to CNN to find not much has changed in the world except they're wearing different clothing.

With the world in its place and the cheerleader happy with her glowing future, I'm ready to get the day going. After a quick check of my email to make sure my world in North America hasn't imploded, I have some breakfast before heading out for my Three Island Tour.

I've gotten quite attached to cold oats, raisins, walnuts and milk, the great coffee, and the compassionate way the hotel restaurant staff help me make my breakfast. I'm still being shown how to use the toaster, how to pour the milk, things like that. If I don't get the spoon to my mouth in one clean motion someone will emerge to put a bib on me and help me through this phase of breakfast as well.

My tour guide arrives on schedule and escorts me around the corner to the Big Purple Bus #3. "Don't forget," he says, "at the end of the day, if you're not on the #3 you'll end up going somewhere else tonight." No pressure then.

We speed off down Syngrou once more. I've gone back and forth on Syngrou every day except the marathon day; it always looks crazy. We're off to the Port of Piraeus to board the 'Giorgis' for the one-day cruise. It's a spectacular day with blue sky, a full sun and legs that are beginning to feel like legs again.

Because it's at the intersection of Asia, Africa and Europe, Piraeus is the busiest port in the Mediterranean, and the third busiest in the world. Tourists and marathoners like myself make it even busier. It was once an island, once fortified, and once a city unto itself, but these days, like all major urban areas in the world it really feels like part of the sprawling metropolis nearby.

With thousands of years of history it would be a great place to explore. Today though, the important thing to do here is to get off Purple Bus #3 and board the Giorgis. About 200 complete strangers disembark from buses and head for the boat. I make an immediate impression by smashing my head on the door frame as I step onto the boat to enter the lower level indoor dining area. In fairness to myself the height of the doorway was about five feet – most tourists are smaller I suppose – and I wasn't expecting to do the limbo at 8am.

I'm in a daze from the collision but within seconds I'm ushered over to pose for a photo with a girl in traditional Greek costume. I'll be able to purchase this photo later in the day for 5 Euros. It could be a good one, but at this point I'm not sure whether my forehead is bleeding or not.

I take my concussion over to the nearest seat I can find. It turns out I'm not bleeding, but my head is throbbing. In part that's also because the saxophone and synthesizer ensemble has seen the audience and started playing North American and British music from the 1950s. It's a very surreal moment right now, made even more surreal when people get up and start dancing. It's not even 8:30am. We haven't left the port yet. An accordion makes an appearance. It's all on.

We get right into some Greek music. There is much clapping and more dancing. And those who are paid to do this sort of thing are plucking visitors away from their cooked breakfasts and cornflakes and up onto the dance floor. Fortunately I'm cowering in fear at the furthest table from the dance floor, otherwise I would be picked up and whisked into the flurry of movement and clapping. Saxophone Man becomes Tambourine Man; there's no way of knowing what's going to happen next. This could be a New Years Eve Party. If I wasn't awake when I got on the boat I certainly would be now.

I look over the tables while festivities continue and see Jack, the Clydesdale who I'd sat with on the flight from Frankfurt into Athens. I know next to no-one in Athens so it's great to see a familiar face. We get up and say hi and shake hands. Within seconds I'm sitting at his table with Laura and Tracy. They're there with others from Jeff Galloway's tour group with the same idea – to see as much of the place as possible in the limited time available.

Jack and Laura both finished the marathon – Laura's first, despite an ankle injury. Originally Laura was going to run the marathon with another friend, but her friend got married, and then pregnant, so the run became less of an option. Fortunately Tracy decided to come for moral support as well as a holiday, which is soon to be extended by a few days in Crete.

Amidst the dancing and singing, and sometimes even a smattering of silence, we talk about running. Jack tells us about a previous Athens marathon he ran. It was a tough run so by about halfway he decided enough was enough; at the next water station he'd get a bus or taxi back into Athens. He sat on a chair and waited. Then, taking the run-walk approach one step further, he fell asleep. Another member of his tour party woke him up soon after. He told Jack it was unlikely a bus or taxi would be around soon, so why didn't Jack get up and run to the next water station where he was more likely to get a ride. So the two of them ran together. They took it slow and steady. Whenever they got near a Water Station there was always the thought that Jack could go a little bit further to the next one. By the time they reached a Water Station where there was definitely transportation available, Jack said to his friend that he was so close to the finish now he may as well keep running. And so he did, and was able to finish the marathon, with a sleep included, which you don't see too often in the training manuals.

The sun is brilliant this morning as it shines on a Mediterranean Sea made of glass. Our first stop is the island of Poros, which is an hour out of Piraeus. But you could be fooled into thinking it's in the middle of nowhere, the Sea of Nowhere. I'm feeling incredibly spoilt as we gently coast into the harbour. We'll be here for an hour. Poros is about thirty-one square kilometres, which is plenty of room for its 4,000 inhabitants. Even if there were lots to see, which there's not really, we can't see it in the time we have. That's okay though because meandering around the town centre and along the docks by the fishing boats is quite relaxing and enjoyable.

I'm instantly struck by a strong desire to not return to the boat and instead settle down, grow olive trees and a beard, fish, climb the mountains with the sheep, and escape from the rest of the world.

But there's no time for that, not today anyway, so we wander in and out of stores looking for gifts and souvenirs, peer into fishing boats as if we've never seen them before, and simply relax in the sun. I can't find anything worth buying except a bottle of orange Fanta. It's Sounion all over again. The Fanta costs 80 cents, compared to 3 Euros on the boat. If I buy several dozen bottles and sell them on the boat I'll have enough to live on Poros for a few months.

Henry Miller once lived here, but I'm name dropping really. So too did Demosthenes, the famous Greek orator, but he was exiled here (tough life). One day, as legend has it, he poisoned himself when he was surrounded by his enemies. I'd really like to see the Monastery of Zoodochou Pigis because I love the name, but it's too far to drive, or even run, in the time remaining.

We leave Poros after an hour of ambling around thinking life wouldn't be too bad living on this island. But no sooner are we away than we're arriving at our next destination – Hydra. The Greeks had sold me on the concept of island living as soon as we arrived in Poros, but the car-free Hydra is even more spectacular.

As one tourist guide described it, arriving at Hydra is like stepping into a painting. I've got to agree. Cars are banned from Hydra, which is only fifty square kilometres anyway, most of which is either uphill or downhill.

It matters less if you have a donkey because they do all the work for you. Just 3,000 people live on Hydra, but probably just as many donkeys. In the summer Hydra is a haven for contemporary art collectors, many of whom have houses on the island.

The sun is in its full command now and the sea is still made of glass. As we enter into the bay, which is a bit like a Greek amphitheatre, I'm struck by the neo-classical stone buildings virtually stacked upon one another up the mountainsides. I'm struck again as we arrive in port and see the cobblestone laneways and the donkeys. If it's even possible, I'm struck yet again – it's almost hurting now – when I see the slow pace of life that envelopes us as we step off the boat.

We have about an hour and a half here, which I know already is not enough time. I spend about five minutes looking in shops for unique and interesting souvenirs, which again aren't there, and decide enough is enough and disappear into the cobblestone laneways to walk up the mountainside. My stove is wider than some of these laneways. My escape from the docks is the best idea I've had in a long time because in the hour I'm seeing, without being nosey, the everyday life that occurs away from the waterfront; people going about their day, children playing, donkeys discussing the latest news from down the slopes and sniggering as they watch their buddies carrying loads up the lanes. I'm getting an appreciation for life here, and I love it. Maybe there's a touch of Greek in my ancestry. Maybe there is a part of Greece in everyone. There should be.

I almost miss the boat; it's with mixed feelings that I get back in time. Then again, being stranded and missing my flight home tomorrow is probably not the best idea.

Home? It seems so far away – physically, mentally and emotionally. I've got to come back to Hydra one day.

Back on the boat I sit up on top to take in the views, and soak in the sun and the sea breeze. It's one of those moments that I want to last forever, but at the same time I can't wait to visit the next island.

And eventually we do, only this time it's not just a stroll around the waterfront. We've arrived on the island of Aegina. Aegina is only forty minutes away from Piraeus, but it feels like the other islands – almost a step back in time, even though it is much more developed than either Poros or Hydra. With 10,000 people it has much more of a busy feel about it in its town centre, creatively called Aegina Town. For all that, it still has that endearing island getaway charm about it. There are cafes and tavernas all around the port, itself a picture perfect image with fishing boats gently rocking in motion with the sea.

We're placed in buses and taken to the Monastery of St. Nektarios about six kilometres inland from the harbour, in the middle of the island. Monasteries are not the sort of things that put the skip in my step, but the Monastery of St. Nektarios is impressive.

It's an imposing complex that was built between 1904-1910 on top of the ruins of a previous Byzantine monastery. The main church is located at the front of the monastery. It's a large bronze and white structure, one of the largest places of Greek Orthodox worship in the Balkans region.

Saint Nektarios, the protector saint of Aegina, helped to build this monastery himself. There have been over two thousand miracles attributed to the intervention of St.

Nectarios. I wish I knew this earlier as I would've quite liked a sub 3-hour marathon the other day.

The story goes that even after he died in 1920, St. Nektarios continued to perform miracles. The first occurred right out of the blocks in the hospital room when he died. A hospital nurse and a nun immediately began to change his clothes. They threw his undershirt on the next bed. Lying in this bed was a man who was paralysed. Instantly, it's said, he jumped out of bed praising God for his miraculous healing. St. Nektarios body remained completely intact for twenty years after his death and emitted a 'magnificent fragrance' over this time. In 1961, the Ecumenical Patriarch of Constantinople blessed St. Nektarios with a proclamation of Sainthood.

Again, I'm struck by the fact that I'm here experiencing this (although not the miracles, at least not that I'm aware of), and I feel privileged to be doing so. I've almost forgotten that I ran the Athens marathon. By now many of us are getting to know one another on the tour and enjoying this experience together. It all finishes too soon, even for non-monastic enthusiasts like myself. I'm sitting on the bus again, this time with Susan, a sports instructor at a school in Lafayette, Florida. We've both been fully consumed by the day. Tours like this inspire her in her work and life more generally, and the fact that she can share the experiences with children when she returns makes the trip even more special.

Back at the port we're given half an hour to wander around and, well, who knows, look at souvenirs perhaps, all of which we've seen before. Nothing leaps out and says "buy me" as a unique memory of this island. It's okay, I'm getting used to this. I wander anyway; it's just fun. I bump into others from the boat. By now we're greeting each other like old friends.

Our instructions are to meet at a small restaurant near the water. Eventually we all arrive and clamber around a few tables. There's a range of drinkers in our group; From those who abstain for whatever reason to those that drink because there will be no tomorrow. One day these people will say "see, told you so," but for now, most of us are somewhere between abstinence and over-indulgence – we have a glass or two of wine or some other special island concoction – enough to be laughing at jokes we don't get, talking to people who don't understand what we're saying, and making the most out of the night.

We've barely noticed, but it's night-time now. How quickly the day descends into dusk. Again, it's too soon, but we have to go back to the boat. That's when the party really begins.

I sit with Jack, Laura, Tracy and a few others who we've got to meet over the day. It's a replay of the early morning arrival on the boat, only this time we are more awake, more sun burnt, have taken on some alcohol and have gotten to know one another. The live music is all go again and people are dancing. Others are watching, drinking and talking loudly or screaming to one another over the sounds coming from the dance floor. Some folks are trying some innovative and possibly dangerous dance moves likely not seen before. It's a good time.

There are some attempts to get me on the dance floor but I explain that my World War Two wounds are playing up again, along with the debilitating injuries suffered in the marathon. I use the "I don't know how" line on occasion, but I've got to be careful with that one as it can work against me – all of a sudden I could be receiving instructions on how to line dance, for example. There's more chance I'll crack a sub 2-hour marathon than line dance.

And then, much to everyone's disappointment, we arrive back in Piraeus.

We're still making new friends even as we leave the boat and find our designated buses. I meet a fellow New Zealander in the parking lot who is now living in the United States. We exchange our life stories in about one minute. There is the promise of meeting up some time in North America but come morning we will likely be distant memories. But if, for some strange reason, you are reading this, please get in touch.

I find my Big Purple Bus # 3, which eventually takes me back down Syngrou and drops me off. I don't have to cross the road, which is a huge, perhaps life-saving, relief.

It's been a great soul-cleansing day. A pang of guilt presents itself when I notice Homer now collecting dust beside my bed, but I quickly get over it. I lie in bed wondering what crazy hour I'll wake up at. But I don't mind any more. Tomorrow I'm off home. Before I leave though, I'll spend the morning wandering around the Acropolis.

**

As I could've predicted I wake up early, although not as early as previous mornings. They've changed their clothes again on CNN, which is comforting, and it seems the world is pretty much as I left it and awaiting my return to North America.

I pack in preparation for a quick departure after my visit to the Acropolis. It seems I've accumulated enough t-shirts to last the rest of my life, along with several other gifts and souvenirs. It's a tight squeeze.

I'm out of the hotel as soon as I can to maximise the time at the Acropolis. It's a crisp, clear sunny morning. Within minutes I'm at the gates. It should be a simple thing to pay entrance fees but two ticket ladies and I are having considerable trouble communicating about instructions and getting the right fee sorted out. What transpires in those five minutes is unexplainable, but it involves me being asked to go through a different booth, right next door, waiting, no, entering, no, waiting, money being exchanged, passing papers back and forth, conversations which I am involved in but have no idea what they're about, and some hand signals to indicate, finally, I am free to enter. I think. I receive a smile in there somewhere but it's likely meant for someone else now that I think about it.

It's all well worth it though. I'm walking through antiquity, and have a strong yearning to be experiencing this with someone else. It's truly inspiring.

The Acropolis sits defiantly on top of several hundred souvenir stores, replica pottery outlets and various cultural symbols and gods showcased in chess-sets and backgammon. We tourists keep buying these things, not because of the quality but because of what it means to us – our experiences. My $5 vase will have as much meaning to me as the $1,000 vase to someone else.

It's hard not to think of Athens without thinking of the Acropolis. The Acropolis, meaning "High City", The "Sacred Rock", stands about 150 metres (490 ft) above sea level. A more accurate timeless definition would be "Rock of Reconstruction." Today, as I begin my ascent, it's feeling a lot further above sea level than 150 metres. I can feel my marathon legs. Solid as, well, rocks, really.

There have been artefacts upon artefacts discovered at the Acropolis that go back to a few thousand years. Maybe I'll find some today? These days it is a UNESCO World Heritage site. The Guidebooks struggle to sort out how much information they can squeeze into a few paragraphs.

I'm not going to attempt any sort of synthesis of the Acropolyctic history here, and I think I just invented a word, but some things are worth noting all the same. Like, for example, the continual reconstruction of the site, complete with layers of scaffolding that could be an architectural achievement in itself. Who knows, some of the scaffolding could have been here for decades and no-one's really noticed. Actually, because of the smog eroding the marble works there have been international teams at the Site for the past twenty years trying to restore and protect what remains. That means, strangely, that the scaffolding is almost permanent, like the cranes and equipment that also look as if they're permanent residents on the site. Conceivably, a labourer could begin and end his career doing nothing but working on the Acropolis. Hundreds of years from now future writers will comment on what appears to be remnants of scaffolding around the Acropolis, which will then be placed in museums, and the strange crane-like artefacts, as they too construct and deconstruct the physical and historical site.

None of which has anything to do with running marathons.

The Acropolis has had thousands of years of continual use as a defensive citadel, Seat of Royalty, burial ground, administrative hub, and religious center, not to mention colourful moments when it's been invaded variously by Spartans, Persians, Nazis, Ottomans, Tourists and Stiff Legged Marathoners...oh, and those other moments when it's been recognised as the cultural hub of the world. It's been a great place to build, demolish, build again, demolish, and, well you get the idea, new and bigger and better temples.

One guidebook describes the Acropolis temples as "the greatest achievement of classical Greece, combining mathematical proportion with a glorious aesthetic to create an effect both human and sublime."

Well, after the Happy Dances subsided following the victory over the Persians at Marathon the powers that be decided to erect what's known as the Old Parthenon. So they cleared the south part of the rock of older archaeological relics and treasures, and made it level by adding 8,000 two-ton blocks of limestone. Imagine.

In other words, out with the old and in with the new; we still do that today. They never managed to finish it because the Persians came back a few years later in 480 BC, got to Athens this time, and got their own demolition teams busy. The Athenians returned, of course, and a new era of temple building and worship ensued once more.

And so it went for many a year afterwards, the prevalent theme being renewal. We can see some of the artefacts from these ancient years in the Acropolis museum, which is where I'm heading as I begin my trek around the base of the Rock.

Along my way I'm entranced by the scale and scope of the Odeon of Herodes Atticus and the Theatre of Dionysus. Especially the Odeon, built in AD 161 by Herodes Atticus in memory of his wife. Looking down into it from above, with a touch of vertigo, I'm looking over a seating capacity of 5,000. It's a magnificent amphitheatre in which concerts are still performed today, especially during the Athens Festival which runs through the summer. At one time, hundreds of years ago in 5th century BC, the Theatre of Dionysus, home of Greek Tragedy, could house 15,000-17,000 theatregoers; it's where the tragedies of Sophocles and Euripides were born, as were the comedies of Aristophanes.

I slowly meander my way around and up to the top of the Acropolis. As it's so early in the day I'm not fighting hordes of tourists as many people have told me about, so it's doubly enjoyable. My legs know they're getting a good work-out, but really, if you're of average fitness the Acropolis is not a problem. It seems almost every piece of rock that is standing was once, and still is I suppose, a major temple or something with significance. Close to the top I enter through the Propylaeum, essentially a gate, built in 437 BC but never finished due to the Peloponnesian Wars. Great views, though, and it alludes to the grandeur that was once present here. It teasingly sits at a point where you can't see the Parthenon ahead. But I can see the scaffolding and cranes all around. And the construction workers, some of whom look as if they're just a few years away from becoming national treasures themselves.

The Temple of Athena Nike, for example, built in 424 BC to honour the Goddess of Victory, was demolished in 1686 to make way for gun emplacements. Its reconstruction, most recently begun in 2000, is because two previous reconstructions in the 1830s and 1930s were done wrong. I doubt the Acropolis will ever be free of reconstruction.

I'm at the top now and directly in front of the Parthenon – it's surrounded by clear blue skies, which, given the publicity surrounding air pollution in Athens, should be something I take pictures of just to prove it really happens.

Originally started in 447 BC to honour the Goddess Athena, it was completed in just nine years, which even in those days was seen as a miracle. Even moreso because it was done right the first time. Besides its sheer physical presence, and impressive project management, it's famous for the advanced mathematical calculations – a ratio-based geometrical system of proportion which has every column bulge a little and lean slightly a few degrees inward. Mathematicians are still preoccupied with this today. So am I, but not for too long. I can't actually go in and around the columns as it's cordoned off for reconstruction, but it's as impressive up front and personal as it is from miles away and below.

Eventually I make my way to the Acropolis Museum, which is tucked away almost on the edge of the rock. With hardly anyone around it's a perfect time to look at the treasures within. A few words here can't adequately describe my sense of awe as I walk through the various halls, although I can imagine how, at this point, some people might be pleased to simply do a quick fly-by, colliding with hundreds of other tourists with their heads already full of antiquity.

There's many amazing facts, but the one that hits me as important is the fact that the Acropolis had been plundered significantly by antiquities collectors for many decades, but especially in the 1800s. National Greek treasures sit in other museums and collections around the world, including the British Museum, which just doesn't seem right. So some treasures displayed are, in fact, replicas of originals that live somewhere else. Why don't they just switch the replicas with the originals? If feasible it's conceivable that the entire mountaintop would have been taken away as well – perhaps to make a theme park somewhere that could do a better job of getting the tourist dollar.

I could easily spend a whole day up here wandering around but I'm increasingly conscious of the fact that I have a plane to catch and there's plenty of things to be done between now and then.

I'm glad I waited until the last morning to see the Acropolis because it's felt relaxed and my mind hasn't wandered off thinking I may have an injury before the race. Even though I can feel my leg muscles today, they're definitely in much better condition than they were the previous two days.

I've cut things pretty tight in order to spend as much time as possible at the Acropolis. I bid farewell to the Hera Hotel and plummet into the depths of the Metro. Fortunately I get on the right train and off I go to the airport. As the train moves into the rural area beyond the city limits I sit there looking out the window with that WOW feeling – that everything has gone so smoothly when something could easily have gone wrong. As if on cue, a man the size of a Clydesdale Runner but not as svelte looking, places himself directly in front of me.

It's Hemi from Athens Metro SS, brother of Helga perhaps. He's in no mood for anything other than death to all foreigners or left-handed New Zealanders who don't understand Greek. It was always a short-coming of my schooling days. It's a simple request though – he wants to see my ticket. I give him my Athens free transit pass that I received with my marathon race package – a nice touch for the event. What I don't realize, but he points out, he's getting quite excited now, is that the pass expired yesterday.

I must pay him the fine now.

Now.

"How much?"

He doesn't reply immediately, partly because he's writing furiously on what becomes my pink ticket. Partly, also, I suspect, because his English is about as good as my Greek.

"Fifty Euros."

"Fifty Euros!!! You're kidding," I say. Which means nothing to Hemi. I try to explain the misunderstanding and ask if I could just pay the fare instead. And by the way, I don't have fifty Euros on me and I'm leaving the country in less than two hours.

At this point he's getting pissed off with me and I'm wondering if I'll be locked up somewhere. In very fragmented English – and I'm being generous – he says I must see the Metro officials at the airport and pay it; he's sounding as if I won't be leaving for anywhere until the fine is paid. He hands me the ticket and points at it, muttering something about something; I haven't a clue what he's trying to tell me. There is not a speck of English on the ticket. In a more jovial time it could've been a fun charades moment, but I doubt Hemi ever plays charades or any games or fun things for that matter.

In the quickly decreasing time available at the airport I resume marathon training running around the place looking to pay this pink thing. Two airlines, two information booths, two wrong directions, two stores and the police station in the basement later and I'm still no closer to solving the problem. The moments spent with the police are very special though. It's a bit intimidating sitting there with five officers talking about me and laughing. I've seen movies that start like this and turn into nightmare prison cells for the lead actor.

I'm no further ahead. Meanwhile, my departure time is quickly approaching. It occurs to me that maybe I should go back to the train station to see if I can find someone there. I'm becoming a deodorant commercial running around this airport.

I find someone! They're wearing a Metro jacket so it's official. And they speak English. "Don't worry," he says. I can pay it when I get back to Canada, and I will be able to get on my flight. I'd change my underwear but there's no time right now because I may miss my flight. Back I run. Thank goodness for the 42.2km training the other day.

I make it, just in time. I slink into my seat relieved and exhausted, wondering if this is deserving of a medal in its own right. Off to Frankfurt first, then London and home. Traveling home should be much simpler now.

**

It should be. The thing with travel though is that plans and thoughts can change in an instant. I wander once more through Frankfurt's airport, which, like last week, maintains its very sterile image. London, however, is filled with surprises.

I discover I have to change terminals at Heathrow. I'm still not quite myself from the loneliness of the long distance running at Athens Airport, and now I have to take on another epic challenge. Time is not on my side either. Wish I was wearing my Asics.

But first, as I exit the arrival gate I'm told by an elderly British gentleman who looks like Benny Hill (well, a Heathrow staff member about 80 years old, and wearing an elderly British accent), that, due to a new policy, I will only be allowed one carry-on bag and not two, which is the opposite to what I was told and allowed to do in Athens. I have two gob-smacked, jam-packed, carry-on bags that I must now compress into one.

I point out to Benny that there is no way the Law of Physics will permit the mass of the two bags to magically evaporate into one. We scratch our heads for a while, our own, but not for too long because I'm under a bit of a time crunch you see. Benny's got a plan. "Do I have a computer in there?" he says. "By Jove I do," says I. Benny says I can take it out and carry it on separately. It just might work.

It does, and we are just seconds away from doing cartwheels of excitement. But there's no time for that – not only do I have to get to the other terminal, I've got to find it.

I'm running now, wondering if one day they will host a

real marathon event in the halls of Heathrow. Novel, but it would bring back desperate sad memories for many people. About five hours later, it seems, I arrive at the other terminal. A slight exaggeration perhaps, but tell that to my body. I've made really good time – panic will do that sometimes. I ease my way through security and feel I've finally arrived. I just have to get to Gate 28 now. Phew.

I can amble around for a bit. Relieved, sweating still. There's a small room that has computers with Internet access so I sit at one for a while and catch up with my work world and friends. But I'm so conscious of the craziness I just went through I decide it's better that I get to the gate as soon as possible. Smart move really because as I head into the unknown hallways once more I see a sign that tells me it will take ten minutes to walk to my gate.

The pride I feel knowing that I've almost made it as I walk into the abyss starts to diminish for some reason. I can't work out why. Something is not right. I keep walking but I'm getting worried, right up until the moment when I panic realising that I don't have my computer with me anymore. I've lost my computer in Heathrow Airport.

If I keep walking I'll get to my gate just in time, and make my flight, but my computer – with all my work, photographs, correspondence and music etc - will remain in England. If I turn around I will accept the challenge of trying to find my computer in Heathrow, and risk, big time, missing my flight.

I'm running again, getting used to this, retracing my steps as best I can remember. Where did I leave it? A store? On a seat somewhere? At the computers? Even if I did, what are the odds it's still there? Maybe Athens Metro 5-0 got in touch with Interpol who have confiscated my computer in lieu of the 50 Euros fine? The Athens marathon seems a very distant memory right now.

My laptop is nowhere to be seen. In one last desperate hope I run around to the security section. Good grief! There it is! Sitting on a shelf along the side wall. I've no recollection of even being there, but who cares, there it is. Before I pick it up I look around to see if it's some sort of trap. I'm quite conscious of the fact it's going to look strange that someone walks up to a computer, grabs it, and runs away. So I walk up to it as if I always place my computer a huge distance away from myself. I sort of pat it as if to say, yep, you're where I left you, like usual, and then I quietly walk away to a point where I think if anyone is watching me they would have stopped by now. I turn into Eric Liddel, put my head up and chest out, and race away to my flight. I'm horribly late for my flight, I think I've missed it, but at least I have my computer once more, and at least I know where my gate is.

I arrive at the gate absolutely knackered. It's as I left it. No-one has boarded. In fact no-one boards the plane for another twenty minutes. Which is okay, because it gives me a chance to take my shirt off and squeeze the sweat out.

This time, I figure, it finally has to be really simple from here. Surely.

Surely Yes, and it is. The flight is spectacularly uneventful which suits me fine. Enough excitement and miles run for one day. By the time I get to Toronto the day has pretty much gone, but I still have to drive three hours home. It takes longer, because that's the sort of day it's been, due to the London pea soup fog enveloping the 401 freeway. Regardless, it still feels really good to be home.

Even though I don't get in the house until about 4:30am.

I'm up around 6am so I can get some work finished and send a report away. One day I will catch up on some sleep.

My next race is the Cayman Islands marathon on December 3rd. It's likely to be warmer, with fewer Metro officials and a smaller airport.

I hope.

Runners at finish line, Athens Marathon.

Runners fimishing the Athens Marathon.

What author's watch looks like at minor 10° Celsius..

John Dawson, Linda Major and Jim Mundy in Athens on a clear day.

Athens legs
before
Athens Marathon.

Athens legs
after Athens
Marathon.

Coming into
Hydra, Greece.

Dave Major and
friends celebrating
his 200 in Athens.

Hydra, Greece.
Thin donkeys only.

Author immediately after receiving concussion.

Metro
Infraction
#4871

ΑΤΤΙΚΟ ΜΕΤΡΟ
ΕΤΑΙΡΕΙΑ ΛΕΙΤΟΥΡΓΙΑΣ Α.Ε.

ΣΕΙΡΑ 19
No. 4871

ΠΡΑΞΗ ΒΕΒΑΙΩΣΗΣ ΠΑΡΑΒΑΣΗΣ ΚΑΙ ΕΠΙΒΟΛΗΣ ΠΡΟΣΤΙΜΟΥ
(Ν. 1214/1981, 2207/1994, 2669/1998)

ALPHA BANK

785

ATHENS CLASSIC MARATHON 2006

23

WHY IS THERE A TRANSFORMATION?

In the 1970s the running boom was exemplified in the marathon world by predominantly male runners pounding the streets in attempts to run their fastest times possible. They pushed their bodies as hard as they could. Although some were gifted and almost genetically programmed to run these wild distances, for most runners, the distance extolled suffering and hardship making it a sport only very few could entertain as possible.

We are currently witnessing the transformation of the marathon experience. The social movement to get moving is transformational at the individual level – people like myself, the organizational level – the various marathon events, and at the commercial level – a point I'll come back to shortly. The inter-relationship of the three levels, all of which are enabled by the Internet, is contributing to marathon running becoming mainstream, not just in North America but in Europe and many other regions in the world.

Why? Kansas City Star reporter John Hanc talked to Amby Burfoot last year about marathons in the mainstream. Amby, the former Boston marathon winner and now one of the best writers and most engaging speakers on the sport, observed that the marathon has become "Everyman's Everest". Run-walk programs in particular, have made this possible.

Joe Henderson, who has assisted thousands of runners in their marathon experience and who has written numerous books on marathon running over the decades, told me the other day that he thinks the biggest reason for the current growth is "that it became okay to be slow". The race data support this – they show that median finishing times have dramatically increased, and so also have cut-off times. Joe gave the example of a five-hour finish – it was once rare but is now quite common. Back in 1997 Joe was quoted as saying "These new marathoners don't want to kill themselves for a fast time...they just want to finish. Twenty years ago, people were training for fast running. Now, they are more relaxed."

Other key important factors for the recent growth, he said, have been the acceptance of walk breaks (which has made the 42.2km distance within reach of many more people), the rise of group training (which often occurs through running with a charity organization), and the huge increase in the number of women running marathons. In some events the majority of runners are women.

A major proponent of the walking break phenomenon is Jeff Galloway. Jeff is a former US Olympian who has been group training since 1978. He has trained over 200,000 individuals over the years, with particular focus on running with walking breaks, and minimising injuries.

He created the Galloway RUN-WALK-RUN™ method. He's also an inspirational speaker with over 200 running and fitness sessions each year. He himself has run over 100 marathons. When we talked over the telephone the other day, I asked him about the growth.

Jeff feels we're actually at the beginning of the curve; that there's going to be ever-increasing numbers of new marathoners coming into the sport. His fundamental training philosophy is to work with people so they can run injury-free, enjoy every run, run faster when they want to, and conceivably, run until they're a hundred years old (the subject of his new book). Walking breaks are crucial, he explained, especially as we get older. We're not putting relentless stress on our bodies by doing so. Walking breaks help to reduce injury. Jeff was quoted in *Marathon and Beyond* in 1997 as saying "It is my belief that we were not designed to run very long distances continuously, but we were designed to go almost indefinitely by running and walking when we put the walking breaks in early and often."

Equally significant, and perhaps a surprise to many people, is the fact that runners are recording faster finishing times when they include walking. The doors have opened up for everyone to enjoy the benefits of training and running a marathon. In a health-conscious age of baby boomers who look to improve their fitness, health and well-being, the 'marathon' has become a very viable place to focus energy. Add to that the multi-faceted social side of the sport and it's no wonder Jeff considers we're only at the beginning of the curve.

Other legends in the distance running world echo these views. Although they're both dead at the moment the New Zealander Arthur Lydiard, who revolutionised distance training and coached several New Zealanders to Olympic gold in the 1960s, observed that, "You can never run too slowly. But you can run too fast." The famous influential German doctor, Ernst van Aaken, a trainer and advocate of women's distance running, wrote, "Run daily; run slowly; don't eat like a pig." Encouraging words of wisdom.

It may come back quite simply to what you, the runner, want to achieve with your running. Although there are marathon traditionalists who insist on never walking, and others who will walk only if they have hit the wall or their limbs are like silly putty, there are increasing numbers of runners who now strategically incorporate phases of walking, even just a minute every few minutes or a minute every mile, into their marathon races. If you're running ultra distances, unless you are not quite human, as some top ultra-runners may make you think, the walking 'breaks' are a must.

Another explanation for this new social movement could be that some of the older baby boomers are also the same people who were involved in the running boom of the 1970s. Now with their families raised they may be coming back to the sport, seeking bigger goals – longer distances perhaps, and are introducing their families into the sport as well.

I asked Bill Rogers why he thought there had been a growth in the number of marathon runners. Bill is an icon of marathon running. Bill won the Boston and New York marathons four times each in the mid to late 1970s. He ran for the US in the 1976 Olympics, and was ranked by *Track & Field News* as the #1 marathoner in the world in 1975, 1977 and 1979. He won 22 of the 59 marathons he ran, with 28 marathons under 2:15 (with a PB of an astonishing 2:09). He still holds the US record at 5 different distances. At 51 years of age he ran the half marathon in 1:11.

Bill said he thinks the growth in participation has been fuelled by the "unique person to person quality of our sport" - friends are examples to other friends. "People discover how they feel after beginning a running/walking/fitness program; that is, compared to their inactive life style; they feel great!"

Unlike our jobs, and healthcare, Bill said, "Marathons are a quest, and in the achieving one does something that can't be taken from you." The other observation he made is that there is a growing desire, and indeed, need, from corporate United States to encourage healthier lifestyles and activities as a way of reducing health care costs. This is a point on which John Hughes, Race Director for the Disney marathon weekend, concurs. John said people are taking more control of their own health. The media is also covering marathon running much more as the number of participants increases, which in turn further fuels the interest in the sport. When Oprah Winfrey runs a marathon, people watch and listen.

Other countries such as China and India are witnessing a growing middle socio-economic class and it is in this bracket that running is becoming increasingly popular. So we can expect to see even further growth in marathon running internationally.

There is a ripple effect when the older and the newer runners have positive experiences running marathons. They talk about the experience with friends and families and encourage others to join them. They may encourage their sons and daughters to get involved. This sharing of positive experiences, coupled with the large number of extremely well run marathons – that is, marathons that pay attention to detail to maximise your marathon experience, like great pasta dinners, social interaction, the goodie bags, excellent logistical instructions, fashionable event shirts (free with registration) and other merchandise, and plenty of drinks, has further stimulated the social movement.

The social movement has been propelled by a growing social consciousness. Thousands of runners raise money for various charities around the world by taking part in marathons. As we'll see later, this has had enormous implications for runners, the marathon events themselves, individuals requiring health care and social services, and volunteer and not-for-profit organizations around the world. There are a large number of organizations that, in exchange for individuals raising money for them, provide training programs to assist runners to meet their own marathon goals. Most runners in the annual London marathon in England, for example, are running to raise money for charities. It seems incredibly mutually beneficial to everyone who is involved.

The business world is increasingly involved. Jim Lafferty in the May/June 2007 edition of *Marathon and Beyond* reports, for example, on Proctor and Gamble, which created a training program for its employees, culminating in 306 individuals running the Geneva Marathon; 10% of the total number of finishers for the marathon. Not only is it a public relations coup for such companies, it also builds corporate morale and team mentality, and contributes to building those individual values and aspirations that can be directed to more positive work environments and performance.

Running marathons can be considered as part of a growing trend to battle the superficiality of modern life. In her book *'Zen and the Art of Knitting,'* Bernadette Murphy talks about the hunger in culture right now for meaning and for connectedness with the world; to do things for our souls and rebel against the speed of living which many of us have been caught up in. Like running long distances, knitting is not something that is completed in a short period of time. It takes patience; it's a slow process, but by the time it's completed there is a sense of accomplishment, and all the while there is time for contemplation and for ideas and thoughts to swirl around unencumbered by the rapidity of modern life. Knitting with others adds a beneficial social interaction. According to Bernadette, knitting helps us to be more in control of the *rhythm of our own life*.

So too with running.

Why? Because there is nothing superficial about starting a marathon and finishing it a few hours later. It is a very real, tangible activity that rewards patience and commitment. You either do it or you don't. And you may have to fight your own demons, however they're defined. It's all about you and your body, and your mind. That's why it's so rewarding. Running marathons is a counter-balance to the many things that affect our lives these days.

This can be referred to as *tempo giusto*, which, in a general sense means, going along at one's own chosen inner tempo. We do this in running, and we *can* do it in our everyday lives if we decide to. We take our lives into our running experience, but we can also take the essence of our running experience and apply it richly to our lives.

24

AND NOW FOR THE CAYMAN ISLANDS MARATHON

DAYS 37 – 56
Planned Distance: Don't Know

"Sure, you could run just about anywhere in the world! But wouldn't you prefer to run on a safe, beautiful Caribbean island, surrounded by tropical flora and fauna, with magnificent views of the sea? Well, come run with us in the Cayman Islands Marathon!"

Perhaps he's just feeling the need for exercise. Or maybe I've inspired him. Whatever the case, the kitchen is shaking seismically as Gordon the hamster sprints up a storm on his wheel. Who knows what would be possible if he was given proper running shoes and a training program.

My running computer is working again. Why? And why did it not work at precisely the most important time I wanted it to work?

Some books say that after having completed a marathon, especially if it's your first, you may not want to run one again too soon, if at all. I'm nearing the end of my 'down-week', post Athens, and I can't wait to get going on the next one. Early signs of addiction perhaps.

It's Friday, 10th November. I've checked the Cayman Islands marathon website. There's 48 runners now registered for the Cayman marathon. With so few runners, there's a really good chance I'll be running completely by myself for most, if not all of it. I'll have two more days off running then I'll get back into it.

People are congratulating me for my Athens achievement and asking me how I feel. I feel proud. The biggest buzz of all is when I show Callum and Jack my medal. It's a good looking medal, which helps. The boys are much less interested in my pictures. As Callum said, "I knew it was going to be boring, but not this boring."

**

After a quiet weekend my Monday begins with me feeling something in my left foot, just beside the ankle, with my first step out of bed. Muscle? Bone? Paranoia? I don't know, but I'm leaning towards paranoia. After doing some very early, early morning research work because I have to travel to Montreal today, I feed the horses and go for a run on the backyard track.

I don't feel any pain in my foot when I'm running but it's there afterwards, and stays with me all day. As does the other foot. No, you know what I mean – it's the pain that stays with me all day. I could go to a doctor but figure after a few days of waiting for an appointment, being referred to a specialist and several x-rays later, I will be told I shouldn't run for a while. I don't want to hear that. Right now, I'm deep listening instead. I may not run tomorrow if I still feel it in the morning.

But the run itself is great. Such a liberating feeling. Besides the foot, everything feels really good. There is little to suggest I'd run a marathon a week earlier. I'm heading into new training territory because I don't know of any training programs designed for regular people running a marathon each month. I think I know what makes sense, to me anyway, so I'll go with that. Well let's face it; I don't really know much at all. At the back of my mind is the advice from the marathon books that more rest is preferred to training too early. But I'm also conscious of the fact that I'm running the Cayman Marathon in less than three weeks from now. I do need to get out for some training runs.

My watch had stopped in Athens. It finally started working again on the second day back home. Now, in my first run since Athens, it seizes again, recording only time and not distance. I'll take it in to get repaired.

I've only been back from Athens for a few days but already I see how easy it is to get caught up in everything and let the running slip away. For that one reason alone I'm really pleased I've got another marathon in sight – one that's not so far in the distance that I could be tempted to put off a training run.

**

Although this first run back home goes well I've elected to use the better-safe-than-sorry principle and have decided to take two more days off. I've just had two days of traveling for work – the Montreal trip and then a full day trip to Toronto (by train; 5:25am to 9:00pm), so it makes sense not to try and squeeze a run into these days, especially given the readjustments my body is likely going through right now. And to be honest, I don't really know the precise contours of those readjustments, but I assume things are happening internally after the pounding my body has been given.

What I do know is that I'm addicted. With a few moments to spare between meetings in Toronto I find myself drawn like a magnet to the *World's Biggest Bookstore*. When I want inspiration on days I'm not running, or even on days that I am, I browse through the running section. It reinforces my focus, keeps me in tune with my goals, and reminds me what I can potentially accomplish.

My mind drifts away as I look through the books. I reflect on that euphoric moment in Athens when I sped up with just a few miles left in the marathon. I should never have opened up my stride thinking I could sprint to the finish. Not only did I come crashing down, it could easily have resulted in injury, and compromised my recovery post-marathon. I guess it's called experience. As I stand there browsing I'm also reminded that my feet feel very tender. This should be no surprise given the way I hobbled around after the marathon.

**

The morning after my Toronto trip I'm doing some stretching exercises. It's raining heavily outside. I watch the Ark float past the house with the horses, cats and chickens, and then go for a run. Or swim really. The weather forecast says there will be four more days of rain.

I email Dave in England to ask about training between monthly marathons. Dave just ran a marathon in Belgium and is set to run another in Cornwall this weekend. Number 202. He replied with reassuring news that I should resume my normal training if possible with maybe one long run between now and the Caymans. The marathon distance, he said, should stay in my legs for about four weeks. I wonder if the rocks will stay that long as well.

Coenraad also emailed me today. I'd sat with Coenraad on the bus out to Marathon before the Athens run. Although he didn't achieve the time he hoped for – 3:45 – he finished in a time of 3:52, and is very happy with the result. He said "the first 32 kilometres of hills just drained too much energy, and towards the end I was just happy to keep moving and finish. When I got to the finish I just sat down in the sun for about an hour and enjoyed the atmosphere while watching the other finishers." Sounds familiar. It's very encouraging and motivating when I hear from other runners that I've gotten to know.

'It comes from within' is the tag line of the Comrades Ultraimarathon in South Africa. This is a race of about 90 kilometres between the cities of Pietermaritzburg and Durban. A race that is also labelled as *The Ultramarathon* to run. A great history. It's fascinating to learn about different runs around the world. I've already started wondering if it's possible I could run Comrades in a few months. All I have to do is find the cash necessary and the training and commitment to run 90 kilometres in June of 2007. It's that cash part that's the challenge; I know I'd be committed and would train for it. It's now on my list of things to do. In fact, the marathon books suggest setting our sights on runs following your intended race. I've not yet done the Cayman or Disney marathons but already I feel the time will pass quickly. I want to have something planned for post-Disney. I'm looking for challenges. Comrades could be it, but perhaps I'm being a bit too big feeling right now.

**

The next day I run for thirty minutes in the rain and cold wind. Whereas a few weeks ago I'd automatically reach for my sunglasses, these days I automatically reach for my jacket. The Cayman Islands Marathon will be a welcome change from training in what is currently a record month for rainfall. At least there's no snow.

I've now become hypersensitive to even the smallest of things that I feel when running. Today it's my foot; a different pain, right on the ball of my left foot. But after ten minutes the pain goes away. I feel tired in my upper body though. The good news is that each run feels like a success. I decide not to run tomorrow – Saturday – when the boys are here. I'll call it a cross-training day as the boys and I will move a cord of wood from the outside and stack it in the basement.

Part of the satisfaction with running is being able to successfully integrate it without compromising other parts of my life that I enjoy. It occurs to me that training for marathons needs to be part of my life, but not something that replaces it. I *am* training and running marathons – it feels like a gift. Balance. Integrate. Be in control of the rhythms of your own life. *Tempo Guisto*.

**

Well, I'd intended to run the next day – Sunday – but it doesn't happen. A crazy day with visitors throughout, including Rob in the early morning who kindly drops by to help work out why I have a burnt out electrical smell coming from the basement. Burning the house down will wreak havoc with a training schedule. I know nothing about things electrical but I'm talented at angling flashlights in the right direction. Rob, ever patient with me, goes through all the possibilities, doing some forensic electrical work. Gord and his three daughters come over in the afternoon and by the time I muck the stalls, goof around with the boys and feed the horses it's dark outside.

I also discover why my running computer didn't work in Athens. According to the manual it won't work in minus 10 Celsius temperature. Vindication of the temperature at the Athens start-line I suppose, but I think they need to rethink the company name 'Polar.'

**

After two days of not running I'm psyched to run even if the farm is hit by a meteor. The burning electrical smell is here once more, so I call an electrician. Burnt out wiring in the hot water cylinder apparently. All fixed now. Importantly, there is still time to run.

I'm feeling some residual from the Athens marathon. The legs are fine and the feet tender, but I'm noticing tightness again, after my run today, in the upper body. I'm feeling tired much sooner and the run is taking more effort. Yet my time today, for 14km, is the same as usual. I also have a strong twinge in the Achilles tendon of my right foot. Enough for me to stop for a few seconds, which I've not done before. I continue running but with a much smaller stride. I ice it after my run and it feels better, and also take some Ibuprofen. Maybe it's too soon after Athens to be doing these distances? I'm pretty much playing it by ear with the training at this point.

I hear back again from the nutritionist today. We're involved in a torturous long, slow telephone tag. At this rate I'll be advised what to eat when I move into a Nursing Home. We're now threatening to meet next week to discuss my diet. Apart from a bit of a blow-out eat-whatever-I-feel-like few days immediately after Athens, I think I'm doing fairly well. I've put on some weight, but with the amount of worrying I'm doing right now I'll be able to get the weight back down.

**

Before I leave for Montreal today I have another massage with Jaz. I lie there feeling quite spoilt for the first 30 seconds. Thereafter I beg for a bottle of whiskey and a bullet to bite on. Jaz finds some major problem spots on my right calf. I can't reply when he asks if his massaging is working because I'm busy wiping the tears from my eyes. I have to believe this sort of pain is good for me, otherwise why am I here? So I suck it up, making sure I at least have enough air in my lungs to get words out. Jaz may be laughing.

After bawling like a toddler whose ice-cream has fallen off its cone, I listen to Jaz telling me that my back and left side seem much, much better than before Athens, and there is little sign of the hip problem I'd been feeling. The bad news is that it seems my right side had taken the brunt of the past two weeks –or perhaps just the race itself; it's far more sensitive to touch than my left side when compared to before the Athens run. Jaz's theory is that my right side has compensated for my left side, specifically, we suspect, my left knee.

We talk about having Epsom salt baths to ease my muscles, and ice for the inflammations. I could be in a bath after each long run soothing my muscles while at the same time contorting myself with body parts out of the water covered in ice; the Mythos beer approach. I'll need yoga exercises to make this possible. Conceivably I could end up tying myself in a knot, which will make getting out of the bath even harder.

An hour of Jas's work costs me $65. Well worth the money. Apart from releasing some pressure points, it's a powerful reminder of the many different parts of my body that need to be in good shape to make running enjoyable and possible. If you want your car to run well you make sure you change the oil regularly, rotate the tires, check the plugs and get tune-ups and so on; you make sure all the parts are working as best they can. Your body is the same, but even more important. Why we, or I, don't look after it better is increasingly a mystery to me as I train for these marathons.

I go for a run this evening after dinner in Montreal. I could've run the streets in dark, bitterly cold windy conditions. That would be the tough thing to do. Or I could proudly wear my newly acquired Athens marathon t-shirt for the first time on the treadmill. And so I do. I discover that size XL in Greece is not XL for me. If I'd bought XL shorts I'd be in the Boy's Choir right now. I'm thinking the shirt might suggest I'm a 'serious runner', but it's more likely I look like someone who has been given the shirt by someone who *really* did run the race.

Once steadied on the treadmill I spend fifteen minutes entering the required information on weight, time, speed, heart rate, toe size, favorite food, dreams, mother's maiden name ... and then ... off I go. Stationarily, if that's a word?

While I'm pounding the daylights out of my Korean War era treadmill a woman beside me is pounding the daylights out of her brand new 2006 Super-Duper XYZ 2000 model. In front of me is some middle-aged guy running on a bit of a tilt, looking like his right leg is about to fall off. The likeness to me is terrifying, but not terribly surprising when I realize it's a mirror. Good God, do I really run like *that?*

How depressing. Never run a marathon with a mirror in front of you. I make adjustments to my stride and gait and the look on my face and anything else that can help transform me into a runner. I can't keep looking at myself any longer so I look over at the woman beside me. She's reading a book aggressively – I'm not sure if that's possible – as she clocks what must be a 1500-metre world record. She looks possessed – driven. And then, just like that, she's gone. At first I think her machine has sped out of control, flinging her into the back walls. Her whole life must be like that. I wonder if she enjoys it. But I see she's okay, she's hurrying off to swim in the pool now, no doubt continuing to read her specially designed water proof book on astrophysics, where she will swim the English Channel. I burn calories just watching her.

My life is slow in comparison. I'm feeling my Achilles, although nothing like I did yesterday. I think the massage has helped, but just in case, I go as slow as I can without falling asleep. With Wonder Woman no longer there to stare at I keep myself busy converting the miles into kilometers, but after a while that gets boring too.

**

I wake up inspired. It must have been a good sleep. I almost leap out of bed to do some work ahead of my morning meeting. Computer on, coffee made, I'm ready to knuckle down and get my work done.

But I ignore my work. Instead I surf the Internet for marathon sites. Wow. So many places to see and run in. Tibet. Sahara. China. Kilamanjaro. The Great Wall of China. Two Oceans, Everest. Antarctica. Marrakesh. Arctic. Under a River in Germany. Toronto.

Hold the phone. Everest?

I shouldn't be surprised that we can run anywhere in the world. The only constraints are cost and timing. Oh, and training, I suppose. We can run wherever we want because we're experiencing a social movement in marathon running. If I was an economics professor I'd rationalize this and simply say that there is a market out there that is responding to consumer demand. The successful entrepreneurs will understand the market, create unique differentiated products (for example, a marathon, or products or services associated with marathon running) and promote them accordingly. If the entrepreneurs have done their market analysis – their homework – they will reap the benefits of this demand, especially if they believe it's growing.

But I'm not an entrepreneur, I'm one of those consumers, currently quite addicted, which explains why I'm up early, ostensibly to do work but actually browsing Internet sites for marathons.

But Everest?

What's next? The Moon Marathon? The Bottom of the Sea 26.2?

A closer look though and I see that it's not just one Everest marathon, but two different events (May or November), *and* a Himalayan 100-mile staged race run over several days that incorporates views of Everest and three of the other four highest peaks in the world. Choices for runners even where you'd think there wouldn't be.

For now, my thoughts are with my own Everest – the next 6km on the treadmill this morning before the meeting. It's now 10am and there's no-one in the exercise centre. I get to use to modern treadmill. What a difference. Thinking how impressive it looked last night as Wonder Woman critiqued the launch sequence for the Space Shuttle, I decide to review a research paper on the importance of upscaling qualitative enquiry.

Geek.

Had I tried reading it last night, I would've been flung off the treadmill. If there's anything that could make you run – away – it's such a paper. I have my earphones once more, listening to the same songs I've been playing for the previous few weeks. I could've watched Regis and the woman whose name I can't remember right now on TV or the news on the latest bombings, assassinations, regular murders, or that Tomcat thing. Instead, for forty-four minutes I ignore the research paper, don't look at the TV, and focus instead on my music and my form. The ugly ungainly guy is in the mirror again, motivation perhaps for my attention to form this morning. I'm pleased to notice his form starting to improve. It's encouraging.

He's still a mess though. As much as I hate seeing myself like that it's a valuable lesson. I spend most of the time straightening up, dropping my centre to my stomach and keeping my legs and feet running directly forward; my right foot tends to splay outwards, a function of being kicked in the ankle too many times playing soccer over the years. The 'new form' feels awkward at first but then starts to feel really good. I'm making progress. As much as I hate to admit it, I really like the treadmill.

Can I afford to buy one? It would be great for a Canadian winter.

Disney has begun formal communications with all registered runners today. An email with many links to things we should know about for the runs in January arrives in my mailbox. Right now it seems very distant. Almost like Tomorrowland. Or perhaps Fantasyland. In any case, after my run I feel really good. I'm mentally gearing up for the Caymans and, gulp, starting to feel much more confident.

25

WHAT AM I DOING TO MY BODY?

I've become increasingly conscious of the physiological knock my body received in Athens. I have a growing desire to learn more about why it feels the way it does and what more I can do to make things better. It's self-exploration.

Exercise researchers say the long runs teach our bodies how to deliver and use oxygen more efficiently – our bodies adapt by creating more blood vessels to send oxygen-rich blood to the working muscles, making more energy producing mitochrondria and effectively repairing any tears that may appear in our muscles from the extra work they are doing. A great system.

Research evidence supports the notion that running, instead of damaging joints, actually helps to strengthen them. This in part is due to the fact that you are exercising your joints (and ligaments and muscles); but if you were a sloth whose activity consisted of opening and shutting the fridge or using the remote, they would become weaker from the non-use. Our bodies are bio-mechanical systems with living tissues always rebuilding themselves. The living tissues and muscles get even stronger when they're being used, and so the stronger the tissues and muscles are around our joints, the better off our joints will be, with greater protection.

What we do need to be concerned about is making sure we are not overweight and that if we injure ourselves, we treat the injury the right way. Stretching is also very important. I've found that there are the right ways of stretching and then there are the ways that I've been doing it. I also don't do *enough* stretching and my aches and pains reflect this.

Fatigue

According to Dr. Jason Carp, an exercise physiologist writing in the journal *Marathon and Beyond*, fatigue is the "inability to maintain or repeat a given level of muscle force production, resulting in an acute impairment of performance". Fatigue, he says, is necessary to protect our bodies from damage. A key element in fatigue for us is glycogen depletion. We have enough stored glycogen to last us for just over two hours of sustained running. We then basically run out of fuel, and as most of us know, two hours is not enough time to finish the marathon.

We also become mentally fatigued. This, says Jason, is due to changes in the levels of the brain transmitters serotonin and dopamine. These changes alter our perception of effort, cause us to feel tired and play tricks on the central nervous system's ability to send commands to our muscles.

It gets worse. When we sweat a lot we get dehydrated.

Dehydration decreases the amount of plasma in our blood, which decreases our heart's cardiac output and stroke volume. With this, the oxygen flow to our muscles is put in jeopardy and our pace slows. Oh dear. Meanwhile, our constant pounding on the road is damaging our muscle fibres, which in turn decreases our muscle force production.

The good news in all this is that it is for these reasons that we train, and run high mileages. By putting in the long distance miles we increase our blood's oxygen-carrying capacity and our body's ability to use the oxygen that is available. Research also suggests that running a high number of miles also helps us to run more economically, by training our bodies to use oxygen more efficiently. By running long – for two hours or more – we train our bodies to tolerate the length of time we are exercising. The other good news is that if we replenish our bodies with carbohydrates immediately after these runs our bodies respond by storing more glycogen, thereby getting us in better condition for the next long run. Continually doing this over a training regime puts our bodies in better and better shape to sustain the distance, and improve our times. We'll also feel better during and after the marathon.

Injuries

Fatigue is one thing, but injuries are another. I think everyone expects to feel fatigued to a certain extent after completing a marathon. It's the injuries incurred training and in the race that are the real downers! You could write a book on all the injuries that can happen and how to prevent them but I wouldn't bother if I were you because they've already been written.

Common sense is the prevailing theme. Sounds simple, but I'm proof that it's not adhered to all the time. What is it that drives runners to over-train? Part of the challenge with marathon running is that it's not what you do if you want instant gratification. Shopping takes care of that. Marathon running, or rather, successful marathon running, reflects patience and commitment, a significant part of which includes a gradual build-up in training to allow your body to adjust and cope with the increasing pressures you place upon it.

The widely used phrase is 'Listen to your body'; that is, listen for signs of injuries or problems that are starting to emerge. We put a lot of stress on it, and this is layered onto the stress it already receives from all those other things we do during the day. Listen to my body sometimes and you'll wonder how I'm even able to do the activities of daily living, let alone run anywhere.

'Listening to our body' may not be the exact thing we need to do. What we're really talking about is a process of self-exploration and constant self-awareness. So far, with training and the Athens marathon completed, I find I already know myself better than before. I'm not going woo-woo here, but I recognise the merit in being more in tune with my body – how it feels generally and when I exercise, how it reacts to different food and fluids, and when it's best to have these, and what a difference a good night's sleep makes.

It's about knowing *cause* and *effect*. By constantly being attuned and responding to changes that occur I'm able to enjoy the training, and indeed, life in general, so much more. We tend to take our bodies for granted, when in fact we are directly responsible for them. Everything we do to, and with, our bodies, will have implications for what we want our bodies to do at a later time. 'Later' could be thirty minutes or six months.

Like life generally, we constantly make choices, even though we don't think of them as such at the time. I know that if I run as fast as I can right now for a one-hour stretch, it's likely going to hurt and I'll risk injury. If I don't run for a month and sit on the couch annihilating a bag of potato chips every night my body will have to work much harder when I run the next marathon, and risk injury, depending on how I run; if I can run at all.

Common sense is the key, along with understanding how my body functions and why. That, in part, is what makes marathon running fun; it's a constant learning process and the person to benefit most is me; and ergo, others around me because I feel I'm a better person – happier and healthier – because of the running.

Massage therapy

One of the best places for getting to know your body better is on a bench receiving a massage and talking to the therapist. Massage Therapists have a wealth of knowledge, can quickly tell you about the train wreck under your skin, and, in my experience, can transform a disaster zone into something still useable.

I had lunch with Karen Raddon, a Registered Massage Therapist here in Kingston one day to find out more about why a massage is so good for runners. Karen is short, slightly built, has a huge smile, and, like Helga in Athens, an unsuspecting vice-like grip that would bring tears to the eyes of a rogue elephant. Unlike Helga, Karen's got a wonderful engaging personality, and is happy to share her knowledge with me.

I'm safe from Karen's vice-like grip for now because we're having lunch and I'm sitting on the other side of the table. She starts to explain some basic kinesiology to me. Seeing the glazed look in my eyes she takes a step or two back from basic, to, I suppose, *pre-basic*, or *pre-Cambrian basic* possibly, and we start from there. As my knowledge level is just slightly past the 'knee-bone-is-connected-to-the' we focus first on why running is a good thing for my body, and everyone else's.

Our muscles are made stronger when we work them. The exercising puts a higher demand on our circulatory system and blood flow, and that's a good thing so long as we don't overdo it, as I found out earlier. If we do too much at once or try and build up too quickly, our muscles will fatigue. Our bones respond to a certain amount of stress by strengthening, again, so long as we don't overdo it.

It's sounding familiar. The running problems that Karen sees with her clients are Iliotibial Band Syndrome, Achilles, Plantar Fasciitis, strains on hip flexors, quadriceps and hamstrings, low back pain, and shin splints. The best way to combat these or simply prevent their eminent arrival, is through a combination of appropriate training (not trying too much too soon), regular stretching, using ice to address any inflammation, and regular massage.

There are many benefits from a massage. Having a light massage shortly after a race helps to flush out lactic acid that's accumulated over the run and bring in fresh blood. A couple of days later the massage can be much deeper and can relieve tense muscles. It's valuable for relaxing our muscles, pushing out any waste (toxins) that may accumulate in the muscles, realigning muscle fibres, breaking up any scar tissue, and getting blood circulation flowing, which is important for ensuring that the most effective flow of oxygen is coming into your muscles. A Massage Therapist will find little niggly problems that you didn't know you had and help prevent them from getting worse, and will address the major ones that explain why you're walking like you've just ridden a horse for the first time across the continent without stopping. Above all else, a massage simply feels so good! I have yet to have a massage where I didn't want it to last another hour.

We can do some useful things ourselves. We're told to take baths with Epsom salt to relieve pain in our joints (although there is limited scientific evidence to support this), lose weight if necessary to reduce the stress on our joints, and eat properly to ensure we're getting adequate nutrients for our muscles and bones.

What many runners may have to think about, Karen says, especially in this new era, is osteoarthritis. Osteoarthritis is the most common form of arthritis. It's caused by a breakdown of our cartilage, which is the tough elasticky stuff that covers and protects the ends of our bones. Bits of cartilage may break off and cause pain and swelling in the joint between bones. Over time the cartilage may wear away entirely, and the bones will rub together. Usually osteoarthritis affects hips, knees, hands and the spine. If the new, older runners coming into marathon running have any injuries from previous sports, there's a chance that at some point these may manifest themselves once more when running.

The good news is that exercising the joints is beneficial – the trick is not to overdo it. Regardless, we need to use our muscles (or they will become weaker and smaller) in order to keep our joints healthy. Keith Williams, a Professor in Exercise Science, says that there is wisdom in the phrase "use it or lose it". In his 1998 *Marathon and Beyond* article he wrote that a commitment to running over the years will slow the rate of decline with age in our physiological functions compared to those who are sedentary. Marathon runners have to accept that as they get older their finishing times will be slower. The rate of decline, in fact, tends to increase in the 55 to 65 age range.

But it's not all doom and gloom for older runners. In ultra-marathons for example, it's well known that the older runners do much better than their younger competitors. Jeff Hagen from Washington State, who is seldom seen without a smile on his face, is a top ultra-runner and frequent contributor to *Marathon and Beyond*, identifies a series of attributes that provide the 'Masters Edge,' as he puts it. These include experience, the ability to pace properly, patience, efficiency, a philosophical approach to the race, trust in oneself and a psychological edge derived from non-running experiences in life. Rich Benyo, the editor of *Marathon and Beyond* puts it eloquently: "It makes good sense to refer to a runner over 40 as a "master." By that point in life, one begins to learn to master the inevitable, not in the sense of mastering it by overpowering it, but mastering it by working in concert with it. And why not? Consider the alternative."

Is running an addiction?

Hello, my name is Malcolm and I have a problem with running. Not as far-fetched as it may sound perhaps. The *New Scientist* magazine examined 'addiction' in August 2006. A number of researchers, it says, stress the need to expand the definition of addiction to include behavioural addiction, of which running is one. Mark

Griffiths, a university psychologist in England, says there are key features of crack, heroin, alcohol and nicotine addiction that can be equally applied to all addictions, and also to many excessive behaviours. First, the addiction dominates people's lives, leading to cravings and preoccupations with the habit. Second, the addicted one has to engage in this activity or behaviour ahead of all other things, even ahead of eating, sleeping or drinking. A third key element is tolerance – as time goes on, a greater 'dose' is needed for the same 'high.' A final key element is withdrawal; when the addicted ones are unable to satisfy their habit, they feel similar symptoms – such as excessive moodiness, irritability nausea, stomach cramps, headaches and sweats.

I'm shaky on the science of all this but the research evidence suggests that behavioural addictions are very similar to chemical addictions, which may partly be explained by the fact that they both trigger a rise in dopamine release in the reward circuits of the brain. The 'high' of this pre-adrenaline rush reinforces the desire for more. In March 2006, a study on depressive mood symptoms and fatigue by Berlin, Kop and Deuster, published in the journal *Psychosomatic Medicine*, concluded that people who exercise and who are forced to be inactive for two weeks feel tired, irritable, sad and self-critical. Those with the highest level of exercise activity felt the biggest drop in mood. These findings, the researchers say, may explain mood changes in response to short-term exercise withdrawal like injuries or recovery from medical procedures that don't require full bed rest.

Talk to just about any runner who exercises on a regular basis and they will relate to this research. It's more than just anecdotes that say many marathoners could be considered in some ways addicted to the sport. What's more interesting as we saw earlier is that the *motivation* for perpetuating the addiction may change over time as the runner runs more marathons.

The research evidence is slam-dunkingly conclusive about the benefits of exercise in general, and walking and running. I may be at risk for simplifying things too much but here goes.

Get moving. It's a good thing.

26

THE CAYMAN COUNTDOWN

I'm back in Kingston after yesterday's trip to Montreal. I take my Running Computer into Runner's Choice; the store where I had bought it. They ship it off to Toronto to be repaired. It's a beautiful November day, warm and sunny; ideal for an afternoon run. I take Fred out back to run 6km around the track. I've not run on the track much lately so it's good for a change. I'm running much slower than normal, focusing on form, and hoping to avoid injury. The books consistently state we should often run at a pace slower than what our race day pace will be. I'm also doing more stretching now and it's helping. No problems with the Achilles today but I've got a feeling it could blow at any time if I try anything fancy like speed or hills.

**

The following day I run 6km around the farm with Fred again. I'd have run 10km but I can't squeeze any more time out of the day due to a lot of very time-sensitive work on the go right now. This bites, but it's my reality. The tired feeling in my upper body is disappearing, which is a good thing as I've been getting worried about it.

I'm looking more closely at the run-walk approach advocated by Jeff Galloway and many others. As Jeff points out in his book, the earliest marathon runners, including those in the first modern Olympics, all used some sort of run-walk strategy. By walking at regular points through the race, and beginning those walk sections early in the run, our muscles are rested for the heaviest burden in the run's latter stages. In the two 30km training runs with Karen in the summer we used a 1-minute walk for every 10 minutes of running and it worked really well.

**

It's Sunday night. I've blown two days off and not run but I'm okay with that. It's been non-stop physical work around the Farm; moving cords of wood into the basement again, cleaning out the garage and sheds, making a chicken coop with Rob (who actually knows what he's doing), working in the barn, and putting away outdoor furniture. Cross-training. Only once did I smash logs of wood against my legs, and I scored some spectacular goals against Jack in our soccer games. All-in-all a great weekend – and the upper body heaviness keeps disappearing.

I emailed ATTIKO METPO in Greece today in a bid to get Interpol off my back. I found the ticket I received for allegedly gypping METRO out of 2 Euros on my way out of Athens. I couldn't see the Greek economy crippled any more. I ask for leniency, compassion and forgiveness. And to not have to pay the 50 Euros penalty fine.

**

It's Monday now. I uhm and aah over whether I should run 14km or something a lot less given that the marathon is less than a week away. I should've run a 20km at some point between Athens and the Cayman Islands but the way I've felt about my body – the heaviness and the niggly things, and the busyness of work – well, I simply haven't gotten out for 20km. Running it now seems silly with just six days to go. I settle for the Colebrook route and a promise to myself to go slow. The day's heavily overcast but not cold. Since I was up at 3am getting some work done and knew I had a nutty day ahead I decide to run as soon as it's light.

It turns out to be a great run. I really do take it slow, and feel no aches, pains or revenge from my Achilles. I practice proper form and try to regulate my breathing with deeper breaths. For the rest of the day my feet feel less tired. I've started taking a salt bath each night. It's a real treat bathing where I don't have to fold my legs behind my head. I've even started packing.

**

After such a good run I decide not to run again before I leave for the Cayman Islands, which is tomorrow. It's been frantic these past two days tying up loose ends with work, getting over project deadlines, and ensuring the house and animals are sorted out and will be in good shape for my return. I drop Fred off at the kennel and speed into Kingston to pick up my running computer, which has just returned from the manufacturers. It's reasonable to assume it won't be minus 10 Celsius in the Cayman Islands so I should be able to pace myself this time. I drive to Toronto quietly optimistic of at least finishing this marathon. I'm less optimistic of a sub 4-hour time.

I get to park for free near the airport if I stay at the Peachtree Hotel the night before I fly south. It's a good deal; cheaper than driving early in the morning to the airport on the day of departure and parking my car in a lot at the airport. I'm sitting with a Caesar salad and a wine for dinner in the restaurant bar. The table of nine beside me are huddled around a 2 x 2 inch video screen camera watching a video of Toronto that's been filmed by the Chinese businessman they are with. Either he is being wooed to purchase their products or the video is a top contender for the Cannes film festival awards. They are completely engrossed, absolutely captivated. I try to sneak a look myself because it sounds brilliant, but their salt and pepper shakers are in the way.

As the epic unfolds and a sale is clearly within reach – I reflect on the past three hours. I left Kingston with a full cup of coffee and an empty bladder. At about midway the pendulum swung. The coffee ceased to be enjoyable and became increasingly painful. I couldn't stop because I had to make it to Toronto by 4pm to be on an important business call that my bladder couldn't care less about. At 3:57pm, I impersonated either Mr Bean or Basil Fawlty, or both, as I stumbled with my legs crossed over the parking lot in search of a telephone and washroom. 'Washroom is Closed' said the sign. The next closest washroom was physically 500 metres away, and mentally about 5 miles away, and I would have had to come back in a fast sprint to get on the call with a pay phone. I didn't have time. There was no option but to call and keep my legs crossed without bursting.

Relief. She wasn't there. I left a message and dashed off

to find a bathroom.

Now I feel I'm finally somewhere. I can relax. Why do I do this to myself? I'm really looking forward to the marathon, but I've hardly thought about it too much with everything else going on in my life with work and another book I'm writing. But come race day the 'other stuff' will be left behind, and in its place will be the sharing of experiences with people who, right now, are complete strangers, but who in a few days will potentially be not only others I run with, but new friends. The marathon event is such as wonderful release.

I have a 6:45am flight so it's off to bed early.

I read a *New Scientist* magazine in bed. I subscribe to this UK-based science news magazine because it's all about ideas – about the possibilities of the imagination and the real work and thoughts that shape the world we live in. I'm amazed at what's possible. And I realise how little I know. It's humbling. Some quotes stay with me. Like this one from Patricia Churchland: "Each of us is a work of art, sculpted first by evolution, and second by experience in the world. With experience and reflection one's social perception matures, and so also does the level of autonomy. Aristotle called it wisdom." I think running marathons creates the opportunity for reflection. Our social perceptions will always be less than optimal if we don't have, or make, the time to be alone with our own thoughts. It's another reason why running long distances is such a powerful experience.

**

On the plane the next morning I marvel at how hassle-free my departure was. Less than 30 minutes. Bodes well. Directly below me right now is the United States. It's big. Directly opposite me on the other side of the aisle is a man struggling to open his yogurt container. He succeeds. I know this because half of it flies onto my lap. It's an impressive distance for flying yogurt. He hasn't noticed. I'm not sure what to do, so I do nothing. What can I do? Except clean it up of course. He does nothing either, and the plane keeps flying, like we want it to.

The yogurt takes my mind off my calf muscle, which is now aching, I suspect, from the 14km run. With just three more days to go, plenty of time in which to change my mind, I decide to try the run-walk strategy in this marathon. Although I feel I could run the entire distance, with Disney still to come I have to be sensible about my capabilities. And besides, I'm quite curious about how the run-walk strategy will work. It occurs to me mid-flight that I want to finish the three marathons without damaging myself. It occurs to me mid-flight that packing a huge container of sea salt for a visit to the Cayman Islands was not the smartest thing to do.

I stop briefly in Miami to board another flight for the Cayman Islands. No yogurt in my lap this time, but the lady on the other side of the aisle provides new entertainment. The flight attendant hands the lady, who must be in her late forties, a Cayman Islands magazine, with a "there you go Sweetie", which was quite endearing.

"My name is Doris," Sweetie replies sternly.

"Okay," replies the flight attendant.

That should have been the end of it, but for some unknown reason the flight attendant returns and asks for the magazine back. A blind and deaf attendant might have sensed this was not the wisest thing to do to Sweetie. Sweetie has clearly had a bad day up until now and is ready to blast a hole in the fuselage. We are all involved now, and sensing an imminent May Day call. Sweetie mutters for all the plane to hear some insightful but not repeatable comments about choice, customers, price, and the fact that no-one cares. She is proven wrong within a couple of minutes as three copies of the magazine are handed to her by other passengers. It doesn't matter though because Sweetie is now focusing intently on her *People* magazine.

The fun portion of the flight begins as we land. No-one had told us the runway at Owen Roberts International Airport on Grand Cayman Island is actually a trampoline. The first bounce is big enough to cause half the aircraft to shriek as if they've been tied unwillingly in a roller coaster. The other half shrieks when the plane swerves from side to side. The passenger behind me speculates that there are actually bends in this runway, but most of us are too busy keeping our heads between our knees to look out the windows as the pilot, we assume, pulls on the brakes.

We step down onto the tarmac and are welcomed by that Caribbean burst of heat and humidity that will never leave me for the next few days. We then join in that other Caribbean tradition of line-ups for immigration and customs. We are one of the lucky aircraft. Another plane's luggage compartment door won't open, and for reasons known only to the experts on these matters the aircraft has to be flown back to Miami, whereupon the door will be opened, the luggage set free, and returned to the Caymans the next day.

We the lucky ones exit the airport and begin to assemble at the next line-up for taxis. I never seem to be at the front of these line-ups. There are no taxis, of course. I wonder how Sweetie is doing at this point. It's 80 degree heat so I think she may have melted away. It's quiet anyway.

The Cayman Islands Marathon organizers have arranged for an information table outside the airport entrance. I meet Jerry Harper here. Jerry's a retired teacher in his late fifties, short and stocky, and not who you'd immediately think would be an athletics coach in the Cayman Islands. But he is a fixture of the Cayman Island athletics scene and volunteers for the marathon each year. He's friendly and sociable, and along with other volunteers welcomes us, the runners, as we arrive. A nice touch from the marathon.

Eventually a taxi pulls up, a minivan. I sit in the front with a very large Caymanian. We make polite chit-chat about the islands. Within minutes his thick Caribbean accent is rubbing off on me. We start laughing quietly with one another as we listen in on the Minnesota businessman's critical Wall Street calls to colleagues at home on his cell phone.

The waiting at the airport has conditioned me to waiting at the hotel, but it's a big tease as I catch glimpses of the beach through the glass doors. My VISA cards are being declined. The receptionist goes back and forward to the card machine seeking approval. This has been happening with their machine apparently. Fortunately I have enough cash for one night's accommodation, and even surprising myself, I'm able to show email proof that Arthur in Marriott's US office – or perhaps India, who knows – has me booked here for five nights.

I brought my computer with me, as these days I'd feel naked without it. I've work to do (did I mention 'geek') and I want to keep in touch with everyone at home. I've been told the hotel is wireless. The waiting at the airport conditioned me for waiting at Reception, which conditioned me for my wait with the VISA saga, which created the Zen-like trance that helps me as Luke and I spend the rest of the day setting up my wireless Internet connection.

By this point I'm ready to throw myself through concrete walls to get to the beach. Instead, I run. It doesn't take long to get there, even at my pace, because the hotel is right on Seven Mile beach, which isn't seven miles, but may as well be. It's long and sandy; the water so warm that I'm looking for the cold tap.

And buoyant. I sit in the water without sinking. It feels great. No more waiting for one thing. I look around to see mainly brown or red bodies everywhere. In these moments I'm compelled to treat myself, partly because no-one else will, so I go to the outdoor bar and restaurant for an early dinner.

According to my Canadian waitress there are large numbers of Canadians, British, South Africans and other foreigners working in the Caymans in the hospitality and banking sectors, especially between November and June. I can see why. I'm sold on the view from this beach-side restaurant alone, aside from anything else that may attract people to live in the Caymans.

It's Thursday night and I'm feeling a lot like I had when I arrived in Athens. I'm really pleased, and proud I've made it this far. Many things can go wrong when traveling, and they still might. Tomorrow I'll look around, swim, do some work I've brought with me because I'd feel lonely without it, and swim again. 'Poolside' sounds like the perfect office.

I could've packed everything I need here in a large toiletry bag. Shorts, t-shirt (optional), sandals, swimsuit, sunglasses, and a toothbrush. Running gear would also help, I suppose.

Which reminds me, I have a marathon to run on Sunday. While Athens was challenging because of the hills, the Caymans run will push the envelope with its heat and humidity, despite starting at 5am. I've been talking to other runners I've met so far; some have decided to pull out of the full marathon due to the heat and humidity and run the half marathon instead. That way, most if not all of the run will be completed before the sun rises.

I'm whistling Dixie thinking I'll do a sub 4-hour run. My running computer may decide it's too hot to work. A study cited in *Runners World* notes that if the temperature is around 88 degrees F, endurance runners should add 5% to 7% on to their expected finish time. With humidity factored in, I may be better off hoping for a 4:25 time, assuming I don't melt away first. Regardless, it's great to be here.

27

HISTORY, HEAT AND HUMIDITY

It's Friday now. I had a great night's sleep and woke up ready for the day an hour earlier than I needed to, due to a one hour time difference. I should probably know these things. It's the kind of place where you want to spend as much time as possible outside exploring or relaxing. I barely have my clothes on and I'm walking along the coral-sand Seven Mile beach, which, not so long ago, was awarded the honour of "The Caribbean's Best Beach" by the *Caribbean Travel and Life Magazine*.

I amble along the beach picturing myself living here quite easily. It's no wonder people have a different view of time. The warmth and the sea are a calming influence. I can feel myself mentally and physically dropping down a few cogs, relaxing as I try not to trip over in the surf that rolls in around me. A beach this long doesn't feel crowded. Exhausted from my attempts at not tripping over in my 20-minute walk, I see an outdoor patio beachside, which seems a perfect place for breakfast. Breakfast overlooking the ocean for $6. I'd pay $6 just for the view; it's a bargain no matter how I look at it.

On my rigorous, hectic agenda today is a visit to a grocery store, possibly a light run, some work, and a meeting with the race organizers. It's sounding pretty busy don't you think? I decide to rest some more while gazing out into the distance.

I'm looking for pirates. This is the place that Jack Sparrow, Will, Elizabeth, Captain Barbossa and the others made famous recently – the Tortugas – as the Cayman Islands were once called. I doubt I'll see any pirates, although this is a major offshore financial center with no direct taxation. Replacing the pirate ships are 60,000 registered companies, including almost 500 banks and 800 insurance companies. The Cayman Islands is now the fifth largest financial center in the world.

In search of the first destination marathon perhaps, or possibly a route to the Far East, an inept Christopher Columbus 'discovered' the Islands in 1503. There was no-one living here at that time, but there were thousands of sea turtles swimming around the islands. And so the islands were initially named *Las Tortugas*, after the sea turtles, one of whom is the current logo of the Cayman Islands marathon.

By the end of the 1500s the islands had been renamed the *Caymanas* – the Carib word for marine crocodiles (likely the lizards on the islands). No-one lived permanently on the islands but they were a popular destination for weary pirates looking for some vacation time, and for folks interested in tasting sea turtles. Even then there was a holiday spirit. The first known permanent settlers were two deserters from the British Army who obviously knew a good thing when they saw it, who arrived in the 1660s from Jamaica, 268 kilometres away. Cuba is not far away either, just 248 kilometres north of the Caymans.

As it was fashionable around those times to own and occupy another tropical paradise, the British Government formally said the islands were possessions of the Royal Crown in 1670. The islands were administered from Jamaica, where the British were creating the foundations of one of the top cricket teams in the world.

Meanwhile, the Cayman Islands continued to be a safe haven for holidaying pirates, and cricket-free. Blackbeard, in fact, bored with cricket, organized the first marathon in the area as a way of competing with fellow pirates to see who had the ship with the most athletic prowess and endurance.

Well, anyway...

By the 1730s, permanent British settlements had been established. Over the next hundred years or so the main activities, besides doing very little at all, were cotton farming, turtle hunting, and salvaging ships that had gone aground around the islands. There is the famous, hard-to-believe-but-true Follow-the-Leader story of the 'Wreck of the Ten Sails' when a ship hit a reef and was then run into by nine other ships that were following it.

In 1937 the first cruise ship, the Atlantis, visited the Islands. In 1953 the first airfield opened in the Cayman Islands, and tourism had arrived as a viable – very viable – industry. A destination marathon can do much for tourism.

Today, tourism accounts for about 75% of foreign currency earnings. And it's doing well this weekend. The tourist industry focuses on the luxury market. Over 2.2 million tourists came to the Islands in 2006, half of whom were from the United States. Most of the tourists – 1.9 million in 2006 – came in a cruise ship. A big ship I suppose. I've just contributed $6 to the statistics for this year.

In September 2004, the Cayman Islands were hit by Hurricane Ivan, which is ranked as the 9th most intense Atlantic hurricane on record. With wind speeds of about 170 miles per hour it caused enormous damage to the Islands as well as loss of life. A quarter of the buildings on the Islands were reported to be uninhabitable. The costs of the destruction totalled over 1.8 billion US dollars.

About 46,000 people live in the Cayman Islands. I've not met them all, but those I have met are very friendly. A large number of residents are ex-pats from all over the world.

These days you can still get your share of pirates, parrots, skulls, treasure and plundering in the Pirates' Festival Week held each year. It's a thirty-year old tradition – a week of costume competitions, parties, street dances, 5km and 10 km runs, swimming competitions, parades, a Landing Pageant and many children's activities. Rum, no doubt, features at various times during the week. There's something for everyone. And I've just missed this year's festival by a week.

**

There's only so much time you can take at a breakfast

table before you either have to order something else, like lunch, or move on. I drag my exhausted body along the beach once more and go to meet the race organizers.

Just down the road from the hotel is the office of Kelly Holding Limited, a small events and communications company that works throughout the Caribbean. The marathon is one of many events they organize. I meet with Rhonda Kelly, Sue and Bev. They have a small office about halfway between the hotel and downtown George Town where the race begins. I want to meet them about another running book, but it's not the best time to sit and chat. Probably the worst actually. So we talk briefly. I welcome the chance to cool down in their air conditioning.

Rhonda Kelly is the Race Director. She is tall and energetic, and like Sue and Bev, on a mission to get the event to run as smoothly as possible in two days time.

Rhonda explains that a tradition has to start somewhere. For the Cayman Islands marathon the tradition started in 2002. A local woman, Tara Tricket, decided to organize a marathon as a way of raising funds for the Cayman Cadet Corps. In the inaugural event, there were 25 marathoners and 69 half-marathoners running, including Rhonda, who ran in the half-marathon. Given the amount of organizing required for any marathon, Rhonda said to Tara that if she wanted, Rhonda's company would be happy to run the event. In April 2003 Rhonda got the call, and since that time Kelly Holding has been the event organizer and Rhonda Kelly the Race Director. Rhonda said, *"We had no idea what we were getting into."*

In December 2003 the second marathon weekend took place. Kelly Holding put its own resources into running the weekend and continued to commit the proceeds to the Cayman Islands Cadet Corp. Although they tried to make the event bigger and better in 2004 Hurricane Ivan had other plans. Ivan swept through the Caribbean in September. Given the magnitude of destruction, especially on the south side of the island where the marathon is run, it was decided to postpone the event. It has gotten bigger since then, thanks to some marketing and promotion on the island and in North America. As a result of the promotions, five times as many foreign runners are competing in this 2006 event compared to the previous run.

Since 2003 the number of runners in the full marathon has increased from 17 to almost 50 in 2006. The number of half marathon finishers has increased from 62 to over 200. As well, there's a 4-person relay event; this year 31 teams are competing. Rhonda says, "It's exhilarating to see how much it's grown." This year, over half of the runners registered for the marathon are from off the islands; 18 Americans and 3 Canadians, and a runner each from New Zealand (well, me), Australia, England, and Denmark. In addition, many of the other competitors are ex-pats now living in the Cayman Islands. Kelly Holding has been organizing the marathon for the past three years; each time it's got bigger and better.

Rhonda says the marathon is held in early December as it's typically one of the mildest weekends in the year (despite what the runners may think). It's also a shoulder season for tourism when the numbers of tourists are lower compared to peak season, and the cost of hotel accommodation considerably less as a result.

It's also lousy weather in many places at this time. It's snowing in Ontario, for example, as I'm talking to Rhonda in her office, just across from the beach. I'm breaking out in a sweat just thinking about breaking out in a sweat when I leave the office. At this rate there won't be any sweat to break out come race day.

It's not easy to grow when there's a very competitive market out there; two other Caribbean marathons are also being run this very weekend. For overseas runners there are plenty of options available, which is why smaller races like the Cayman Islands Marathon go into North America and market themselves. Kelly Holding, for example, was at the Boston Marathon actively promoting the Caymans Marathon. A Destination Marathon, especially in the islands, not only has to entice runners to its start-line, it has to compete to get them to travel to their marathon and not others held at the same time, or any other time in the year for that matter.

28

DESTINATION MARATHONS

Tourism is a major industry worldwide and continues to get bigger and bigger. It's clean, expands the mind and shrinks the world, and provides jobs for people in places which otherwise wouldn't have anything in today's market economies. Similarly, there is increasing recognition of the role that *sports tourism* plays in national and local economies world-wide. A microcosm of the sector is the Destination Marathon. Kurtzman and John Zauhar in their 2003 research paper, observe that each marathon has a unique cultural, natural, human-made, social and economic setting. That's what makes destination marathons what they are.

The word 'sport' derives from the middle English 'disport', which means to divert oneself. Marathoners do this in spades of course. If I look at the Oxford English Dictionary, partly because it's a huge thing sitting in front of me on my desk and I feel compelled to use it, I see many meanings now ascribed to *sport*.

What are the experts saying about sports tourism? Well I'm thinking about the university-based experts here, the ones who think more deeply than everyone else, partly because they can, and partly because that's what they're paid to do.

The first thing the researchers typically do is develop a conceptual framework to help structure their thinking. Some research disciplines take decades to do this and by the time most academics are happy with it, or beyond caring, or dead, another way of thinking emerges, and the cycle begins again.

According to Pigeassou, Bui-Xuan and Gleyse in 2003, there are epistemological issues on sport tourism, which, if we dwell long enough, could manifest themselves in marathon running. Oh dear. In the *Journal of Sports Tourism* they ask the question: Can sports tourism be considered as an independent scientific domain? And, then there's the one that especially gives me goose bumps: *Do the activities of sports tourism fall within the category of sports tourism?* I mention this one because when you are running 26.2 miles, Koan-like questions like this will wile away your time quite nicely, if you don't fall asleep grappling with the answer, or answers, or pose new questions, or bore your fellow runners.

Even still, earlier, in 1997, Sean Gammon and Tom Robinson in the *Journal of Sports Tourism* had observed that "Though much has been written concerning the precise nature of Sport and Tourism, there seems to be little work that discusses the practical side of the subject and its implications." Perhaps the most important point for race directors and local decision-makers from these types of mind-bending discussions is that there are two different types of tourists associated with marathon running: those that visit a destination with the primary purpose of running the marathon, and the secondary purpose of being 'the tourist'; and those individuals that visit with the primary purpose of being 'the tourist' with the secondary objective being the marathon event – the best example being friends and families of the runners who are supportive but likely are just as much or more interested in other elements of the travel experience. For the marathoners, if there are other recreational or tourist activities available and known for a given area, they will be more likely to sign up for the marathon. Runners are looking for something different, while the marathons themselves are trying to differentiate what they have to offer so they can attract more runners, and more friends and families of runners. The marathon 'experience' is much bigger and more varied than simply running 26.2 miles.

Catchy phrases attempt to lure runners to register for marathons. The following spread shows some of the phrases different marathons around the world use to advertise their event.

"Flat, Fast and Festive"! • "A Must-Do 26.2" • *The Most Regal Marathon* • **"More People, More Music, More Fun, More than just a Run"!** • *"The Agony of Victory, The Pain of Da Feet"!* • "Not Just an Event...An Experience. One of a Kind. Don't Miss It." • **"Surf City, Here We Run"!** • **"Exhilaration at every mile"** • *"Breathe in the beauty. Turn up the heat. You are in the 'PARADISE ZONE'"!* • "A New Southern Tradition, Come Run With US"! • "Running in the Footsteps of Legends" • **"...because life is not a destination"** • "Mind Body & Sole" • "World Class Event, Small Town Charm" • **"26.2 Miles of Breathtaking Black Hills Beauty"!** • *"Unleash the Wolf Within"* • "Experience of a Lifetime" • *"The marathon with altitude"!* • "It's not the beginning or the end of the race that counts, it's what happens in between". • *"Probably the most beautiful 26 miles, 385 yards you'll ever run"* • **"a Race for all reasons"** • "Run and get free stuff"! • "Spectacular Views. Great Friends. A Noble Cause". • "YES, YOU CAN" • **"On your mark. Get set. Let's rock"!** • *"A Monster Race.....running alongside the shores of the world's most famous loch".* • "The most amazing marathon you will ever run" • "The Eindhoven Marathon is one of the fastest marathons in the world and by far the most enjoyable"! • "feel the love" • **"Feel the spirit"** • *"The Last Marathon"* • "....Great Race.....Great Location....." • **"World's Coolest Marathon"** • *"The run and the scenery will take your breath away"!* • *"Run Paradise"!* • **"Embrace the Next Step"** • "The RUN that's FUN for everyone"! • **"Achieve your Goals"** • *"It's my marathon! and I'm running for..."* • "Come for the Run, Stay for the Fun"! • **"Cool Caribbean Running"** • "Endless miles, Endless smiles" • "Solidarity Race for the Saharawi People" • **"Cool Running New Zealand"** • *"Friendliest Marathon in the Pacific Rim"* • "An epic challenge that will require an epic strength of mind" • **"Picture a race where your dreams are fulfilled"** • *"Do you have what it takes? We think so"* • "Run. Rock. Relax".

People, places, passion, inspiration, pursuing dreams and goals. There are some big statements, some big claims with some of these marathons, but you get the idea. The marathon experience, quite simply, is a feel-good experience on many different emotional, physical, mental and spiritual levels. If I could, I'd be going to these events continually throughout the year.

The United States National Sporting Goods Association reports that 'marathon tourism' [destination marathons] is on the rise. Part of the reason is the profile of the runners themselves, who tend to have disposable income that can be put to travel. Coupled with the growing desire for healthy lifestyles the future looks promising for marathon tourism. Ellen Creager, a journalist for the Detroit Free Press, writes that large marathons like New York, Boston, Chicago and Honolulu can bring over $100 million into the local economy in a weekend.

In fact, New York does much better than that. A study conducted by Economic Research Associates on the New York Marathon's impact estimates that the race weekend brings in $220 million to the city. Eighty percent of the 37,000 plus runners are from outside New York City. Participants and spectators spend $71 million on hotels, $45 million on food and beverages, $42 million in retail merchandise, over $16 million on entertainment, $14 million on transportation and $11 million on running and fitness gear from the Expo.

Over 2006 and 2007 several marathons released findings of the local economic impact of their events: Washington DC and the Marine Corp Marathon ($31.7m), Miami ($15.8m), Boston ($95m), Baltimore ($14.8m), Portland ($15m). In Columbus Ohio, the Marathon reports that over 5,000 hotel room nights are booked directly because of the marathon weekend. The PF Chang Rock N' Roll Marathon in Arizona meanwhile, surveyed its runners and based on these findings, estimated that the total economic impact on the local county from the weekend was $41 million. Obviously all these data are a function of size but the point is clear – there are considerable downstream economic benefits from hosting a marathon, over and above the buzz and enthusiasm that the running inspires in the community.

What makes marathon events so attractive is that they require next to no infrastructure development. They can bring thousands of tourists to a location, infuse local populations with excitement and inspiration, stimulate the economy and create a weekend of positive experiences.

As more and more of the financial benefits are known, and more dollars invested and donated, we may see the commodification of what, really, is perhaps one of the simplest pleasures of all, running. I wonder if we'll lose something special with this growing commodification?

By the middle of 2008 the Gold Coast Marathon in Australia was considering expanding its event to make it a two-day festival, with 'support events' such as a 10km run and walk being held on day one. The number of runners had risen substantially from the previous year (25%), including increasing numbers of Japanese runners entering over the years. The Marathon Chairman, Kerry Watson, commented that "a lot of Japanese baby boomers, known as *Dankai*, who are about to get their superannuation [pension], are into fitness and travelling." With more disposable income, these Dankai are looking to spend, and combining travel with a healthy activity seems to make sense.

So much sense, in fact, that thousands of Japanese runners travel to Hawaii each year to run marathons (Honolulu and Maui especially). Meanwhile, the 'Oprah of Japan'– Akiko Wade – hosted a show dedicated to the Gold Coast marathon, and the famous comedienne, Hanako Miyagawa, ran in the half-marathon. (Several years ago the *real* Oprah ran the Marine Corp marathon in Washington DC, which heightened the awareness and interest in running marathons. Of course she had the papparazzi follow her every move, but nonetheless she did it).

The Japanese runners are extremely important to the Honolulu marathon and the Hawaiian economy. According to a study conducted by Hawaii Pacific University Professor, Jerry Agrusa, the 2007 Honolulu Marathon and Race Day Walk generated $108 million in spending and $3.7 million in state taxes. Over 20,000 runners and walkers were from Japan (compared to 2,400 from mainland USA). Agrusa calculated the economic benefits based on survey data that indicated 1.06 additional tourists (family/friends) came with each runner. Japanese runners, on average, would stay for 5-6 days.

What's interesting, besides the mind boggling numbers, is the depth of understanding that can, and probably should, be made of the runners themselves; there are lessons for other marathons interested in increasing the number of participants traveling to their events. Jerry Agrusa explains that Japanese tourists purchase *omiyage* – small gifts for friends and family (I know that feeling too). They also buy *kinen* – souvenirs that help to legitimize and commemorate their visit. So from just one country alone we have *Danken* buying *omiyage* and *kinen*, and I feel a second language coming on.

Thom Gilligan was working for a travel tour company

in the 1970s; while he was doing this he was booking his own travel plans to the Honolulu marathon. He convinced six other runners to go on the trip which he planned and ran. He couldn't convince his boss of the potential market so he ended up forming his own company *Marathon Tours and Travel* two years later.

Today, the company offers over twenty package tours to marathons around the world each year. Gilligan says he was in the right place at the right time – Boston in the late 1970s, but that aside, he's made a viable company out of offering a full experience for runners. The tours are wide and varied, offering much more than just a run. In January 2007 he was quoted in *Runner's World* as saying, "People will say that they had no intention of going somewhere like Antarctica until they heard there was a marathon there... But afterward, they are talking about the experience, not the race. So you need a good race and a good destination to make it work." He attributes part of his success to following his gut feeling. He added, "Runners are adventurous, well traveled, and independent type-A personalities. They don't want to sit in the back of a tour bus. They'd rather be running in front of it."

Thom Gilligan says that most travelling runners like to keep busy. Another trend he is noticing is the increasing popularity of half-marathons, which has put distance running, with run /walk strategies, into the realm of possibility for many people. The half-marathoners are traveling too, and more and more half-marathons are springing up around the globe.

There are several points to be made about the likes of the Marathon Tours company. First, I want Thom Gilligan's job. I can't think of many other jobs that would be as interesting, fun and rewarding. Second, it is highly likely the market will continue to expand; there is now an umbrella organization, for example, of tour companies that provide marathon tours. Third, although the core of the sales and marketing is "the run," it is the many other activities available in an area that will also entice runners for their partners, family and friends. Fourth, for people who are not interested in searching for all the flight, accommodation, and other transportation deals, and not wanting to deal with registration, the tour companies are a great one-stop solution. Fifth, if you want to get into a marathon but registration is closed, there are still options open to get access through guaranteed places that the tour companies have. Sixth, as good as your searching and booking skills are, you may want to think twice when trying to book arrangements in remote exotic places where language could be an issue, visa requirements challenging and communications with the marathon races 'spotty' at best.

Many traveling marathoners put it this way: "I have the money to travel and the desire to run. Years down the road the money will seem irrelevant but I will have collected irreplaceable memories."

The cost of traveling to marathons adds up, even domestically, by the time you pay for airline tickets, rental car, accommodation, race fees, and meals, aside from any discretionary spending. About half the marathoners who travel do so with their spouse or partner. Overseas travel is much more expensive again, especially if the desire is an exotic place to run 26.2 miles. Yet the demand is there. A marathon in Antarctica, for example, will cost over $6,000 US, but you'll have to go on a waitlist as the places are full at present.

Not all traveling marathoners are spending thousands of dollars. There are equal numbers of stories of those staying with friends, or camping, and running only in marathons as far as the car can drive them to. The world record holder for the most marathons run – 1,566 and counting – Horst Preisler, has never owned a car. That's right, 1,566. Horst, age 73 and still running strong, and his wife, who live in Hamburg Germany, made a conscious decision years ago that they would either raise a family or buy a car. Having a family won the day.

Then again, if you have a spare US $2,000-3,000 you can travel for a week and run the Great Wall of China marathon. That same amount will get you a marathon and an eight-day visit to Easter Island (including mainland Chile). The sixty-three square mile island is located over 2,000 miles away from the nearest population center. It's one of the most isolated inhabited islands in the world, but you can run a marathon there. Between $3,000 and 4,000 US will get you a one-week trip to Kenya to run in the Safaricom marathon or half-marathon. That $5,000 US that burns a hole in your pocket will take you to a marathon experience on the great Tibetan Plateau in India. The options are truly endless; limited only by your own budget and waiting lists to get to these exotic runs. Running a marathon is also possible in Alaska via a cruise ship vacation, as is running a marathon on Mars.

Well no, not that last one, but maybe it won't be too long.

And I think the word, really, is "Experience." I could run a marathon distance from the end of my driveway and feel like I'd accomplished something, but it's not the same as going to an event and experiencing "it" with others. We'll come back to that later. In Nashville, for example, you'll see fifty live bands playing at 27 entertainment stages at The Country Music Marathon and Half Marathon, which is more than just putting one foot in front of the other a few thousand times.

We should also think about those places, less desirable, that could equally benefit from a thrust of marathon spirit. Many cities use marathons in an attempt to transform their images to the rest of the world, or at least their own country. Cities, for example, that are seen as industrial wastelands, try to establish themselves as a place for pleasure and health. There are several tricks or essential marketing strategies to consider. One is a catchy name or phrase – like the ones earlier – that create something – a theme – that no other race uses. The second strategy is to choose your weekend carefully, because you may be up against some tough marathon events in other places that could limit your participation numbers. The third key ingredient is getting the event 'out there'.

With over 400 marathons to choose from each year in North America alone, there are plenty of marathons to run and only 52 weekends. Unless you do something different.

It's no longer just sufficient to state to the world that you are hosting a marathon, come and run 42.2 kilometres. We're runners, yes, but we're also consumers. The corporate world knows this well, which is why you see global corporations, national companies and small businesses all advertising their products and services at races. They know their market. An older clientele, many with plenty of disposable income looking for new things to do and new places to go. It's a microcosm of the baby boomers in many respects. These corporations pay for the latest fabrics for t-shirts, stylish medals presented to finishers, more freebies in the goody bags, and some amazing prize money.

The Dubai marathon in 2008, for example, is offering one million dollars in prize money. To a sport that has never been one that athletes gravitate to for huge financial gain, that's an enormous amount of cash. Increasingly the major marathons are competing with one another for the elite runners, who may only race 1-3 times a year. When you're that good the financial enticement will influence where you run and when. It's less of a concern for me. Well, it's not a concern at all really. I'm still waiting for the call from New York, London and Chicago to compete for their prize money.

I guess I can compete for prizes at the Cayman Island Marathon. Door prizes perhaps. But although the Cayman Islands has a major tourism market based on large cruise ships, even the smaller number of visitors like me that fly in, enter the marathon and look for great breakfast deals on the beach, help the local economy.

29

PEOPLE, PEACE, PASTA AND ALL THAT JAZZ

I'm still enjoying the air conditioning in Rhonda's office. Now's not the time to be asking Rhonda about destination marathons. I'm clearly going to be in the way so I quietly leave and walk back to the hotel, well, the beach front actually; it's only a ten minute walk up the road. I'll talk to Rhonda later. It's sunny, hot, and humid. I'm sweating 20 seconds into my walk. All the more reason to go to the beach.

But before I do, I decide to test my running computer in the hotel. Not by running though – I seem to have an aversion to that today – but by walking a couple of full laps of the hotel. Inside. I don't have the time or means to do a full calibration at this point but I want to see that it records distance with time. It's a quiet experiment, apart from saying hello to about five hundred curious hotel staff along my route. It seems like a success. Time for a break.

Waves gently lap the shoreline as people sunbathe, relax, sleep, swim and generally have a good time. There's a pale guy sitting beside the pool that overlooks the ocean. He's holding a colourful drink with an umbrella, his laptop in front of him, head phones on and he's busy writing a report. What a geek.

It's me. And I'm wishing that I have fewer, no, hang on ... *no* days in a tropical paradise when I have to work. It's now mid-afternoon. While I'm frustrated at having to write a report, here of all places, I remind myself that I'm actually here and that there are many worse places I could be writing a report. So I could turn these thoughts upside down and say this is the place to write a report.

Eventually I jump into the pool; some evolutionary failing to avoid report writing, I'm thinking. Half of me wants to explore the island, but the bigger half wants to stay off my feet and do everything I can to rest before the run on Sunday. The bigger half wins, so I spend the rest of the day around the hotel and the ocean. There must be therapy coming at me in all directions, most of which I don't fully understand I'm sure, but the combination of salt water, sun, sleep, staying off my feet, and mentally escaping to a different place must be good for me. Given these conditions maybe I'll run a world record on Sunday.

After having a rest from the relaxation in my hotel room, I head to the beach and continue the rigorous conditioning into the evening. I sit in a beach chair by the water listening to my music on my computer as the sun goes down on the horizon. A woman sitting nearby tells me she's here every day at this time to watch the sunset. She can't believe I'm working. I tell her I'm just listening to music but, although true, it sounds a bit flimsy. And then the sun gives up for the day, and the night begins. There's a band playing to the dinner guests at the outdoor restaurant. I sit on a rock nearby; not in the restaurant but close enough to have the bread passed to me if required.

Faced each night with a blended audience from around the world with multiple tastes and expectations, the band plays every possible genre known to civilisation. Bob Marley shares a spot with Elvis, followed immediately by Enrico from Latin America and a couple of those romantic candlelight songs which I recognise but can't name. Fifties rock n' roll features briefly. The dinner crowd continue on as if the band is not there. It's a shame because the band's quite good. The band almost calls for a paramedic for their lead guitarist when I clap after one of the songs.

In fact, I clap after each song, partly because no-one else is. I've now become the unofficial critic of the band this evening. After each song is completed the band members turn to me automatically. I start to vary my clapping to somehow reflect varying levels of satisfaction. It's getting complicated now. I should maybe get a scorecard.

The band is comprised of two male guitarists, a female vocalist and a drum machine on a computer. In the break the guitarists tell me that one of them is from Winnipeg and they've been playing in the United States for the past three years. They obviously enjoy it but you can't help feeling that they'd bring their playing up several notches if the audience were more receptive. Or receptive at all.

In fairness though, the audience is simply enjoying the company of friends, family and new people they may have just met here. There's clearly romance in the air for some, but some couples are spending their romantic night not saying anything to one another. Band or no band, if you're fortunate enough it's a wonderful experience sharing fine food and wine and enjoying one another's company as the ocean shimmers under the moonlight and a warm breeze rustles the leaves.

On my way back to my room I notice marathon types at the Lobby bar. Why not? I introduce myself. We get talking, naturally, about marathons. Lee and Trudy are middle-aged women from Fort Worth Texas, and have run several marathons together. Having gotten bored with the US marathon scene they saw the Cayman Islands Marathon leap out at them from the Internet. They decided to try something different.

Shortly after, Frank arrives. Frank's from Chicago, in his late fifties, and lean and healthy looking. He's been running and doing triathlons for years. He's waiting for his friends to arrive but they're having trouble getting flights out of Chicago due to snow storms. We all feel good that we're in the Caymans right now. Frank tells us of a runner who was having trouble with his feet always feeling crammed into his shoes when he ran. So he cut all his nails off. Still having trouble, he then cut the tops off his running shoes and ran open shoe. Frank's running the half-marathon, but he's also going to the Cayman Islands Jazz Festival, which happens to be on tonight and tomorrow night. There's a number of international performers playing at the Jazz Festival, including Natalie Cole and Arturo Tappin, among others, tomorrow night. Tempting.

Two other women, Rose and Chris, arrive now, and although they're not running and are here simply for a holiday, they get caught up in the marathon atmosphere. They promise to buy me a drink if I finish the marathon. There's incentive for you. It's good fun; there's a special magic for which the alcohol is not the sole cause.

I could stay all night but have to be moderately sensible about things. I doubt a couple of light drinks and a late night will substantially alter my run, and had I opted to go straight to bed I would've missed meeting some fun people. The experiences all count. It's the balance of things.

***

The next morning it's hot and humid once more. It's Race Pack pick-up/ Registration day here at the Marriott Hotel. The weather forecast for tomorrow is in the high eighties. I'm very conscious of the potential effects of the humidity. Obviously so are the organizers, which is why the run begins at 5am tomorrow. I'm motivated this morning. I go out first thing for a light run. Just 2km but it feels good; as far as I can tell everything seems to be working, including my running computer. It had rained in the early hours and there are still the odd drops of rain falling. I'm hoping it's like this tomorrow.

I stumble along the beach to my breakfast spot, managing to step on a piece of coral that sends a jolt of pain through my body. I don't need any coffee, I'm wide awake now thanks. I had better pay more attention to where I'm walking. It's a long way to come to watch a marathon.

Ahead in the distance I think I see another hotel, so in the swashbuckling spirit of Caribbean adventure I go beyond my breakfast spot in search of – well I don't know really – but I'll find out. It occurs to me that I'm passing up something I already know I like for something I know nothing about. I know that this says something deeper but now's not the time to go there. I've got to keep looking out for the coral.

It turns out the somewhere else is not a hotel but a series of new condominiums and construction. This is some of the rebuilding after Hurricane Ivan. I keep walking. It seems like I've walked half of Seven Mile Beach when I finally arrive at what looks like a decent spot.

No kidding. The Ritz-Carlton dominates the landscape and I'm like a bug to its light. Well worth the extra walk, but unlikely to provide me with a $6 breakfast. A $6 glass of water perhaps. How often do you get to have breakfast at the Ritz in the Caribbean? Not often – for me anyway, so I rationalize it's the right thing to do. I look for the restaurant.

I feel rich, and poor, just walking around the pool, and then feel like Tom Cruise in Mission Impossible, spending over ten minutes trying to work out how to get inside the building without blowing it up, or alternatively, like, Paris Hilton, having my staff deal with the inconvenient detail of finding access inside.

Eventually I find an access point, we'll call it a door. I walk in as if I own half of Manhattan. The other twelve people in the restaurant have a collective gross national product exceeding most African countries. The maitre'd shows me to my table, cracks the linen napkin and lays it across my lap, and pours some real orange juice. It doesn't seem like the time to ask for Fruit Loops. After he asks if I'd like coffee and quickly estimates my net worth after tax, he passes me the photocopied abridged version of the latest New York Times.

I'd be wasting space describing my buffet breakfast but you can imagine it wasn't too bad for the $30 Cayman dollars ($36 US), including tip. We'll call it carbo-loading. I didn't really want to leave, but it was going to appear rude if I systematically worked through the Hotel's entire buffet selection over the day. Pulling my fully carbo-loaded body out of the chair I venture into the hotel proper for a while, which opulently straddles over the road away from the beach to its main entrance and golf courses. The richness and vastness are overwhelming. I walk around the Hotel just to look like I should be here and feel important, but I know I have to get back to planet earth and pick up my race kit.

Back at the Marriott there's a buzz in the air as runners register in the mezzanine area; old and new friends and families talking to one another. It's a small, intimate affair in comparison to Athens; we're not in an aircraft hangar, for one thing. Registration is as smooth as I could hope it to be, and there are real goodies in the goody bag, as well as blue and yellow t-shirts with our Marathon Tortuga proudly running with the Cayman Islands flag.

I meet Jerry, who I'd met at the airport, and he introduces me to Marius Acker, one of the top runners in the Caymans when he's not surfing. Marius is in his late twenties, medium height and thin; he has that runner's 'look' that I'll never have. He's entered the half marathon and is considered to be one of the favourites.

I also meet Dane Rauschenberg. Dane is running 52 marathons in 52 weeks in 2006. Fifty-two?! He's almost done; this marathon will be #48. Like Dave in Athens, Dane makes me feel like I'm a sloth. He also looks like a runner. Tall and thin; you would miss him if looking from the side. Very personable and dedicated to raising money for his charity – L'Arche in Mobile, Alabama, a chapter of an international community living organization for people with mental disabilities.

Dane ran alongside Lance Armstrong's group in New York. There were cameras, police and vehicle fumes the whole distance as he kept his eyes and ears on Lance's group. There won't be any of that in the Caymans, in part because Lance Armstrong isn't here, but also because this marathon has about 37,000 fewer runners. There's also no Expo here either, but the goody bag contains t-shirts, a personal fan, key chain light, drink bottle, plastic cup and other assorted goodies. One runner comments that it's the best goody bag she's ever received.

The heat is one thing that the runners have been expecting, but the humidity is a surprise for some. One woman from California tells me she's just changed from the full to the half because of the humidity – the dry heat is fine, she says, but she wouldn't be able to last the full marathon distance in the humidity.

There's a group of friends – Frank's friends – who've made it finally from Chicago; getting away from the snow, grey and cold of the windy city. There are families reuniting around the run, with some of the family members now living in the Caymans. One runner is celebrating his fiftieth birthday tomorrow by running his first marathon. Friends have entered together simply to see if it's possible to actually run the distance. Everyone's excited, happy to talk and simply happy to be here. Surprisingly, it starts to rain heavily and blow a gale – a bit of a relief in some ways but it only adds to the humidity. Perhaps its nature's way of saying take it easy and rest up. I've already walked a big chunk of the beach today. I need to keep cool and stay off my feet.

But I don't do that.

**

I do take it easy for some of the afternoon; checking emails, doing a quiet jig of joy when I see on the Internet that it's snowing back home (pathetic isn't it), and watching a movie on TV.

I'm thinking I might go to the Jazz Festival in the evening, but before that there's the pasta party in George Town at Breezes by the Bay, a picture postcard type of Tropical Grill and Rhum Deck Restaurant/ Bar that looks out over the ocean. Quite spectacular. It's only a thirty-minute walk from the hotel so I'll sweat my way down to the party.

It's quiet in the downtown area, but that's probably because there are no cruise ships in today. If the cruise ships are in, it's chaotic. It's the same old story; passengers from the cruise ships, each of which can hold up to 5,000 all-you-can-eat-and-drink guests, pour into the streets from the ferrying boats, ask which island they're on, it's Tuesday it must be the Cayman Islands or maybe Jamaica, maybe it's Wednesday I can't keep track now, I don't know, it's not important really, let's just get off the ship I'm going crazy, and buy a few dollars worth of products and services that I'll never see again or even use in my life so, oh, I know, and one of those colourful shirts you look so good in, and, oh, don't let me forget this time, let's get a gift for my sister, are you listening. Before they turn into pumpkins and hop back onto the boats they've made their purchases in one of the five hundred jewellery stores, souvenir stores, clothing stores, or the Jimmy Buffet Margaritaville Store and Bar. The fun reaches another metaphysical plane when five or more ships are in port at the same time.

There are three levels and outdoor decks at Breezes by the Bay, but most of us stay inside making sure the air conditioning works. Not being weenies, just being sensible. Complete strangers sit with one another and reveal our pasts, our fears for tomorrow, and other things that seem incredibly important at the time. The food is superb; everything – the fruit, vegetables, salads, the pasta and breads are fresh and healthy, and full of carbohydrates of course. I don't eat much because I'm still pretty full from my Ritz-Buffet-Trough-Binge thing and a foot-long veggie sub I had eaten earlier this afternoon.

I sit with Alice and Thomas, a couple from San Francisco, and Angie from South Africa. Alice runs but Thomas prefers cycling. He cycles with Alice and sometimes cycles ahead and places drinks strategically for Alice along her running route. They're here to have a vacation. Being able to combine it with a marathon, in this instance a half-marathon for Alice, is exactly what they're looking for. Angie is from South Africa and living in the Cayman Islands for two years. She thought, why not try running the half marathon. It'll be interesting, she says, because she's off to an office Christmas party tonight after this pasta party.

All good things must come to an end, but new ones begin. I walk back with Alice and Thomas to the hotel. Well almost. It turns out the Jazz Festival is en route. I can't resist going in. How many times in your life do you get to go to a major Jazz Festival that is ten minutes from your Caribbean hotel? It's $50 admission, which doesn't seem like a great deal. If you would like, it's another $2 for a plastic patio seat, which is a novel way of doing things although unlikely to grab momentum in North America. I was able to get the chair of my choice, a sleek white model circa 1978, from the seat dispensers and take it to wherever I want to sit in the open field. I park my chair at the back of the crowd, yet I'm still within metres of the stage. I'm feeling quite proud to be here, and somewhat surprised there's not more people.

After two hours of sipping water and enjoying the atmosphere, we're getting right into the music with *Swanky* and *Hi Tide*. People haven't stopped coming in, and suddenly it seems that I'm no longer at the back of the audience but right in the front. Thousands have arrived since I got here; there won't be enough plastic seats on the island let alone the concert venue. The festive occasion is just getting more and more festive.

A woman walks through the seated folks up front asking if all the chairs are taken; to which everyone politely says yes – if there is a chair unoccupied it's only because someone is off to the washroom or to get a drink or both. Seeing the futility in asking she picks up a plastic chair and makes a run for it. Immediately a silver haired man, I'm guessing in his nineties, leaps to his feet, balances, and takes off to bring her down.

Or at least get the chair back. He does. The crowd goes wild. There's a new hero in town, and hopefully one that's not in full cardiac arrest right now. As much as I'd like to go to the washroom, well, a portapotty, partly because of all the water I've been drinking, I don't want to leave my chair alone. I can't take it with me either. I'm getting desperate though, so I start crying, bequeath my chair to the couple beside me, untangle my legs, and stumble like a drunk back into the darkness where the portapotties sit quietly waiting.

The music is brilliant. I'm forgetting I have to run a marathon in a few hours. It's close to 11pm when Natalie Cole finally comes on. Her music blasts me into the back fence. Her voice makes sure I stay there. It's an explosion of sound that sets car alarms off in Cuba. I'm increasingly conscious of the fact that I have to get up around 3:30am. It's almost midnight now and I still have to walk back to the Hotel. If I stay too long I'll also go deaf, which may mean I'll miss my 3:30am alarm when it goes off.

I wave good-bye to Natalie but I guess she's busy. And unlikely to be running tomorrow. Better chance of seeing her at the Ritz Carlton buffet.

It's been quite the day. Quite the experience. I listen to the concert all the way back to the Hotel. I'm pleased to finally be in bed, but realise as I turn the light off at 1am, that in four hours I will start running 42.2km.

Hmmm.

Summary

Planned Distance = Dont know;
Actual distance run = 54km

30

THE CAYMAN ISLANDS MELT DAY

This is it. The Day. It starts later than 3:30am because I thought that was too cruel to myself. Instead, I set the alarm for 3:55am, a massive twenty-five minute sleep-in. I'd like to say I feel rested but I'm doing all I can to reach over and hit the snooze button three times. I get a wake-up call. Yes, thank-you. Got it. I've asked the front desk to call me as well, making the point that if I sleep through the beginning of the race it's bad news.

I slither off the bed and drag my happy body into the bathroom, making some coffee en route. More wake-up calls. Yes I am thanks. But I think I'm talking into the coffee cup. There's a lot to do in less time than should typically be allotted for such things. I have a shower thinking this will wake me up. I disappear into a netherworld of alarms going off and phone calls, losing track of the reality that is quickly ticking by. It's a desperate time.

Another call. I assure the front desk that I'll be there for the shuttle bus in a few minutes. I'm multi-tasking right now, hoping that I have everything for the race and that I'm fully dressed – at least shorts and shoes anyway.

I arrive at the shuttle stand with shoes in hand like Kramer arriving in Jerry's apartment. I don't put my running shoes on until the last possible minute in the belief that my feet will be wearing them for a few hours so why make the suffering last any longer. Other zombie-like runners are milling around. The mood is one of cautious optimism, mixed with relief that the day has finally come. We're bold enough, or still in a trance, to tell others what we hope our times will be. Tad and I confess we're hoping we'll break four hours this morning.

It's a nice touch by Kelly Holding to provide the shuttle bus service, even though the start line at the Breezes by the Bay intersection is not too far away. We arrive in the darkness but see we're not the only ones who think it's a good idea to get up when some people are still wandering back from the Jazz festival. I can't hear Natalie any more so I think she's finished.

Some runners, in fact, have skipped the sleep portion of their pre-race build-up. They remained with Natalie at the concert until the very end. By the time they got back to the Hotel they saw little point in going to bed. They stayed up and took their time getting ready for the run. That's experience and confidence for you.

The volunteers and organizers are wearing yellow t-shirts. Jerry wears an unmistakable bright orange shirt as he and the other volunteers usher runners to the start line. Despite Orange Jerry's glow it's still dark. And very warm. Well, hot and humid. Doesn't bode well.

It's a festive spirit again as we huddle closer together at the start-line. Some runners are more awake than others. There is some irony in the notion that you train for months and months and when the time finally arrives you want to lie down on your bed. Some runners look within themselves for inner strength and resolve. Some runners tie their laces for the fifteenth time. Some runners look for the start button on their MP3 players. Some runners look like three-year olds who have just lost sight of their mom at the shopping mall. Some runners congratulate others for making it to the start-line. It's a sincere, meaningful and important moment.

The gun goes off and so do we. There are giggles and cheers from the runners and the spectators. Marathoners, half-marathoners and relay teams all leave at the same time. The serious runners have, within seconds, already disappeared into the darkness. Friends and family members who had no choice but to drive their running partner to the start-line, no doubt are relieved to see us finally disappear into the black abyss, perhaps thankful they're not running a marathon or a half-marathon, and can instead look for another coffee, or the car, or a place to sleep.

Within minutes I'm caught up in my own drama. I'm completely soaked with sweat. It's humid alright. At my very, very best, I estimate I'll be doing this for four hours. I try not to think like that though because that seems like a very long time. Instead, like most runners, I prefer to break the run into manageable chunks – the next corner, the next mile, the first quarter, the half-way mark, and so on. It would help if I could see. Later in the race I'll break the run into more realistic goals like 'the next mail-box' or 'the next step.' Careful not to disappear into a bush, I almost do a pirouette of joy when I see my MP3 player is working *as well as* my running computer. Is this a harbinger for the rest of the race?

Well this is no time to get caught up in woo-woo. I need tangibles to get me through, like talking to other runners. I find myself running alongside Roger MacMillan. I didn't know he was Roger MacMillan of course, but we chat. Like several others I've met, Roger and I still keep in touch.

He's running well; better than me I think, although I'm pleased I'm not running injured at this point. After a couple of kilometres we runners have begun to spread along the route. From now on the distance between us will increase.

Our conversation ebbs and flows over many minutes as Roger uses the run-walk approach that has become increasingly popular in marathons these days. He tails-off for a minute and then a few minutes later we're running together again. Roger says he runs for several reasons, such as keeping fit and living longer, preventing bad habits from creeping into his life, and the simple enjoyment of it all – the fresh air, getting out amongst nature and hearing and seeing the birds and wildlife. And, he adds, it's also about the camaraderie of running.

At age 69, Roger is the oldest competitor in the Cayman Islands marathon. He's originally from the United Kingdom but now lives in Alberta, Canada. He started running in 1989 after asking a fellow worker one day where he got all running shirts he was wearing. His co-worker said from running races, which spurred Roger on to register for a 10km race. Roger got addicted to the running life. Since that time he's run a few marathons and about forty half-marathons.

As Roger explains, being as far north as he is in Northern Alberta, it's great if you can train indoors. He did most of his training for the Cayman Marathon on an indoor track in the Northwest Territories, just 200 kilometres south of the Arctic Circle. Some choices are easy to decide upon. Run outside in the near Arctic winter in snow, winds and minus 35 degrees Celsius temperature with the wind-chill, or ... run inside.

It's been great talking to Roger; the time passes by quickly while I'm covering the distance. Eventually we split up due to different pacing strategies. Mine also includes some walking, which I hadn't done in Athens. I'm hoping it's going to work for me here, because I know the heat will probably suck everything out of me if I run solid. It may do that even if I don't run the whole way, even though I like running in the heat. It's still dark and I'm dripping with sweat. When the sun arrives it'll feel like I'm running in an oven.

The course is a double-loop along the south shore of the island. The start-line is the finish line; for the full marathoners among us, we'll cross the line once – our half-way point, and then repeat the loop. Most of the first half is in darkness, so the second loop in the light of day doesn't actually feel like you're repeating the run. A clever trick.

A quarter of the way through the race I'm feeling good. I've decided to walk for a minute every 2.5km that I run. My pace feels good. Maybe too good. I'm suspicious. At this rate I'm heading for a sub 4-hour time. But it's early still. Orange Jerry drives by on his Vespa and cheers us on. Fifteen minutes later he's further along the course cheering us on; there's speculation he may have a twin.

There are plenty of water stations, which are fantastically sprinkled every mile along the course with bottles, yes bottles, of water, and plenty of them, for the runners. There's a competition being held for the best water station, so there are costumes galore and tremendous support from these volunteers. One station has volunteers dressed as fruit and vegetables, another has a rock n' roll air band, another is hosted by nurses and another is a microcosm of Mexico. The volunteers are really getting into the spirit. Comments from the runners at the stations and in between clearly show it's much appreciated.

I'm close to half-way now and still feeling good, but not as good as thirty minutes ago. I catch up with Tad, who I'd met in the shuttle bus earlier. We run together for a while. It looks like the heat is taking a toll on him as we approach halfway; the end of the run for the half-marathoners, which explains the smiles on some runners faces. Tad says he feels a lot worse than he looks. I start to pull away, or to be more precise, Tad drops back.

I check my running computer and see it's telling me I'm at half-way. The course on the other hand, strongly indicates half-way is about 500 metres away at best, maybe further. This is not the time to discuss distance with race organizers but I roll my eyes, losing my balance as I do so, because a certain déjà vu feeling is filling my thoughts right now.

A certain déjà vu feeling is filling my thoughts right now. I cross the half-way/finish line at the Breezes by the Bay intersection as the day starts to lighten up. While I'm disappointed about the running computer, which also means I'm now behind my estimated time as I try to break 4-hours, I'm still pleased to be half-way and feeling like I'm in control. But boy, those half-marathoners who have finished sure look happy.

And then, about twenty minutes later, it all starts to un-ravel. The sun comes out. I quickly realise how good it was not to have it. It's HOT now. There's little respite apart from the water stations. The runners have thinned considerably, perhaps melted away, as the half-mara-thoners have finished. There's only 40-50 marathoners now spread out over several miles. The MP3 music that helped me get this far when I wasn't talking to other run-ners is showing signs of fatigue. The sound is scratchy and intermittent, at best. I think it's moisture from the sweat and water I've tipped over myself. For the next half an hour I burn valuable calories putting the earbuds in every conceivable position possible, tamper with the wiring like I'm a fine jewel-maker, and turn the MP3 player on and off, at a conservative estimate, a hundred times, thinking this will magically transform things. I'd kick it but it's too small. Nothing transforms except me; I may have developed a repetitive strain injury pushing all the buttons. I'm lousy with remote controls for TV and sound systems as well.

Orange Jerry and his twin come in and out of focus three more times, am I dreaming, one of which might have been a mirage, I'm not sure. My running computer continues to lie, I know it's further than what it says; an electronic conspiracy is taking place. My mind wanders uncontrollably. I'm doing all I can to ensure my feet don't do the same.

The views meanwhile, are great, even though the wa-ter stations are now too infrequent, despite the fact that they haven't moved, or have they, and I'm wondering how can I possibly finish this run. It's a mess. The sun has sapped all my energy. I'm reduced to a waddle, although at unpredictable times, I transform back into a runner again.

But I'm not the only one. Other runners are clearly experiencing similar wonderful feelings. Incredibly, I pass two runners, who must, given my speed, be running backwards. We are redefining the word Run. We're all in this together, but it does wonders for your soul to think you can run just that little bit faster than others at times.

But for the most part I'm struggling. Another runner and I have been running close to one another in run-walk segments and we eventually become synchronised in our efforts. It's John from Florida. This is John's second marathon. For the rest of the race we pull each other through.

We're obviously embracing the run-walk strategy, which looks more like walk-run at this point. Or walk-walk-run-walk-walk ... We're extremely polite about this. "Any time you want to walk just say so, and I'm good with that", is our evolving mantra to one another. At any time one of us could take off, but we don't. There's no point. There are no records to be broken. We've got about eight kilometres left to run and if John can pull me through this I'll be forever grateful.

At 35km I start getting a bad stomach cramp, which is very unusual for me as I never get stomach cramps. At 36km I throw water over me, which turns out to be a bad move because I miss and end up getting a lot of water in my shoes. I'm now Mr. Squishy for the rest of race, developing a blister in record time.

According to my increasingly inaccurate running computer I've now completed the marathon. But I see the taller buildings in the distance, about 2km away, where I know the finish line waits. I posit a theory to John that maybe the organizers have overshot the distance. He smiles in that polite you're-being-an-idiot way that people do, and I change the conversation.

One kilometre to go. The cramps have gone. We're transforming yet again, doing much more running than walking. We've picked up the scent of the finish line. A dog decides to run with us, especially John. He jumps around a bit and so does the dog. John tells me he's been attacked by two dogs when training. He has a scar on his face from being attacked by a sheep dog. On another run a German shepherd jumped on him from behind. Along one strip of his training route he now has a metal bar sitting discreetly by a fence, just in case.

As we wind our way through the last few hundred metres of downtown buildings I can't believe I'll soon stop running. I'm okay with that thought. John, for some strange reason, starts to race ahead of me. I catch up with him. We turn the last corner and see the finish line seconds away.

Or minutes. It feels like minutes. Eventually we get there and cross the line together. I don't even look at my time. We shake hands. A volunteer full of smiles and energy places a finishers medal over my head. I'm barely standing. The weight of the medal pulls me closer to the ground. The relief and release is almost overwhelming. This was a tough one.

I decide I need a massage under the tent. There's a line-up – only about half a dozen runners – but its long enough that I have to sit down, because my legs feel like they're being sucked into a hole in the ground. As I sit down I get leg cramps, and like the parting of the sea, but less dramatic perhaps, those in line ahead of me make way and urge me to go to the free table that has emerged. It's very kind of them. Within seconds I decide to lie on the table for about five years. The massage therapist starts to bring my legs back to normal, which is a good thing as I'll have to use them again sooner or later.

But it's done. The second marathon completed. I'm hungry and thirsty, but if I drink one more sip of Gatorade it won't be pretty. I talk with the therapist but I have no idea what I'm saying. There may be profound thoughts going on through my head but I think they're being pushed aside by thoughts of juicy steaks, lying on the beach, a few cool drinks, passing out and another massage.

I mentally pinch myself, reaffirming the fact that I've really finished. I've run a marathon, and it's not even 10am on Sunday morning. It's great news as now I've got a whole day to rest, relax and replenish, and start the re-education of my legs and all they're meant to do. Some non-marathoners are probably just waking up to continue their vacation.

The sad news is I have to get off the massage table; something about other runners needing help. I surprise myself by getting off without any help in less than ten minutes. I'm hobbling but there's no sense of imminent collapse like I'd felt before the massage.

I see Frank from the other night and we congratulate each other. He never did go to bed after Natalie finished, and looks fine at this point of the day. He invites me to watch the Chicago Bears game at the CARA pub later in the day. Everyone is smiling and congratulating one another, but I seem to have special smiles for the people that I've met earlier or on the run. It's an amazing atmosphere filled with spirit, goodwill, goal achievement and camaraderie. We're truly all in this together.

I see Angie from South Africa. We sit down together on the curb. The euphoria of finishing and the ability to rest my legs, which seem like they are only painted on right now, means the curb feels like a lazy-boy recliner. I don't want to get up, perhaps, ever. The downtown intersection has been cordoned off so it's now a sea of runners, friends and families, with music playing in the background. Angie's quite pleased with her time of 2:11 for the half marathon. Pretty good alright, considering she'd been out at her work's Christmas party the night before. She's not so pleased that she pulled her calf muscle though.

Dane is all smiles as well. Number 48 completed, coming in 3rd place for the men with a time of 3:24. Most of us will be contemplating when our next run might be, but Dane knows his will be next weekend. I see Tad next. He sits down and shares his potato chips with Angie and me. Heaven. Boy, do they know how to put salt on potatoes. I can't get enough of them, but the thought of two grown men fighting in the street over potato chips pulls me from the brink of an embarrassing moment.

The three of us cross the road to the other curb to get a better view of the award ceremony. As we make our way over I meet up with Lee and Trudy from the other night. They tell me they finished last and second last, but it was well worth it because they had five police cars with sirens on and lights flashing behind them as they came into the downtown area and over the finish line.

The organizers had waited until all the competitors had finished; again, a very nice touch. Marathons are for everyone and finishing is always special regardless of where you place. In any case it's still morning and no-one seems to be in any hurry to leave. It's still very festive. I'm creating my own festive feast with a personal banquet of bananas, diet Pepsi, water and a cookie. It may not sound like much, but it's what my body is craving right now. The chips are finished. I'm crushed.

First place overall in the marathon this year is Julie Stackhouse (3:06) from Florida, running in her first ever marathon. Local man and favourite Mark Hyde is close behind in second place in 3:09. Malcolm Anderson stormed in close behind with a time of 4:35, securing 32nd place, with his first half – his split – at 2:06.

The Award for Best Water Station goes to 'The Mexicans', who have now won it three years in a row. Gina Connolly who leads the Mexicans each year said to me that they "not only give out water, they try to share their culture, warmth, cheer and soul". Gina added, "We've learned how to keep a high spirit within our team in order to encourage the runners to keep their motivation levels up, and in doing so, finish the race."

With the awards ceremony over now people are starting to leave. With Tad's potato chips finished too, I decide it's time to drag my body along the street to a waiting shuttle bus.

If there wasn't an elevator at the hotel I'd still be crawling up to the 2nd floor. Once inside my room I lie gently down on the bed with that oh... aah ... feeling; just long enough to feel spoilt. Soon, I get a cold bath ready.

Apparently the high today is 30 degrees, with a relative humidity of 75%! This fact may largely explain why my body feels the way it does. I'm still starving, and would eat a horse if it galloped into my bathroom.

It doesn't, so I resort to chocolate bars and some orange pop instead. I'm getting some feelings in my legs that are unrelated to cramp and anvils; nice to know they're functioning once more. I lie there feeling immensely satisfied that I finished, and looking forward to an afternoon of doing a lot of nothing, and having a massage at the hotel.

That's right, a massage. I simply enjoyed it so much in Athens. I'm in self-spoiling mood because I feel I deserve it. Lisa from England thinks so too, and for the next fifty minutes she manipulates and pulls and stretches my body. Lisa's here on a short-term working stint, as so many people seem to be on Grand Cayman Island. Well my body is pleased she's here today, but almost as soon as it starts it's over. It's easier getting off the table this time.

I hobble over the road to the CARA pub and watch the Chicago Bears with Frank and his friends. If you want to veg out mentally a good option is to park yourself in front of a football game on TV. We're all in a slightly euphoric, exhausted state. The air conditioning is on, which adds to the enjoyment considerably. If I wasn't sitting on a high stool I might be tempted to fall asleep.

Instead, after a couple of drinks I decide to go back to the hotel. As much as I'd like to sit on the beach in the sun my body has had enough heat for one day. It's late afternoon by now. I pull the curtains, order some food, lots of it, sit back and watch Tommy Lee Jones and Robert Downey Junior try to catch the fugitive. I then watch three back-to-back Law and Order TV shows; I manage to solve the crimes. Not long after that I fall into a deep, deep .... sleep.

2006 Cayman Islands Marathon Results				
Place	Name	Country	1/2 split	Finish
1st	Julie Stackhouse	United States	1:33.09	3:06.17
2nd	Mark Hydes	Cayman Islands	1:33.12	3:09.26
3rd	Michael Ridsdale	Cayman Islands	1:33.11	3:18.01
4th	Julie Armstrong	United Kingdom	1:36.24	3:19.53
32nd	Malcolm Anderson	New Zealand	2:06.37	4:35.05

Note: there were 48 finishers.

31

Cayman R&R

A deep sleep maybe, but not that long. It's 5am. I lie here planning the day ahead – it's my last day – a big breakfast I decide, followed by a trip to Stingray City. That will eat up most of the day.

Although there's only one other person in the hotel restaurant, for some reason the four hostesses are watching me. Is there a kick-me sign on my shirt? Am I wearing all my clothes? Every time I look at them they either give me that I'm-about-to-laugh smile or look quickly away. It's like I'm playing a game with them, but I don't know which one.

Maybe I look like a marathon runner about to take a financial wrecking ball to their buffet breakfast. That would be closer to the truth. Maybe they think I'll start eating the table. There's an enormous amount of buffet breakfast food waiting to be eaten. My body is craving anything and everything all at once. As much as I'd like to, I can't eat all day because I'm off to Stingray City shortly.

It looks like there's a few of us from the hotel going to Stingray City, including Chris and Rose who I'd met a couple of nights before at the hotel's Lobby bar. We pile into a minivan and head-off for our adventure. After a few minutes by the water looking at the typical array of souvenirs we're boating out towards the reef and preparing to throw ourselves into the water with killer stingrays.

Unfortunately stingrays have received some bad press lately after Steve Irwin, the Australian Crocodile Hunter, was killed in a freak accident with one a few months ago. We're assured that nothing like that is going to happen here but you can't help thinking about the possible can you? Alcoholic drinks are available on the boat.

But what are the odds, really? Let's face it, if they were a real danger it's highly unlikely that the Cayman Islands would take a risk that could crush their tourism market.

So after a pensive few minutes where some folks get the last minute jitters about being killed by the stingrays or worse, most of us tumble off the back of the boat, or walk down the back stairs to walk into the water, to swim with these creatures.

Stingrays can grow to up to 6.5 feet (2 metres long), and up to almost 800 pounds in weight. There are over sixty species of stingrays but none of us could tell you the difference. The key facts we're told is that they're harmless, and to stay away from the barbed razor-sharp spine – the stinger grows from the stingray's tail. Sounds like pretty good common sense. They're related to sharks but that doesn't worry me. Their venom provokes muscle contractions, but we'll not be concerned about that.

At all. For today we will put all that fear-thing aside and swim with them, hold them and feed them. Maybe even adopt them or sneak them home in our bags. Puts the marathon in new perspective.

There's about a dozen of us swimming in 15-20 ft deep water. Initially the Rays are camouflaged on the sandy bottom where they spend most of their time, but hey, this is feeding time now, so they swim up to us. They brush alongside us like little kittens, except these are distinctly wild animals – hell, stingrays – and I can't believe I'm really doing this.

What a buzz. The stingray's eyes are on its side, but its mouth, nostrils, and gill slits are on its underbelly. The first one that sidles up to me looks like I could use him as a surfboard. He lets me touch him; at least that's what I think is going on. It's like stroking a pile of portobello mushrooms – soft and velvety. Our tour guide, meanwhile, is picking them up, carefully, and encouraging us to come and pat them.

After a while I'm getting used to them brushing up alongside me; always wary of the stinger. Feeling invincible now, I decide to feed them – some concoction that the tour operators know works, as stingrays typically eat clams, oysters, mussels, and humans.

No, not humans, just kidding, but funny things go through your mind in these moments, especially if you're like Jill, another tourist, who has decided to sit on the back of the boat and swim with the stingrays from there.

With my hand holding this magic fishy stuff in the water, Tex – I call him Tex because he's huge – comes along with his mouth on his underbelly ready to suck the food from my hand. Or maybe my hand from my arm. We're told that their suction is quite powerful. If they think we are food by mistake we can end up with a hickey on any part of our body, which is exactly what a few of us end up with. Explain that to your partner who's not there with you.

So Tex glides gracefully up to me. Within a split second the food is gone. It's like a high powered vacuum cleaner. I lift my hand out of the water to see if Tex also swam away with a finger or two. I'm relieved to see everything intact.

It's one of those once-in-a-lifetime experiences. I swim around for about an hour or so with these wild creatures. Rose passes her camera to me and I start clicking like I'm Jacques Cousteau, except he's dead right now too and I can't take photos underwater to save myself. I snorkel over to the reef nearby. The water is quite choppy but I manage to take several blurry photos of what I think are fish; mostly I snap award-winning images of blurry rocks. I've inherited my mother's photography skills. (Rose later sends me the photos so I can vouch for the high ratio of blurry images.)

Back on the boat with everyone and their digits accounted for, it's celebration time. We cutting-edge adventurers have survived the wild. The stories are flying, the drinks spilling, and the hickeys are proudly displayed as if we've just survived shark attacks. The sun is shining and you'd think this was the best day in the world.

I've forgotten that my body is still recuperating from the marathon. But as I say good-byes to everyone back at the hotel the various aches and pains come back to remind me of the previous day. The salt water swim was excellent therapy, so much so that I figure I better get some more and head for the beach.

Not too much of a good thing though. Later I do a bit of shopping for friends and family at home. I'm struck by the vista as I walk into town. That's a lie. I take a taxi because the humidity is off the charts and the temperature is in the 80s. I'm melting as soon as I go outside. The vista is of six huge cruise ships lying menacingly just off the coast. They must have arrived overnight. I mentally prepare myself for the swell of people. Just as well because when I get to town it's like a shopping mall on Christmas Eve.

Where am I? But then I remember that this is what it's all about. I've never been on a cruise ship so I don't understand the attraction of going port to port to pre-arranged destinations with thousands of strangers to buy similar souvenirs in each spot. I'd be hoping to miss the pick-up time.

I had been thinking of spending a relaxing few hours ambling quietly around the downtown area but I'm so overwhelmed by the jostling cruise ship people – especially in Jimmy Buffet's *Margaritaville* where thousands of dollars are being exchanged to buy products that have virtually nothing to do with the Cayman Islands – that I just want to go back to the beach. Any beach. There are dozens of free beaches that will soothe and relax and provide memories for a lifetime.

**

The people.

I met a lot of people that were involved with the Cayman

Islands Marathon. Jerry 'Fatcalves' Harper, an athletics coach in the Caymans is a tireless volunteer who has coached countless successful runners there. These days he is a large man; an imposing figure on that motorcycle when he drives around the course to ensure everything is going smoothly on race day. He seems to know everyone and everyone knows Jerry.

Mark Hyde, a Caymanian who was the first male home this year, is one of the local favourites. He always registers late, which gives the organizers heart palpitations. Several other Hyde family members run in the marathon day races. Mark commented in a local paper that he runs the marathon every year because he wants to inspire other people to run. He added that "Each footstep allows one more problem to fall away, and when I finish I have a great feeling."

Julie Stackhouse, an athletics coach from Florida, won the overall marathon this year. Incredibly it was her first ever marathon. "The victory was surreal," Julie said to me afterwards. "I can't believe the sense of accomplishment. I'm hooked on marathons."

Maria Mays is an ex-pat from the United Kingdom. Maria won the half marathon (again) in a time of 1:26. She actually had the flu on race day. While all of us were sweating through the race Maria was cold from start to finish. The great thing about running, she said to me, is that all you need is a really good pair of running shoes and the rest is over to you. It's what you make it. Maria runs to and from work every day, for a total daily distance of about ten miles. She's become quite visible in the community. Maria said one day a stranger came up to her in a store and asked what they should be doing with their hands when they run. What she also likes is that you can run and get to see some great places.*

And this, really, is at the heart of destination marathons. It was my motivation for running New York in 1985; how else was I going to see Harlem, the Bronx and Yonkers and come out alive with all my limbs intact?

Winners and fast times are only part of a marathon. In fact, they're a very small, almost insignificant part. Most of us don't break land speed records. Running marathons is about many things, like commitment, sense of purpose, overcoming adversity and building self-worth. We all have reasons for running marathons, and often the individual stories are inspirational. The Cayman Islands marathon was no different.

Stephanie and Mike Jones of Clippity Clop Farm (really) in Richards Landing, Ontario, Canada ran the half marathon. At exactly the same time their friends back in Ontario showed their support and shared the experience by running the same distance in darkness and snow. Canadians do that sort of thing; snow is just freezing cold and wet, but otherwise it's pretty much like summer.

Lyn Elvins, a South African now working in the Caymans who has run over 60 marathons, ran with a piece of carved driftwood that fit perfectly in her hand. Lyn was given this by her father in South Africa, when he was unable to see her run and shout words of encouragement at the Two Oceans ultra in South Africa one year. Lyn runs with the driftwood now. As she says, when she went to the Caymans it was "the next best thing to packing Dad".

---

*The following year, 2007, Julie Stackhouse, the overall marathon winner this year, ran in the half marathon, as did Maria once more. They were neck and neck the entire race with Maria edging Julie out to win in a time of 1:28:14, just 15 seconds ahead of Julie.

Another marathoner talked about the passion and satisfaction of running in the Caymans. She said that the sense of accomplishment that running brings is like nothing else and living in Grand Cayman surrounded by its beauty, especially during a run, is almost too breathtaking for words.

Some of the other finishers had these words:

"Running has made me stronger, more confident, and has proven that I have within me the dedication and commitment to accomplish any goal or challenge that stands before me"

"During the marathon I realized how much courage everybody can have in order to succeed"

"Through running I have learned about myself at the deepest level"

"Running has inspired me to accomplish more than I ever imagined"

"The reward to me is truly much more than the effort expended"

And about the Caymans specifically, they told me:

"I found the Cayman Islands marathon on-line and simply couldn't resist going on vacation AND running a marathon in one of the most beautiful places on earth"

"I felt the weather was perfect, although a bit more breeze would not have hurt anyone. The course itself was spectacular and the people along the course could not have been more motivating"

"At 4am my 4-year old was asking "why are you going for a run now Mummy? It's dark outside." Then she ran around the living room showing me how fast she could run. It was a great feeling lining up at the start line in George Town with all the competitors. In the pitch black"

"I have to say how impressed I am with how this race concluded its festivities. As every runner came across the finish line, the announcer would announce them by name and a huge roar would erupt from the crowd. I am not kidding. Runner after runner, all the way to the last two finishers at just over 6 hours were spurred on by a crowd which had hung around, talking and chatting and cheering. It was an awe-inspiring sight for me and one I am sure every runner was happy to be a part of"

"I have never before attended a race that gave anything to the spectators. Again the size and intimacy may have worked in our favor but I very much appreciated the free pastries, fruit and really decent coffee. Breezes by the Bay also let folks sit on their balcony and watch the race even if you weren't buying anything. It made me feel included and I appreciate that"

"The race course was simply outstanding. It was a runner's dream. While the heat and humidity presented a challenge, especially for me coming from a much cooler climate (i.e. leaving a snow storm) the course support was beyond outstanding; the organization was the most effective that I have seen and I would highly recommend that anyone who enjoys running and wants to see paradise sign up for the next marathon or half marathon"

"I am in the personal habit of collecting a running hat from each marathon or ½ marathon that I run ... as a memento. Cayman did not offer that option

because minimal participation did not make
such efforts economically viable to vendors.
However, one of the marathon organizers
took my information and specifically ... JUST FOR ME ...
had two running hats made with the logo
used on the finisher's medals"

"Our adventure to the Cayman Islands Marathon
actually started as somewhat of a joke. Jim, who is
almost retired and spends a fair amount of time on the
computer, found the marathon while he was surfing the
Internet. He sent it to a few running friends and asked
"How about this one?", not thinking any of us would be
seriously interested. When we weighed the options, a
winter weekend in Chicago or a winter weekend in the
Cayman Islands, we decided it would be a great idea!"

"The atmosphere of camaraderie and the festive mood
which was taken to the volunteerism
and other participation was very evident"

"The course support was beyond outstanding"

"I think Cayman is one of the most
beautiful places on earth"

"The intimacy of the race
may be one of its best aspects"

"It is an exhilarating atmosphere
from beginning to end"

So, without trying to sound terribly biased, plenty of
good things were said about this destination marathon.
But what didn't I like about it?

I wasn't so keen on how they made the sun rise so
quickly. Sure, it's the Caribbean and all that, but with

a bit of planning they could've convinced whoever is in charge of The Sun, to delay its arrival on race day. A new thermostat to regulate the heat would be good. Some cloud might be useful.

It finished too soon. With the race beginning at 5am, it was well over before noon. Yet no-one really wanted to leave. The festivities were just beginning. With a few more additions – showers, jacuzzis, more food, open bars, dance floors – this could easily have turned into an all-day street party.

Maybe some thought could be given in the future to finishing on the beach. That way, tired, exhausted bodies could simply collapse into the salt water.

Maybe have the Jazz Festival after the marathon.

**

I regret having to leave the Islands on my last day. Actually I felt that way every day. But there does have to be a last day, and now, this is it. I'll be back.

I pack my gear, take another look at my medal, smile and limp out of the hotel to the waiting taxi. I ask the driver if we could do an emergency run in to town so I can pick up the souvenir types of things I'd been jostled away from the day before. The Cruise ships are in again, so it's like driving in New York City at rush hour, but only inside a half mile radius. Fortunately I don't need any of the jewellery stores, but it's still just as crowded in Margaritaville where I have to fight for, and squeeze into, a countertop position in order to buy a unique gift that no-one else ever bought from the store.

My taxi driver meanwhile waits patiently and illegally outside the store, ready for the quick getaway. We laugh because that's not going to happen. In the meantime she tells me about an argument between her boyfriend and herself. When she asks him if he will arrange for some work to be done around their house he says, "What am I? Do you see contractor written on my forehead?" She replies "What about the bathroom?" He responds again, "What am I? Do you see plumber written on my fore-head?" Later that day he comes back to find the plumbing work all done and a smile on her face. "I suppose you baked him a cake as well," he says as the jealousy builds up inside. "What am I," she replies, "Do you see Betty Crocker written on my forehead?"

I really need the Caymanian accent to carry that story but we're laughing all the way to the airport about that and other life experiences. I peel out of the taxi, race to the check-out counter thinking I'm late, I am, and then stand there for several years dripping half my body weight away. Like the tourists, the plane is in no hurry to leave, or was sleeping, so I still have time to buy more souvenirs to clutter up the place when I return home.

Just when I think I'll have to make my third sweep of the four airport souvenir stores, I get a huge "Hey there" – it's Rose and Chris. They're leaving within half an hour of my departure time. As if our lives depend on it they usher me over to the bar, and sure enough, there we are again, chatting away as if we've known each other for years. They're buying the drink they promised me for finishing the marathon. It's so much fun that suddenly I get this heart palpitating feeling that I've missed my flight. About a minute later my name is called over the Intercom and I sober up very quickly.

Turns out I haven't missed my flight but instead I'm fortunate to be given a free random search of my suitcase and effects. It takes thirty seconds to unzip my bag in a small sterilized room and another thirty minutes to wait and have it looked through. I'm not terribly happy because it's cutting into my time with Rose and Chris, but eventually I'm cleared of trafficking, well, anything, I suppose, and able to return to the bar. No cavity search either and that's always a good thing. Rose and Chris provide more stories and buy more drinks for me because of the ordeal I've just been through.

I'm already flying high and I haven't even boarded the plane. It's a great way to leave the Island. I'm feeling proud yet again, although this time it's because I discover I've boarded the right plane.

It's a short uneventful flight to Miami, where I wait several hours for my connecting flight to Toronto. It's not supposed to be as long as it is but we, the airport and thousands of stranded passengers, have to wait for a major storm to blow through, grounding all the aircraft. I'm getting exhausted from souvenir hunting and can't face another store. I get a cool drink and people watch instead. A high school basketball player about twelve feet tall leaps up and touches a sign as he passes under it – the sort of spontaneous thing I think that the likes of Michael Jordan would have done at that age, although I wonder if Michael's pants would've fallen off like this guy's pants did.

I think destination marathons are perfect for the body, mind and soul. First, I'm seeing a place I've never seen before. And not just passing through it like a nine-European-countries-in-five-days sort of thing. For 42 kms I'm really seeing the place and meeting locals, tourists and other runners. Second, I may ache a bit, or a lot, but I feel great. I also know I have time after the race to relax – justifiably relax – and take in the sights and sounds of the destination. I'm feeling proud, I'm on a high, and the experience is almost complete.

I say almost because what would make it complete is if I'm here with family, or a partner or friends – others that I know who I could share the experience with and have some fun doing so. Being by myself is still fine because I've met many others and had a great time, but it does feel like something is missing. Something special.

That's got nothing to do with the Caymans or destination marathons in general, but it could well be a feeling that's shared by many others like me.

What I do know is that if I want to, I can go anywhere in the world and run a marathon. If the timing is right, you love running, and if your motivation and training – your readiness – is 'there,' you almost have to ask yourself why you wouldn't run a marathon and have a vacation at the same time. Of course having money to do this will make a huge difference as well. And I've been very fortunate in this respect as I've been able to use air miles I've collected from traveling with my day job.

These days there is almost always a cost incurred, a possible profit to be made and a very real financial bottom line. Marathon running has become a major industry in and of itself.

Speaking of which, on my last day in the Caymans I get an email from Athens. I'd gotten in touch with them begging that they put a harness on the Interpol team and to please forgive me for my indiscretion of not paying the two Euros subway ticket as I left Greece. Sympathetically they wrote back:

"We regret the fact that your visit to Athens ended with the bitter experience of being fined in the Athens Metro. However, we assure you that all cases are being carefully examined one by one, so that passengers are not mistakenly fined.

Thank you for communicating with us.
Fine Collection Office"

So at this point, I'm taking this as a No; that I still owe the Athens Metro some hard cash. I only hope the city hasn't folded financially in the meantime. I should feel good, I suppose, knowing that I wasn't mistakenly fined.

**

I finally get home around 3:00am after a long day of flying, hanging around airports, and then driving my stiff but sunned body from Toronto through intermittent snow flurries. How quickly 30 degree memories can change when you're hit by a good old fashioned Canadian snow storm. The memories disappeared completely at 2:00am when I was pumping gas in the middle of nowhere somewhere far from anywhere along the 401 Freeway. The sun may lift the spirits in winter but it doesn't stop the wind chill from scything through my body. Certainly not at 2am. Why do people live here in the middle of winter?

**

It's the next morning and I'm back in the real world again. I'm up and at it at 6am, feeding the horses, cats and chickens. Fred's still at the Kennel.

I'm feeling in much better condition compared to how I felt after the Athens run. There is still a general overall tiredness, but I feel like I can start running any day already. That should mean the training for Disney will be that much better. My knee has held up throughout, the Achilles has not become my *Achilles*, and there appear to be no specific pain points anywhere. Or maybe I'm just not very good at spotting where the problems exist. I'm already quite excited at the prospect of running the Goofy Challenge.

And so I'm back, and my mind is recalibrating the important things. Like getting a treadmill. Without mirrors alongside it. Absolutely a pure indulgence, but given Canadian winters, maybe it's simply common sense. Can I afford to buy one? Not a chance. There are purists out there who would claim there's no need to have a treadmill if you are smart and dress appropriately. That may be true, but the idea of running and not freezing at the same time appeals to me. Cracking my head on ice doesn't.

It seems the more I run, the more I enjoy it. The more wonderful people I meet, the more I want to keep those friendships, meet more people and continue enriching my life with the camaraderie of marathon running. If that sounds goofy, then it's time to talk about the Disney experience.

Race organizers, race day Cayman Islands marathon.

5 am race day, Cayman Islands.

"The Mexican" water station.

The Mexicans. Winners, again, of the water station competition, Cayman Islands.

Mike and Stephanie
Jones and friends
Clippity Clop farm
Canada.

Author stealing
Tads potato chips,
Dane Rauschenberg
and Derek Larmer
foreground.

Frank receives
finishers medal.

Breezes By The Bay

Post run festivities, finish line Cayman Islands.

Fun with stingrays takes my mind off tired body.

Roger MacMillan, Cayman Marathon.

Not a bad way to
finish the day,
any day.

32

ALL ROADS
LEAD TO DISNEY

DAYS 60 – 90
Planned Distance: Still Don't Know

I've now run two marathons in a month. Although I've not secured a place in the history books for land-speed records I'm feeling proud. I'm thrilled that my body, especially my knee, is holding out. The training manuals often say that 2-3 marathons at most in a year is all you should attempt. I think I should be careful with whatever I do. That said, I'm meeting people who run marathons much more often than that.

The more I run, the more people I meet, the more I read, and the more I see, it's become blindingly apparent to me that there is more to marathon running than I'd ever imagined. I've never put the word *more* five times in one sentence before. Maybe it was six?

The Disney marathon will be different in many ways, but in one way that especially pleases me is that I'm going with a good friend of mine – Karen – and we'll be able to experience it together, which to me is a welcome change.

It's been a long time coming. We bounced around several websites a few months ago and were simply drawn into the Disney magic like a moth to the light– something completely different, not to mention the enormous medals. And for people living in a Canadian winter, a trip to Florida in January seemed like a good plan.

You need to register early for the Goofy Challenge because there are limited spaces available. In fact the spaces were already filled when we leapt up with excitement seeing the medals on the computer screen in the middle of 2006, but we were able to get in through booking with the travel company Marathon Tours, based in Boston.

The two main reasons we're embarking on this trip to Disney are the medals, and the fact that the Goofy Challenge is something different. I say this unashamedly because everyone talks about the medals and for running two races we'll get three. A marathon medal is special enough, but when it's a huge gold plated medal shaped like a Disney character or three, if you're a successful Goofy Challenger, and you know your children's eyes will pop-out when they see them, they take on greater significance.

So we're off soon to do the Goofy Challenge; a Donald Duck medal on the Saturday if we complete the half-marathon. A Mickey Mouse medal if we complete the full marathon on the Sunday. A Goofy Medal for both runs if we complete the full marathon in less than seven hours. Our training will require strengthening exercises so that our neck muscles will be able to take the weight of the three medals.

When you wish upon a...

Three and a half weeks from now I'll be doing the Goofy Challenge. These past few days have been officially classified, by me, as REST DAYS. It's been very tempting to get out and run, as my body has felt great considering the Cayman meltdown, but the Book Wisdom suggests that more rest is better. I've put a little bit of weight on in the week I've had off running but that doesn't worry me.

Between Athens and the Caymans the furthest I ran was 14km (twice). I probably should've had a longer distance in there somewhere, but I went with how my body was feeling. This time, because I feel much better than after Athens, I hope to do a couple of 21km runs at least.

There's a good chance the weather won't help me. It's now December. We could get snow any day. At a minimum we'll have very cool days and quite likely rain. We may also get fiercely cold winds and icy conditions.

**

Well, it's been nine days since the Caymans marathon. I finally go for my first run. I meet Karen at the trail over by Sydenham, about a ten minute drive from my place. We run a leisurely, chatty 6km. Karen's trying to ramp up the distances for Disney but as she hasn't run much lately, she's concerned she may not be ready. At all.

I was ready to eat anything that moved after our run. Perhaps that's my body still adjusting. Apart from a small blister on my big toe that felt like I was running with a water balloon on my foot, everything felt fine. There's an immense difference in my body post-Caymans when compared to post-Athens. I ran about thirty minutes slower in the Caymans and that may have made a difference. While I pushed myself in Athens, in the Caymans I simply couldn't because all my systems seemed to shut down due to the heat and humidity.

Karen and I go for another 6km run the next day on another part of the trail, talking the whole time once more. The weather for most of the day is torrential rain and strong winds followed by strong winds and torrential rain. Until we run; then the clouds part and the wind drops away. Perfect running conditions. Karen has brought along her four dogs, and with Fred along as well we all charge down the trail as if in hot pursuit of a fugitive. Lilly, the cushion-sized dog, is the biggest concern because she's hard to see and runs into us unpredictably. But it's fun running with the dogs because they're so happy to be on an adventure. They're great company. Our 6km time is ten minutes better than the previous day, which probably means we were exceptionally slow yesterday. But the important thing is that we are out training. Especially Karen, who needs to put the time and distance into the running with Disney so close.

**

Today I go out by myself around the back fields for a 4km run. I only run 3km because I feel a heaviness in my upper body again. Pity too, because it is a balmy warm day. I'm a bit concerned that the heaviness has returned. I should probably find out what's going on but I'm afraid of what the answer might be. Not very mature is it? Instead, I've decided to rest again for a few more days.

I may not be running, but I'm thinking about running. Karen and I decide the best strategy for Disney is to walk-run the half marathon in order to save our energy for the full marathon. We get a big psychological boost today when the Disney registration and brochure arrive in the mail. It's full of information about the weekend, colour maps of the courses, plenty of colour photos, and some great shots of the Donald, Mickey and Goofy medals.

With Christmas fast approaching I'm trying to be very careful about what I eat and drink. It's difficult with friends and neighbours dropping in and winding down, or up. I've also got some ridiculous foetal position work commitments that have me getting up at 1am for a few days. Yes, *getting up* at 1am. If you don't think that's sick then *you* should be seeing someone. Every now and then different work projects conspire so I have no option but to find the time to write reports for multiple different projects. The easiest place to find the time is when most of the world sleeps. It must affect my running and it can't be healthy. But it seems there is no other option because, I don't know, getting paid is important.

After a few days of not running, but getting up when many people are still going to bed, I decide to run again, and meet up with Karen and the dogs for another 6km. It's a highly pleasurable run, with us nattering away to each other once more. When we finish the 6km we walk for another 1km, continuing to talk throughout. I'd definitely recommend having a partner to run with – someone with whom the conversation is effortless. My body feels good again and the heaviness is gone.

I'm glad I've run today because tomorrow I'm off to Toronto on the 5:25am train and not back till the evening. I'll call it a rest day.

**

The day after Toronto I'm back on the backyard track for another 6km run. Cool but sunny conditions. I've replaced my earphones with older ones that loop over my head so that I look like Radar from M.A.S.H. They're huge and ugly, but they don't fall out, the sound is great, and the best part, in the cooler conditions, is that they keep my ears warm.

The other 'high tech' equipment I have – the running computer with the footpod – is still giving me grief. When I was running with Karen the other day we did some simple calibration between my running computer and her Garmin I-Hope-the-Falcon-Lands-Here GPS system. While my running computer's footpod just looks like a Borg-like warty growth on my shoe, Karen's Garmin looks like she's running with a small table on her wrist.

The first time we calibrate over 6km we're within 10 metres of one another, at most. That seems odd given it was so far out when I ran the Cayman Islands marathon. We run again the next day though and we're two hundred metres out after 6km. I don't get it, and I'm getting disillusioned with the gadgetry. Is it really that necessary?

What I need is something that simply records the time that I'm running, and maybe the splits. Distance and pace are handy, but my life will not be altered substantially without them being recorded. People have been running for thousands of years, doing fine without music, knowledge of splits, pacing, heart rates, and calories burned. I doubt *Pheidippides* would have improved his time decked out with a Garmin and MP3 Player, but maybe his job satisfaction would have risen significantly.

**

Another day, another 6km. This time, out the back with Fred – who again stops part way and watches me run the remaining distance. The run feels good, but I still feel a general tiredness in my body. The good news though is that my legs never feel very tired or sore. My knee, despite inflammation at times, is much stronger than ever before, and I have no serious Achilles, calf or groin injuries to speak of. I've been very lucky. Maybe I've done some things right? Like the salt baths, for example, which still feel like an indulgence.

With Christmas quickly approaching life is starting to crash into training and training is starting to crash into life. But they're becoming one and the same in many ways.

Last night, for example, we had a band practice – our first 'gig' of sorts – about twenty people coming to Jeff's place for a pot luck dinner and drinks and listening to us play. My legs get a work out from all the nervous shaking they are doing as we perform in front of what was, we think, a very generous crowd. Lots of fun and laughter, but a very late night – well OK, very early or late next morning – 4am, I think. The pressure of the night wasn't helped by the fact that I'd completely lost my voice that morning. As the band's singer this is a major problem.

I drove into town to ask a pharmacist for something to help. He said, "drink lots of water."

"That's it?" I replied. He shrugged his shoulders, paused for a few seconds, smiled and said 'good luck'. For the rest of the day and early evening all I did was drink water and tea. I may as well have just stood over the toilet for the day but at least I got my exercise in going back and forward. Right up until the first line of the first song I had no idea whether I could sing or not. I was a wreck. I tried telling the other guys in the band but they didn't believe me – they thought I was just trying to get them worried.

For reasons I don't know or understand, my voice came back – not the way it typically is, but enough to get it, and me, through the night.

Besides the five hundred bathroom visits there was no running that day. And none the next day either as I recover from the night before. With two days to go before Santa completes his own unique ultra, Karen and I plan on doing a 21km early in the morning of Christmas Eve. But it's getting far too complicated to coordinate our schedules. We take the easy way out I suppose, and decide that running in the bitter cold and dark doesn't make much sense.

**

There are two more rest days planned and I'm feeling good about it. I'm near total exhaustion from the band performances, as we had another one last night, just three nights after the first one. I'm cross-training, running around like a nut as we all do at Christmas time. I 'cross-train' some more with the boys, playing soccer and going for walks with Fred. It's surprisingly very mild weather, so it's a feel-good time.

The boys are staying with me for a few days. The day before Christmas we have own Christmas Day with Fred. On Christmas Day their cousins from Toronto come to visit for a few days, so it's just me and Fred again. I'm in bed as early as possible with the boys on our own pre-Christmas Eve night. I'm even in bed by 7:30pm on the real Christmas Eve. I'm exhausted. If nothing else over the holiday season, I hope to catch up on some badly needed sleep. Good indications of this are my eyes. They quickly grow styes, then grow whole barns, if I don't get enough sleep. I've been battling the onset of these all week and feel them just one sleepless night away.

If I was a zealous fanatical regimented person adhering to a defined training program including all the specifics with nutrition and sleep there's no way I'd be including late band nights in the mix. But that's the thing; we're always making choices with our time. Given the sheer enjoyment of playing in the band I would never trade it in for a stringent running program. I'm realising that my enjoyment with running is in part due to the fact that I've been able to integrate it with everything else I do.

As Karen pointed out one time, running is not about making *sacrifices* with our time, it's about making *choices*. There's a big difference. I don't have it all worked out and some days it's totally crazy, but somewhere in my jumbled existence it seems like it works. It's a symbiotic relationship, a happy co-existence that strengthens everything I'm about.

That realization alone is a great Christmas present in itself.

Christmas Day

With Disney less than two weeks away I feel the need to do at least one long run before then. Today, I've decided, Christmas Day, is a long run day. Conditions are right for a long run – good weather (no snow or rain, just overcast to sunny skies), no work commitments, and actual sleep the previous night. I've no excuses not to run. I'll run this morning because I'm off for Christmas dinner later in the afternoon. I'm going to alternate nine minute runs with one minute walks over 21km.

I do my familiar Colebrook loop with the remainder of

the run on the trails. It's a good run. I stick to the plan except when it looks odd that I stop running and suddenly walk when someone is beside me. The battery on my MP3 dies after an hour of running. But I discover for the next hour that I become much more attuned to how my body feels when I'm not distracted by the music. It's quite an A-ha moment for me. The music is clearly a distraction, but one I like, although it probably limits my ability to fully understand and learn from my body while I'm running. I should probably always be recalibrating my running – listening to my body – to improve my form in particular.

Maybe I need to ask what the real reason is for running with music. Is it that I get bored, or perhaps scared, in the company of my own thoughts? Is it because I don't want to know how my body feels? Is it that I can't conceive spending so much time by myself without some form of external stimuli? Or am I simply making too much of this?

I run the 21km in 2:06, which includes the one minute walks along the way. I'm really pleased about this; equally pleased that I was able to run it without any major side effects or injuries. I feel more tired on the hill sections than usual, but other than that everything feels good.

The rest of Christmas Day is quiet. I manage to successfully do nothing until later in the afternoon when I go to my friend's (Liz and Rob's) sister's place for Christmas dinner. Liz and Rob have a large family and have sort of adopted me. I'm hopeless with names and it doesn't help matters when they keep moving around on me. I eat too much and it's roasting hot inside. But they're a wonderful friendly family and it's a great way to end the day.

As the night goes on I'm almost getting giggly thinking

about my 21km in the morning and yet now not feeling any effects at all. And that's without alcohol. A few months ago I would have been horizontal feeling the pain aching through my body. I've come a long way without realizing it, although the fact I'm saying it now must mean I've noticed something. It's another great Christmas present.

**

Two days of rest later and I'm out again running my scheduled 6km, this time in 22 minutes! That's just under four minutes per kilometre. It was absolutely amazing. I was flying. Sometimes you can reach deep within and pull out the reserves to do something special with your run.

Well, it sounds good but it didn't happen. It was going to be a 6km day but there were a ton of things on the go – work, for example, and cleaning up for visitors coming over and going into town and ...and ...and ...well, I have no major excuses really. I'm not sure if it's simply a convenient excuse or not, but the fact that I continually hear or read that its preferable to have more rest than less, especially in my situation between marathons, the better it is for you. So I don't push myself at all to get out and run. Deep down I feel I should run, hence this fall-to-the-knees admission of guilt in front of you right now. But common sense tells me I should be smart and rest. It's an awkward spot for sure.

The next day is a spectacular day with the sun shining, the air warm, and the ice melting. I haven't heard from Karen for almost a week now – I'm hoping she's been able to run. For some reason my mind flashes back to the beginning of the Athens marathon. I can remember it in vivid detail – the cold, the camaraderie, the adrenalin rush, the sheer elation of being there. You can't replace memories like that.

I was in the same frame of mind as yesterday as to whether to run or not. In the end I did this time; a short run – initially to run 6km, but part the way through I decide to just run back and forward on my own road instead of a longer run out to Yarker Road. So just 4.66 kms today instead of 6, although it feels like 10 km! Maybe it's the snow and ice covering the ground that influences my decision. I feel tired today with one of the slowest runs I've ever done. I've got band practice tonight, which means another late night – not part of the training regimen. Oh well.

As you're probably thinking, this has been a fairly extended and apparently successful rest break. Despite the lack of distance – well okay, running period – I've been thinking about the Goofy Challenge more and more. I'm thinking twice about anything physical I do in case of injury – like playing soccer or rugby with the boys, tobogganing, moving rocks and wood around the farm, brushing teeth, folding laundry, and of course thinking twice about the running, and where I run. I've been doing more stretches, making bigger expansive movements as I get out of bed, and I continue to take baths. Overall my body feels good but I still wonder about the heaviness in my chest that I've felt running lately.

I'm pleased to say that New Year's Eve passes without incident. The Band plays again for a few folks, and we do that whoopee sort of thing at midnight. Well, close to midnight. Most of us have completely forgotten it's New Year's Eve, so it comes as quite a surprise when someone remembers it's midnight, or some time near it.

I'm probably a prime candidate for a running-style New

Year resolution, but I don't make any in the end. After a few drinks it was going to be too deep and existential, and I'd likely forget it anyway.

And before you know it, the New Year begins. No resolutions made but I won't be losing sleep over it. I'll be losing sleep over other things anyway. I do know that in 2006 I started the year struggling to run fifteen minutes without stopping; it was a train wreck, that first beach run back in January. What a difference a year makes.

New Years Day. I just got an email from Coenraad, the South African I met in Athens. It was Coenraad who first mentioned the 90km Comrades ultra run in South Africa. He was telling me about two New Zealanders he'd met after he and I split up at the beginning of the race, and who he met again by coincidence after the run. Turns out this was Robyne, who I'd finished the race with, but who I never saw again afterwards. A small world. And last night when I was playing with the band, I was talking to Martin (acoustic guitar) who is South African and his wife Susan. Before emigrating to Canada they lived most of their lives in either Pietermaritzburg or Durban (the start and finish of the Comrades race), and know the Comrades route really well. They're off for a holiday there in a week's time. Susan's sister actually lives on the Comrades route. I'm now getting an even stronger urge to run there. Synchronicity. One wonders how these things intersect when they do, and why?

**

The countdown to Goofy is on. I go for a light 2-3km run today just to keep moving. The weather over the past few days has been unusually warm (seven degrees Celsius yesterday, which for winter is incredible). I've started to put clothes aside, and mentally run through the *Magic*

Kingdom and alongside the *Expedition Everest – Legend of the Forbidden Mountain.*

**

The next day I twist my left knee moving posts around the farm. I land awkwardly on some wood. I'm not limping but I can feel the twist every time I put my foot down. There's no point being a hero hobbling around a light 3km. Even 1km. Or ten metres. If there's the slightest doubt about my knee, then I won't run until the half marathon a few days from now, and even then I'll take it easy.

The good news today is that Karen and I have connected again. She's been running over the Christmas/New Year break which is a relief, including a 15km run and acting as a pacer for a friend in a 5km Fun Run. We both realize the Goofy Challenge will be tough. We agree we are both 'determined and tenacious' enough to make it happen, so long as we have no major physical showstopping injuries.

**

The day before we leave I contact Disney directly to confirm our room bookings and shuttle service from the airport. The first lady I talk to wishes us a 'Magical Experience.' The lady she then forwards me to wishes us a Magical Experience. Not to be outdone, the gentleman who I'm then referred to wishes us a Magical Experience. The most important magical thing is that eventually I get the magical information I magically need.

I'm thinking it will all be a fantastic magical experience. I'm hoping to find some magic somewhere in my legs. A 2:04 time in the full marathon would be quite magical, for example. Even a 4:04 time would be quite magical.

I drop Fred off at the kennel for his own magical barking resort experience then get my hair cut. Even though it doesn't take long to cut my hair Bunny cuts it as if she is leading contender for the World Sheep Shearing competition. I'm just getting comfortable in the chair and she tells me we're done. I've always wanted to say "It's too short" when they show you in the mirror what the back looks like, but I won't do that today as Bunny is clearly on a mission which doesn't include small talk.

Meantime, I'm hungry and letting myself eat what I want, except junk food. I'm drinking lots of water, tea and orange juice and have cut back on coffee. I'm doing lots of stretching. Mentally, I'm getting on my game.

I've also packed, the day before I leave, which is unusual for me. Packing now is much different from packing for the Athens run. I'm more laid back, more relaxed, and I have a pretty good feel for what I will need. I pack lightly this time, including no computer. Already I feel a sense of withdrawal.

I look at the program we've been sent. If running the marathon at Disney World doesn't scare me enough I can follow in the footsteps of fellow New Zealander Sir Edmund Hillary, and take on *Expedition Everest*. It's new at Disney's Animal Kingdom Theme Park. I won't be climbing on hands and knees like Edmund to an altitude of 28,000 feet, where no one had gone before, not even the Enterprise. Instead, I can take a "high-altitude (so it says), high speed train" through hair-pin turns to reach the peak. Why? Because it's there I suppose. But if that doesn't thrill my pants off – or soil them – then the fact that I'll then be hurled backwards from the summit just might. A Yeti will apparently be lurking somewhere 'up there' to create all sorts of havoc. While Ed Hillary and Tensing, his Sherpa colleague suffered altitude sickness, among other discomforts, as they *'knocked the bastard off,'* I'll focus on keeping all my bodily fluids and solids where they should be.

In comparison, running 42.2 kilometres seems pretty straightforward. Even the half-marathon the previous day doesn't seem that intimidating any more. This is obviously big feeling talk.

My last mission today is to drop Gordon off at Gord's place. He's a hamster, so he doesn't understand what's going on. Gord and his Dad do though, and to celebrate my leaving for the marathon weekend they insist we toast a few drinks to one another. There must be a lot of us in the kitchen because by the time I leave it's almost time to get up and drive to the airport in Toronto. As I stumble into bed to see I'll be up shortly it feels like I've just run a marathon. Maybe I should stay up.

Summary

Planned Distance = Still Dont know;
Actual distance run = 59.7km

33

IT'S MAGICAL

DAYS 60 – 90
Planned Distance: Still Don't Know

We're off. We put on our Mickey Mouse Ears, sing Disney songs and dance to the airport ready for adventure, fantasy, frontiership, and tomorrow. Well, we go to the airport at any rate. Karen picks me up early and we drive three hours to the Toronto airport to catch the American Airlines flight to Orlando, Florida. Along with us are Scott and Jordan, son and girlfriend of friends of Karen's, who instead of running somewhere, are flying out of Toronto to a Caribbean adventure on the same day. We're staying at the Caribbean Resort at Disney, but I doubt it's the same thing. We're staying in Trinidad apparently.

Of more immediate concern is the fact that we'll have to fly to Florida. I'm stopped at the security check in Toronto. Although I avoid a cavity check again it's made clear I will lose my little plastic jar of Vaseline. I'd been planning a smearing rampage over all the passengers at 30,000 feet, so I'm a bit disappointed.

While flying is not a major concern for me, Karen has moved beyond white knuckle status, even though she's flown thousands of miles in the past few years. You don't realise how much turbulence there actually is until you've sat beside Karen on a flight. She has instant religious epiphanies, seizures, paralysis, bouts of hysteria, vice-like gripping moments on other passenger's legs and arms and moments of trying to sell her children if it will influence the flight in any way.

It's worse when the plane takes off. To compensate I say useless things like 'it will be over soon', or 'its blue sky now', and, what must rank as the most pathetic, 'can I do anything?' All of which do nothing to make Karen feel good. I suppose my yammering at least takes her mind off the marathons. I'm still going through my own torment with the loss of my Vaseline, but I don't think Karen cares.

It's a rough flight, no doubt about it. We toss and turn while Will Ferrell does the same on Talladega Nights, showing above us. Lucky for us, and the airline, the plane lands, and right where we were hoping it would. Once in Orlando's airport we search for Disney World. There's a shuttle waiting to take us away on our magical experience. It's not hard to find, especially when we can see the white of the Disney staff teeth from several hundred metres away. We're placed in the respective corral to indicate which resort we're heading for. We're happy waiting inside because its twenty-seven degrees outside and brutally humid, and stinky where the buses arrive.

It's not long before we're sitting in our air-conditioned bus listening to Disney tunes repeatedly playing on the overhead televisions. For some unknown reason there is no image on the televisions, just the relentless cheeriness

– call it music I suppose – of the noise coming through the system. The same music, over and over again. We keep looking at the screen. Transcendental Disney moments. Part 1 of an indoctrination perhaps. M-I-C-K-E-Y ... M-O-U-S-E ...

We have no idea where we are going, but then we're not expected to. When we do get 'there', we're ushered out of the bus, put in a line-up (get used to this), and eventually get our room assignments. At this point we now *actually* walk, in the fresh humid air, to our rooms. It's getting dark but it looks like we have some sort of Lake in front of us. I'm guessing it's the Caribbean Sea. Man made. We've come from a Canadian winter to almost the Caribbean. Nice to finally arrive.

We'll have to think about running at some point.

We're Here

Apart from marvelling each week during my childhood at the black and white TV Disney show on Sunday nights, my first 'live' experience of Disney was in the 1980s when my friend Colin and I came over from New Zealand to study in Canada. After receiving unlimited drinks on an American Airlines flight into Los Angeles from Tahiti, dropping vertically, and instantly, a few hundred metres as we flew directly over LA, and being told to take as much wine with us as we liked, we stumbled out of the airport and headed excitedly to the Youth Hostel, knowing that we'd go to Disneyland, the 51st State, the next day.

What an introduction to the United States. Two very green, just-off-the-boat New Zealanders who thought the Americans had an accent, not us. Driving on the wrong side of the road was no major problem since in LA we were pretty much gridlocked on the freeways anyway. We were far more dangerous in shopping mall parking lots where driving rules are guidelines at best. With relief, pride and an undamaged rental car, we arrived at Disneyland, which is not far south from the LA Airport in Orange County. There was no chance of being dangerous in this parking lot as we were ushered into our spot by about 100 smiling, clean-cut Disney Parking Staff making twenty cents an hour. We saw the entranceway over on the horizon, got instructions, packed our compasses and proceeded to spend as much time walking from the parking lot to the entrance as we had driving there from the Youth Hostel.

Our mouths were wide open virtually the whole time at Disney. We quickly adopted American accents, which we continued to use for the next few days until our jaws started to hurt. The only ride we took was a roller coaster inside Space Mountain. Neither of us had ever been on a roller coaster before, which was part of the fun. The horror was that we sat at the very front. With it being pitch black inside the mountain we had less than a split second to work out whether we were hurtling down the tracks at the speed of light, about to be derailed, or come blasting out the side of the mountain like a Disney styled Mt. St. Helen's eruption. The animated cartoons make it look quite funny but we couldn't laugh. The G-force, I think. While kids behind us were screaming with apparent joy, our mouths were flopping around with speed wobbles as we speculated on the condition of our underwear.

I've not been on a roller coaster since.

Organizers of the Athens marathon would fold into foetal position if they came to Disney for the marathon. The events are so different you'd think you lived in a different world. And you do, really. For one, there's the language. While we all understand what a fictitious, ageless duck called Donald might be saying, we'd be clueless if someone mentioned *spanokopita, podikos or papia*. In many ways, Disney will feel a lot more familiar to me than Athens ever did. That's partly why I'm here; to experience the differences.

I'm reading the brochure for the Marathon Weekend again. It's a glossy feel good brochure with everyone smiling in the sun. The banner phrase for the weekend is "Make it a Tradition," encouraging us to come year after year for this weekend. There must be something quite magical going on because over 115 marathoners have run the Disney marathon every year since it first started in 1994. I also learn I'm in the running to be the 100,000th finisher of the Walt Disney World Marathon. It's not a race, as the Vice President for Disney Sports Attractions explains, it's now a *Running Tradition*.

Everything, it seems, is a celebration of some sort this weekend. Over three days, the Expo is celebrating Health and Fitness. Not just dozens of booths selling or promoting their wares, but appearances by celebrity runners, seminars on training, racing and nutrition. There are autograph sessions, music and dancing as well. I can already tell it's going to be a feel good place.

Morning comes around after a restless sleep. We get into the groove of taking shuttle buses everywhere and before we know it – well around 11am actually –we've mastered the connections and successfully arrive at the Expo. We want to "do" Expo anyway, but for Disney we don't have a choice since this is where we must pick up our Race Numbers and Packet Pick-up. To identify runners we all are given exclusive plastic wrist bands – for the weekend we're wearing blue wrist bands with *Goofy's Challenge 2007* written on them.

You can tell it's a bit of a badge of honour for runners – it seems that being a Goofy Challenger puts you into another level. Of what, I'm not sure. Perhaps it's just you're goofy enough to try two runs in two days, which is fair enough.

The Expo is huge. John Hughes, the Disney Race Director, tells me there's about seventy-eighty vendors at the Expo spread over an area of 110,000 square feet. And it's absolutely jam-packed crowded – not surprising when you consider there are 15,000 runners registered for the full marathon and another 12,000 for the half marathon. It's hard to move sometimes, but it gets your adrenalin going. We can buy pretty much anything we can think of that's associated with running. Any company that's anything is here selling their products, giving away freebies, and providing demonstrations.

Other marathon races are also here advertising their events, which includes displaying, and, oh-my-gosh, letting us hold, their finishers medals. Nice marketing touch. There are some big honking Hard Rock marathon medals chiselled out of dumbbells that will require more weight training.

The Hard Rock Franchise is proudly promoting its Heavy Medal 2007 Series – through an intricate arrangement of race dates and associated medals, runners are being coaxed into registering for the Hard Rock races. There are six different medals possible depending upon which combination of marathons runners select. Complete two marathons in 2007 and we'll get a Silver Note

Medal, shaped, of course, like a large silver note. We'll get a Golden Note if we do back to back marathons in 5 weeks. A Grand Slam medal will be ours if we finish 4 of 5 Hard Rock marathons in 2007, but the crème de la crème of all the Hard Rock medals is the *Rock Star Medal* where we will "earn star power with the hippest, most coveted medal to adorn your trophy case". We'll get this by completing all five musical marathons or half marathons in 2007. It will have to be a well built case. There are more medals of course, but you get the point.

Some races promote their events by offering 'free' runners caps and t-shirts with the race logo if you register there on the spot. We can't help ourselves, and if only to prove that this sort of marketing and promotion works, we sign up for a race that I know we probably will never run, but it's a really cool, free red running cap all the same.

There is so much Disney marathon merchandise that I could have a good burst of shopping here and never have to buy clothes again. I'm already walking around wearing my cool red cap and in my bag are two long sleeve technical Disney marathon running shirts we got when registering. There's thousands of dollars being exchanged at this Expo.

It's now getting tiring – shopping does that to me – and we have two races coming up this weekend. We go upstairs to get away from it for a bit only to find ourselves in front of the free wine tasting area. By this point we can't help but smile with our chardonnays as we peer over the balcony and watch the Expo unfold below us. We almost drop our drinks in shock as the dance group over on the other balcony explode under a kaleidoscope of changing lights, doing a creative dance/ warm-up/ rap/ cheerleading thing to the sounds of a funky be-bop something that is blasting over the speakers inside this stadium. I think we're in an indoor basketball stadium, but there's little room on the court to even bounce a basketball today.

The gyrations are impressive and entertaining. If I wasn't tired before I'm certainly tired now as I watch them burn more calories in a few minutes than I've burnt in two months of training. I marvel at their flexibility because I would snap like a wishbone if I tried even a quarter of the moves they ease through.

Or maybe I'm tired because of the wine. I'm not sure, but it tastes good. We know we'll look like lushes if we just stand here and drink all day, and that kind of preparation won't help for the half marathon tomorrow. We head back downstairs to the Expo for the speaker sessions.

There have been some great speakers lined up. Nancy Clark, the nutritionist with best-selling sports and nutrition books is here, as are Hal Higdon and Jeff Galloway, among others, and Jon Hughes, the Disney Race Director. We catch the end of John Bingham's talk, which has the room giggling and laughing. The hallway is also laughing because there's not enough room for everyone wanting to hear John talk. We sit on the floor against the wall like everyone else.

But we are here now specifically to learn more about Chi Running – in a session led by Danny Dreyer. We're curious as to how it works – partly because it seems to make so much sense, especially when you want to minimise injuries and run as efficiently as possible.

It's a fun and packed session as Danny takes us through the basics, including our own attempts to find our core and, as he put it, tighten our asses. It works. And without knowing too much about it we feel like we are converted. He's a very personable and engaging speaker. Later I buy Danny's book and he signs it, with a written note wishing me the *best of luck with The Goofy*.

Fearing too much of a good thing, we muster the courage to do one more round of the booths in the arena where the Disney merchandise is displayed. There's so much to choose from I'm almost paralysed. I could easily spend a few hundred dollars here, and I guess that's the point. Eventually I buy a Goofy Challenge coffee mug and a black fleece-lined Goofy windbreaker jacket. The important thing is the Goofy logo on the front. Karen buys another big chunk of their store, including an orange, yes orange, tracksuit top, which will ensure she never gets shot accidentally on the trails.

We lose a few pounds sweating our way back to the shuttle bus with our merchandise. The bus will take us back to Port Royale, where we are staying at the Caribbean Resort. We get into a conversation with Hank – a large 170-year old man who refers to himself as a Truck and not a Race car; I feel like I'm a Mini in comparison. He too is doing the Goofy Challenge. He's full of confidence, which gives us renewed hope.

Back at Port Royale we decide it's time to relax and reflect on our shopping day. We wander by the Lake/Sea/ Water thing, noticing the magical sign telling us and other Disney experience people that we can't swim there, even at the sandy beaches. A tough one, we think, to explain to the kids.

But wait a minute. This is Disney World. We can't just sit around here. We have an opportunity to experience new things, so we should make the most of it. Buoyed by our unusual string of success with the shuttle buses we take another one to Boardwalk. A step back in time to New Jersey, we think, in the good old boardwalk days.

The sun is hot and the sky is clear – a perfect day for a boardwalk. If it's an accurate replica, they really struggled to find good coffee back then. We settle for a salad and sit on a park bench to watch the world go by. I guess it's the Atlantic Ocean we're looking over now. It's complete with ferries transporting people that can't, or don't want to, walk around to the other side, and others that will disappear down the canal into another part of Disney World.

The world, or part of it at least, does walk by. Most of the passersby show they're not short of money. There are a lot of beautiful people strolling past us and there's a large number of marathoners, many of whom are showing off their gear, or flexing their wristbands to show which event they're here for. We're all looking at everyone else – working out who is running and who is not. We try to simply blend in and look as if we're not, but the goofy wristbands are a bit of a giveaway. It's easy to strike up a conversation with others.

The whole place is spotless – most likely because of the Disney staff all around enthusiastically picking up garbage, if they can find it. Who knows, maybe they work on commission.

All in all, it's a relaxing day. We've come out of it filled with the buzz of the weekend to follow, infused with new knowledge about Chi Running, mentally tipsy with the success of finding our way around, and loaded with material things to take back home. We hop on a shuttle bus and head back to the Caribbean, where we wait in line-ups at the cafeteria-style takeaway section at Port Royale to get loaded up with carbs. We could've gone into the formal restaurant but like the idea of sitting outside as the sun goes down. It's an early night because we'll need to be up very, very early tomorrow to get to the half-marathon on time.

On the pursuit of the Donald Duck medal

It's early alright. 3am to be precise. The race starts at 6am and we have to get on a shuttle bus to get to the start-line by 4am at the latest, so we are told. I'm not sure if I'm awake or not but I make moves to indicate the day has begun. I didn't sleep that well anyway, so maybe waking up at 3am is a good thing. At least I'm relieved I haven't slept in, although I do feel a bit like one of Barbossa's crew.

I think of the ritual that I seem to be getting into. Coffee, eat something, in this case some sandwiches, and a power bar. I make sure I put all my gear on the right way and pin the race number to my shirt. In short time I'm all set. Karen meanwhile is doing the same, and drops in for coffee as we make last minute preparations. The coffee is not great, but it's hot, coffee-like and has some caffeine. It also helps the bowel system, and if I can take care of 'that' before the race I'll be quite pleased.

We're quite conscious of the instructions that state the last shuttle bus will be at 4am. Seems too early. It's pitch black and we have no idea where to go and no other transport, so our options, short of changing our minds and going back to bed, are limited.

We get to the bus stop well before 4am. The bus comes, phew. And it's full of runner-like zombies, some of whom are still sleeping, and others who have clearly just finished their tenth cup of coffee. "It's going to be a hot one" is the primary topic of conversation. But regardless of the level of sleep deprivation we are still smiling.

Karen and I talk about our race strategy, as if we haven't done this before. I'm more than happy to run together but Karen's equally happy if we run our own separate races. For perhaps the twentieth time, we finally agree we'll run together.

There are two strategies we kick around for the half-marathon. One is to go very slowly, recognizing that we have that full marathon thing the next day. The second approach is to run strong, be proud of a good time, and be careful all the while not to injure ourselves to the point that it will affect our full marathon tomorrow, or worse, mean we can't even run.

We end up doing neither. We say all the right words about taking it easy, but get caught in the moment. Or rather, the tide, with over 12,000 runners entered for the half marathon. It's almost beyond comprehension. We are all shapes and sizes, ages and genders. So many of us, in fact, that it takes fifteen minutes to actually get over the start line and get the chip timing underway.

By 4am we've arrived at a giant parking lot at the Epcot Centre. There are thousands of us, plus friends and families. The rock band 'Brothers' are playing live, and there's tons of music and commentary over the large speakers and Jumbotron. The only place to sit though is on the asphalt, which we sit on, because in two hours we'll be running 21km. Two hours? That's a long time to wait. We could run a half-marathon in that time.

Hungry? Well there's a concession stand selling all the typical hot dogs and things if we're interested. Seems an odd thing at the start of a race but this is what it is here at Disney; maybe it's for family members? Some runners think its fine as I see they're buying the food, but I'm not sure how that will feel at Mile Five. There are dozens of portapotties around in any case.

Eventually we're ushered through bag check then corralled into Sections A, B and C according to expected finishing times. This is to help avoid congestion, trampling and general chaos at the start-line among the faster and slower runners. And the walkers too, as there is going to be a large number of runners who will deliberately walk the distance today. We're in Section B.

Off we go. Not running, but on a 1km walk to the startline. It's still dark but we're kept entertained by Jumbotrons along the walk, and music from the loudspeakers, and they *are* loud, ranging from rap to the Beatles. We're all getting pumped up now.

It's hot and humid already, with predictions for temperatures going into the eighties. We've heard some complaints about the 6am start. I'm not sure what all the other 12,000 runners think because I've not had time to talk to them, but I'd prefer to miss some sleep and start at 6am to avoid the heat of the day - any time. My experience in the Caymans sealed that thought.

The half-marathon route will take us from the Epcot Centre up World Drive to the Magic Kingdom. Once there we head into Tomorrowland and Cinderella Castle, before turning back to the Epcot Centre. We're running in Disney World, yes, but we won't be running in the theme parks all the time.

We're almost ready now. Good thing too, as a number of us are peeling off the road looking for nature's toilet. We find it in all sorts of places of course; trees, bushes, anywhere. But mostly not in portapotties as there are not many of these along this walking routeway. Oh well.

Donald, Mickey and Goofy each have something special to say but I'm not sure what it is really, although I could probably guess. The national anthem plays, and huge fireworks explode in the air as the gun goes off somewhere in the distance just ahead of the wheelchair competitors and Section A. We'll be at the start-line shortly we think.

We get there. Some runners suggest we receive a medal for reaching the start-line. We take off, well sort of. Actually, amidst the fireworks and pumping music we stumble across the start-line, careful not to trip into the folks in front of us. We start running as if we're all members of the Nineties and Over Running Club. It's a long slow shuffle for most of the first mile or so simply because there are so many of us. If I was looking for a PR this wouldn't be the place.

We're making good time. Both of us are quite capable of a sub-2 hour half marathon if we push ourselves. But in these early moments there's no push option available, except perhaps pushing the people in front of us out of the way. But we didn't come here for personal bests, we came to enjoy the experience and have some fun. If you think like that, and take Disney for what it is, then it's a great weekend.

It's pretty crowded though for the first few miles. I say miles because that's how the races are signposted in the US. I prefer kilometres because it feels like I'm making more progress passing them more often than mile markers.

We're running on roads for almost the entire half-marathon, which is fair enough because you need some way to get to the theme parks. Karen and I are focused on the Magic Kingdom, between Miles 5 and 6. When I think of Disney, I think of the Magic Kingdom, and not the Epcot Centre, Everest, or the Animal Kingdom. To us, the Magic Kingdom is what it's all about. As the castle looms closer and closer, the thought that we are running disappears, even moreso when we start seeing the Disney characters. I realise at this point that we made a big mistake not running with a camera.

But dozens of other runners have brought theirs and stop to pose with the stars of Disney. Who cares about their finishing times anyway? At a minimum we're saying "hi" and waving to the characters as they wave to us. It would be a bit rude if they didn't wave back I suppose. In some cases we're high fiving them. Of course they're paid to do this sort of thing, and waving thousands of times each day is probably in the Employee Policy and Practice manual. But we feel special nevertheless.

Some people are quite sceptical of the whole Disney/Marathon thing but it's really quite a buzz running through the castle, and knowing we're on the return leg of the half marathon. By now the runners have finally spread out enough that we are not tripping over one another, or into Disney characters. Karen wants to run harder, while I'm constantly looking at my running computer suggesting we slow down. Eventually we do, but it's not until about the last mile. It's still a slower pace than what we can normally do, so I should be pleased we haven't gone all out.

We run in fog for the final mile through the Epcot Centre. It's quite an eerie feeling. We cross the finish-line relieved that everything is still intact, and we're not injured. We're given our huge Donald Duck medals and thermal sheets, and shown where to collect food and drinks should we need them. The medals are gold plated in the shape of Donald's head, with a full Donald etched running within the head. Another gold plate dangles below Donald's head with the year 2007 etched on it. The medal is attached to a red ribbon with images of Donald and Mickey both running, smiling and enjoying themselves. It's a feel good look obviously, and those who are strong enough are proudly wearing them.

Everything is extremely efficient at the finish line. We're out of there very soon afterwards. Karen thinks she has pushed it a bit too much, and is now even more wary of the race tomorrow.

I feel fine and very pleased that the half-marathon is out of the way. The phrase 'half' doesn't do the distance justice, because it's still 13.1 miles, which is a credible, serious distance whether you are running it or walking it. As we look around at the finish-line there are plenty of very happy people milling around.

Later, on the Donald Duck Certificate I receive in the mail, I find out I (we) have run a chip time of 2:33 – which is not that fast really, but for my effort I place 5,478th out of 12,293 runners. If you're into the statistics, I finish 370th out of 603 for my age group. The stats are a bit meaningless. The important point, as the certificate notes, is that I've "Conquered the most magical 13.1 miles at the Walt Disney World Resort."

It was certainly magical as we went through the Magical

Kingdom, but less magical on the roads. It was crowded for one thing. If you don't like running with thousands of people for an entire race this may not be for you.

But we can't be too anal about this. We all knew what we were getting into. There is a lot of 'nothing' in between the theme parks but the maps we were provided showed us this. It was crowded, yes, but what do you expect when 12,000 people run a distance together of 13.1 miles.

One of the good things about starting so early is that there's still a big chunk of the day to enjoy. That's a relative concept of course, especially when we've been up since almost the day before, and we've got a marathon the next day. I'm still intimidated by the marathon distance, but less so now after Athens and the Caymans.

Running with Karen has also confirmed for me that it would have been a lonely experience here at Disney by myself, much moreso than the previous two marathons. There is so much to absorb here, and I'm not even a Disney buff. We decide to take the rest of the day easy. As soon as we get back to Trinidad we shower and freshen up, take on the transit routes once more, and head to the boardwalk again for a nice lunch. We're a little stiff, but hungry and feeling like we should celebrate.

It can be quite tiring getting up at 3am and running 21km. And it can be quite tiring doing nothing. Put the two together and you have yourself an afternoon of quiet strolling around, going nowhere in particular. Before you know it, the day is gone. It's sunny, and around us we see countless runners wearing their Donald Duck medals, some of whom are walking with that characteristic 'I've-Just-Run-A-Marathon' gait.

It's an early night for sure. But first, some light fare back at Port Royale – still hungry – and a celebratory glass or two of wine, as if we needed anything else to ensure we slept well tonight. We sit on the patio and watch the Disney World around us. I'm living life on the edge eating a Bacon Double Cheeseburger. I don't know what a typical one of these costs but here it's costing me $7.88 US. But to a certain extent it is my *dream come true*, as my receipt states, because in my current craving state, a BDC seems like the most wonderful meal I could possibly imagine.

There's no need for any other entertainment; I provide part of it eating my burger. We're both very content sitting back watching everyone, and saying anything that comes into our heads. It's a great calm, relaxed feeling. Later, back in our rooms, we get our kits ready for the next day, recognizing that tomorrow will be no cakewalk, or boardwalk, for that matter. The longer we're on the course tomorrow, the hotter it will get. We'll try to finish as soon as possible, but regardless, we expect to be out there for at least 4 ½ hours, even with everything going well. It'll be good to get tomorrow over with.

In search of Mickey

It's 3am. Groundhog Day. Here we go again. I'm woken up by my phone alarm, which reminds me I might be running a marathon today.

Besides any tiredness due to lack of sleep, I'm feeling a bit stiff and my periformis/gluteus maximus feels like going back to sleep. It's tight, like a big sailor's knot has been tied while I slept. I'm feeling good about today though because if successful it will mean the completion of a goal. I didn't really know if I could run 3 marathons in two months. A year ago I would've said not a chance. But here I am, spurred on by the prospect of a Mickey Mouse and Goofy medal, close to achieving what I set out to do.

Karen and I meet up again as we did yesterday, and make our final preparations. We're less concerned about the bus, but we're thinking more about sitting for 2 hours waiting to run. It's already hot in the dark, with expectations of temperatures up to 85 degrees today.

Today there are only 11,000 of us waiting to run these 42.2 km. Runners are either coded as Blue or Red starts, and as such, begin in slightly different places from one another. Again, we'll begin at the Epcot Centre and run to the Magic Kingdom. From there we'll head down Floridian Way and Bear Island Road for a few miles until we reach the Animal Kingdom at about Miles 16 and 17. That's a long stretch of road. We"ll run a couple of miles around that Kingdom and then head off to MGM Studios at Miles 22 and 23. We'll run through Washington Square Garden, see the Big Apple on New York Street, and wander, possibly drag ourselves by the Sorcerer Mickey Hat before leaving MGM heading for a final push, or crawl, through Boardwalk and around the Lake at the Epcot Centre.

It all seems straightforward when you write it down or look at a map. But that changes as soon as you start putting your feet on the road and consider the prospect of making thousands of steps continuously over the next few hours. In the heat. In the humidity. Add a blister or two, lack of water, some tiredness from lack of sleep, a bowel system that may or may not be a star performer when you want it, and you start to see that time is emotionally and mentally, perhaps spiritually, elastic. Yet the physical distance remains the same.

And so with these confident thoughts in our minds we catch the bus as usual, arrive at the start-line/ parking lot in the darkness once more, and like the other 11,000-plus runners listen, watch, stretch, chat, sit, drink water, listen, watch, stretch, chat, sit, drink water, and ... well, ... you know ...

And eventually, away we go again, herded into the appropriate sections once more. We're all just waiting to explode out of the gates, well, over the start-line, but we must be patient ambling up to start our magical experience. In yesterday's pre-race time we posed for photos with Woody and Jessie from Toy Story, but we've not had that opportunity this morning. We'll make sure we high five the characters at the start-line again.

I suppose the walk to the real start-line is a good way to mentally prepare, although I think I can confidently speak on behalf of 11,000 runners that we just want to get going. There are about 1,000 non-Americans running. Not that I counted them; the Race Director told me this (there were 908 in the half-marathon). John also told me that 48% of runners are female, whereas for the half-marathon the figure was 63%.

Booom! After the speeches from Mickey and others, and spectacular fireworks, away we go. I high-five Mickey as I cross the start-line. He'll have sore paws by the end of this.

Like yesterday, it's crowded over the first few miles. We keep a steady pace early on even though it's somewhat chaotic. One man drops his water bottle which causes six other runners to fall in various directions and angles.

The narrow bits of pathways are causing problems and later, so too do the roundabouts that link the respective roads. The camber is heavily angled on the tight turns, with the slope quite uncomfortable to run on, especially at a fast pace and if you have knee troubles. It's easier for runners who are mountain goats that have evolved with one leg shorter than the other.

Actually it's uncomfortable on these cambers even at a slow pace. These turns create more verbal and visible dissatisfaction for many runners later in the race. It's a talking point.

For the first few miles though we are in a groove. The pace is slow but suits us fine. Every ten minutes or so, we walk for a minute. So far, the run feels relaxed. Everything seems to be in control.

The scenes along the route feature the same sort of hoopla as yesterday. There's much excitement as the Disney characters come into view. I'd like to think it's an inspiring scene for the characters also – to see 11,000 runners on their way to completing a marathon.

We still don't have a camera but think yes, "next time" – yep, should bring one. It's one of those kick-yourself-in-the-pants sorts of things.

The most enjoyable part of the race is the Magic Kingdom. If the race just went around the Kingdom a few hundred times I'd be quite happy. Everything is, well, Disneylike – it's like I'm really there. Who knew? It's a fun feeling which lasts for several minutes, with the biggest buzz being able to run through the castle on the footbridge.

So for several minutes my mind is taken off the run; the diversions are brilliant. Unfortunately for us they are not long enough, and soon after the Magic Kingdom we continue running for many miles along what should be called Emptyland. We're heading for Animal Kingdom. It's not as though there's nothing to see, it's just that there are no theme parks. If I try to be objective about it, it's still a nice run.

But our energy levels are dropping. Our ten minute run – one minute walk strategy is slowly transforming into longer walks and shorter runs. We reach the halfway point in a time of 3:02. Not fast at all, but not too, too bad. If we were able to sustain this pace it would still only be a 6:04 time, which certainly puts us out of the prize money, definitely, but keeps us in the race and assures us of a Goofy medal. Dozens of runners have no doubt already finished.

Our problem though is that we are declining rapidly as various body systems decide to slow down or potentially cut out completely. Karen is tiring because of a much limited training program – a function of a heavy work overload, but she is gutting it out with tenacity. We're sticking together, and although I'm not feeling it as bad as Karen, I'm absolutely fine with the drop in intensity.

As we get closer to the Animal Kingdom we're effectively running around the backside of the Disney properties, discovering interesting sewage smells (we think it may be animals at first) and the places where all the 'stuff' is kept (machines, garbage dumpsters and maintenance equipment). Let's face it, it's got to be kept somewhere. It almost feels like another theme park, Maintenance World perhaps.

Fortunately after several miles of Emptyland and our brief encounter with Maintenance World we arrive at the Animal Kingdom. I remind myself not to get too excited as there's unlikely to be many, if any, actual animals here. It's an amusement park, remember. I don't want to disappoint myself with high expectations, because everything here is 'made'.

Disney staff allude to our imminent arrival at Animal Kingdom with a real parrot and real rabbits sitting alongside the road along with other real furry animals. That's as exotic and dangerous as it gets. What's more interesting is the by-now very-tired-and-slower runners coming through the park and passing by 'real people' visiting it. If you didn't know we must look like a bunch of crazies running in what is now even hotter sun than before.

We're crazy?

People are paying a lot of money to experience Dinoland, Jungle treks, Discovery Island and the many restaurants and stores throughout the park. It's odd that the name of the park has 'animal' in it, because really, if you were to count, there's not many animals to be seen.

Our walk-run ratio continues to shift. We're walking much more now, and although I'm not saying anything to Karen, I'm looking at my running computer and estimating and recalibrating time to completion based on our current pace. The cut-off time to still be awarded a Goofy medal is seven hours for the full marathon. I don't know when we will finish, but at our current rate of decline, and if a speeding train was passing another speeding train but moving at a different speed, and if Tommy has six apples and Betty has four oranges ... and oh ... anyway,

I'm hallucinating now ... we're definitely slowing down. I'm not saying anything about this to Karen because we don't need that added pressure. In the back of my mind, creeping up quietly along the side actually towards the front, is the thought that maybe we won't get inside the cut-off time.

No Goofy medal??!!

It's getting hotter.

If miles 11 to 16 were Emptyland, with a hint of Maintenance World, then miles 18 to 22 were Nowhereland, characterised by totally unremarkable nothingness. It's where we falter most, where the chain comes off the bike. We almost grind to a halt. Those who have run this stretch will know it's the Osceola Parkway – a long stretch of mostly straight highway where – unfortunately, and much to the shock of runners still going - the water stations have run out of water. That's right. The highest temperatures ever at a Disney marathon, and despite the weather forecast heads-up of heat and humidity the water stations run out of water – drinks – for the latter runners and walkers.

We reach Mile 20 in a time of 4:47. There's still 6.2 miles to go, which seems like an awfully long way. Conventional wisdom talks of dividing a marathon into two sections – the first 20 miles and the last 6. I'm wondering more and more if we'll make it under the 7-hour cut-off. We should, even if we just walk at a good pace, but you never know what can happen. It's hot, our bodies are tired, there's no water and the heat of the day is coming into full force.

The mood of many runners by now is irritable at best.

Disbelief is running rampant. Many runners are now reduced to walking, some of whom have just had their last stuffing pulled out of them with the disappearance of the water supply. Our walking is still interspersed with runs, but not many, and a few runs are simply straight to the portapotties.

As the physical distance that remains gets smaller, the emotional and mental distance expands. It's hot. Did I mention that? Did I mention the water has run out? The Osceola Parkway is a psychological bomb that annihilates many runners in miles 20 to 21 because it loops onto itself. We run – walk – walk – run for one mile then turn around and come back over the same road. Even then we still have a mile and a half to get to the MGM Studios for some distractions. We're looking for distractions anywhere we can find them. There's not many people running now, and those that are, are doing the shuffle thing. Looking from the sidelines we do not look like a group of elite athletes at the peak of their careers.

But wait. Who cares? Really, what does it matter if people are slow, or even walking? If you're a purist there's a chance you'll object to walkers in a marathon no matter what. But turn it around and much more refreshing thought emerges. Anyone who covers 26.2 miles running *or walking* should be commended because they are out there doing it – experiencing, being healthy, enjoying others, feeling alive, and *in the moment*, sharing – while the bulk of the population is not. Peak fitness and a beautifully carved body may not be the most important goals for many at the back of the pack, but regardless of what position you are in the race, you still have to lug that body of yours over the full distance.

And 26.2 miles is a long way, especially at the end.

This is where the magic is – the latter runners. It's a very, very social scene. We strike up conversations with runners who are raising money for their own charities, or to remember a family member who has recently passed away due to an illness, or a combination of both. There are runners who have recently had heart attacks and who are determined to put themselves back into a condition that will contribute to a better, healthier, longer life. There are mother-daughter teams, friends bonding together to run a marathon and share a special experience, others who are simply there to prove to themselves, and others, that they can succeed if they put their mind to it. And then there are the TNTs. We'll come back to them shortly.

People in this pack of the race are not disappointed that their times will be slower than thousands of others. They don't care. It's not a race for most people; it's a challenge. A personal challenge. If you overcome the challenge that you set for yourself – like completing a marathon – then you're well on the way to facing and overcoming other challenges. Let's face it, the challenges in life will inevitably come; that's partly why completing a marathon is so important. It's about tenacity, confidence, self-worth, commitment, resilience, perseverance – all those things that help you face down adversity.

And it's fun to be out here, in the moment, as these people can attest. People are hurting, or are tired or both, but most are still smiling and chatting away. Friendships are being made. There's plenty of time to think as well. Just as a healthy diet improves your brain functioning, skin colour, hair quality, attitude towards life, and all the benefits to your internal organs, as well as help you lose weight, completing a marathon distance helps you get to know yourself, and to get to know others, as well as help you to get, or to stay healthy. Again, the more you know yourself the more you are able to cope with what life puts in front of you. Being physically fit and healthy makes it even more possible.

So here we are. We've resigned ourselves to a much, much slower than anticipated finish, but along the way we've become immersed in a social clique that has already mobilised itself through 23 miles. People are more interest in talking than they are running. In a different race, with a bit more training, we'd be finishing in around 4 hours. Today, we're doing much more talking and significantly less running. It's now looking like we'll finish somewhere between six and a half hours and seven hours. But I'm still not sure, even at Mile 23. I'm keeping quiet about it. We have to keep moving if we want that Goofy Medal. And we do want that Goofy medal.

Run or walk, I'm feeling the sun; it has no intention of leaving. The upside is that it's a truly spectacular day. We're coming into the last mile or so now, as we walk around the Lake at the Epcot Centre. We *are* going to make it under seven hours as we've kept a steady pace. I'm really pleased I've not had to show any angst, or ask that we run hard to get under a time. Frankly, I'm not sure we could've but we'll never know. And it doesn't matter.

Karen and I have constantly recalibrated our expectations during the run. We definitely wanted to run a good time in the marathon. To us that was somewhere between 4 and 5 hours. But we won't flog ourselves for not achieving that goal, because overriding that was the fact that we were here to run for a Goofy Medal. *And to enjoy it*. Let's not forget we ran a half marathon yesterday. Sometimes we have to remind ourselves what it is we really want in life. So for us, yes, disappointment that we didn't run better (well, a faster time). Moreso for Karen, because she feels strongly that we should be running strong; as best we know we can. Less disappointment for me - not really a disappointment at all actually – for although I'd prefer to run as much as possible, I'm okay if we walk. We'll come away with a Goofy Medal and lots of great memories; and likely with me feeling much better about it than Karen.

And so as we walk and talk our way around the Epcot Centre on a beautiful sunny day. We take the final turn towards the finish line, and I realise I'm achieving my goal of running three marathons in two months. I'm thinking that this is not the end, but in fact the beginning, as I'm still experiencing my own transformation. This is just a phase, one that started with training for Athens and is finishing with Disney. Karen meanwhile, is fulfilling her goal of the Goofy Challenge, as well as fulfilling her commitment to come with me to Disney to do this; and I'm very grateful that she's done so.

We cross the finish line running, with different emotions and feelings, just like the thousands of other runners today. We all have a common purpose but our reasons for completing the marathon can be so different. That's at the very heart of the transformation of marathon running today.

More to the point right now though, our bodies are tired. Really tired. The distance always commands respect. As we walk through the chute, picking up our bag and, of course, our Goofy medals, I look around at the faces of runners and family and friends. Some people are crying; overwhelmed by an achievement perhaps they never thought was possible. Others are crying, because they are in some serious pain as knees or ankles have given out, or they're dehydrated, or the blisters are now huge and bursting, or the shin splints or Achilles are becoming the body's 911 calls.

Some people are on stretchers; never a good sign.

Some people though, and some of the same people, are immensely happy with smiles; maybe they're actually Disney characters themselves. Deep inside the finishers I can see a sense of satisfaction – the "I've done it look"- slightly hollow, slightly exhausted, and maybe with wobbly knees and muscles that feel like jelly, if there's feeling at all.

I've not broken any records, but not broken any bones, and there appear to be no signs of internal organ failure. Like working physically anywhere for a length of time, my body is tired but feels 'full' – a rich feeling of having been rejuvenated – that the energy expended will do wonders for the body tomorrow. The more I do now in the time immediately following the marathon the better I'll be recovery-wise.

We don't mull around too long at the finish line; we're now cutting into relaxation time. But we do opt for a post-race massage, provided by Florida Hospital Celebration Health. We can get ten minutes of massage for $10, with the proceeds going to the Leukemia and Lymphoma Society. It doesn't seem like much time but it makes a difference. Most of my ten minutes is spent either getting up or getting down, but I'm pleased to say I don't fall off the bench. Actually the fifteen minutes I spend lying on the floor waiting for my treatment inside the makeshift tent/massage room is therapeutic in itself. I'm seconds away from nodding off when I'm offered the chance of a rub down. There are hundreds of runners lining up through the day so it's hit and miss really as to how long we will wait. Karen is lying down somewhere else in the tent, no doubt pleased to be doing so.

The quick rub down is such a tease it's almost certain you'll try to prolong the activity somehow. A good strategy is to ask the therapists about their lives, their pets, school, goals in life, travel, their favourite colour ... anything to keep them talking and you on the bench. But they know these tricks too, and show deft skills as they finish conversations with a smile, and a final move with their hands to say that's its time you're on your way. Another strategy is to tell a long story, talking very, very slowly, near the end of your time. Not that I use either strategy. In any case, my ten minutes last fifteen minutes, my therapist may have taken pity on me, with the beneficiaries of that extension being my calves, thighs and feet. Karen somehow manages a twenty-minute massage, but then she's a gifted conversationalist so it should be no surprise.

We stumble our way across the parking lot, a marathon in itself, congratulating the many other runners we pass as we search for our shuttle bus. We're congratulated as well, and our Goofy medals somehow elevate people's perception of our achievement. Despite our slow time, we're proud too. Our Caribbean resort awaits, but we've not set any plans except for finding our rooms, showering, gussying up and joining others in the evening post-race celebrations in Downtown Disney on Pleasure Island.

After showering we meet up for a drink and something to eat on the patio at Port Royale. I can't face another Gatorade product now until the next marathon, wherever that may be. The sun is still out and there is also some wine waiting. Well alright, we ordered it, it's time to celebrate.

For all our running, and walking, we're in fairly good shape. We're not stiff like boards and we don't have to walk backwards up stairs. We're moving into that contented, tired phase of the day. Sitting there looking out into the vast fake Caribbean Sea with a real glass of wine and some real salty fries we sit in the sun and reflect upon the day. Like yesterday, we've been up since 3am, so we can feel tired for that reason alone. We drift in and out of conversation through the rest of the day as the fake world of Trinidad passes by.

**

We decide to skip the 5:30pm Awards ceremony on Pleasure Island, but look forward to the celebrations, which begin, it says on the program, at 7pm. We sit on the bus with Willy from Kirkland, Washington State. Willy is recently retired and has extreme difficulty hearing, along with some other significant health problems over the years. But that's not prevented him from running marathons in Anchorage, London, Rome and Portland. And also running for Team in Training in the 2005 New York marathon. Willy gives me the URL to check his NY marathon photos out. (I look at them later, and they're great – especially the photo of Willy with the three NYPD Officers posing for the camera in the middle of the intersection – if you're reading this, thanks!).

The *Team in Training* is an amazing phenomenon.

In 1988 Bruce Cleland was training with friends and then ran the New York City Marathon in honor of his baby daughter Georgia, who had leukemia. They referred to themselves as the "team in training" (TNT). Since then, that one act of commitment and recognition has evolved into a huge organization committed to generating funding to support cancer research and help blood cancer patients live longer and better lives. In exchange for a training program and support to complete endurance events, participants raise money and awareness for the charity. It's a win-win situation.

Over 130,000 people in the United States are diagnosed annually with leukemia, lymphoma or myeloma. These new cases of leukemia, Hodgkin and non-Hodgkin lymphoma and myeloma account for over nine percent of the 1.4 million new cancer cases diagnosed in the United States alone.

The US Leukemia and Lymphoma Society is the home of TNT. It's the world's largest endurance sports training program, assisting people to train and complete marathons, half marathons, triathlons and 100-mile cycling events. Since 1988, over 360,000 participants have raised more than $850 million. The TNT runners are easily identifiable with their purple shirts, and are even known or referred to as the Purple Shirt People. At times it looked like a sea of purple in the Disney marathon, and sometimes sounded like it too as they supported one another over the 26.2 miles. Information provided by the Country Music Marathon and a Half Marathon in Nashville states that Team in Training, the race's official charity, has raised $148 million (net) in the past 10 years, with $16.3 million coming from the Nashville marathon weekend alone.

It's been good to talk to Willy, and inspirational too, when you hear how people manage to overcome adversity, and yet still commit to supporting others, such as Willy has done with the TNT. We say farewell to Willy when we arrive at Pleasure Island soon after 7pm. The shuttle bus service is brilliant. I can't imagine driving anywhere around Disney World; it would be a nightmare.

After half an hour of walking aimlessly we realise that The Party is actually everywhere – at all the clubs on the Island. What we have – our ticket – is a card that will get us free admission into the clubs, "valued at $23.38." We're disappointed, because meeting up with fellow marathoners would have been fun. We're not into the club scene at the best of times so it's unlikely we'll be blazing the dance floor anywhere tonight.

Well let's face it, it's the last thing we want to do. And seeing line-ups at the clubs only furthers our resolve to avoid them entirely. Instead, we window shop and try out a Harley Davidson at the HD store. There's quite a lot of 'Disney' on Pleasure Island, which shouldn't be a surprise, and plenty of other places for us to spend our money. *Mickey's Pantry* is where we can go, for example, to buy Disney Home and Kitchen products. If it's toys we want then where better than the *Once Upon a Toy* store? If you're one of those people who need Christmas all year round, you're in luck as the *Disney's Days of Christmas* store is here for you. In fact, pretty much everything is here – 'here' being at one end of the Island.

Across from the Christmas store is *Goofy's Candy Co.*, which I'm guessing, sells candy, and I can trade Disney Pins at the *Disney's Pin Traders* nearby. I don't have any of course, and it may not be my thing, but never mind because maybe the *Disney Fine Art Gallery* is my thing? Too expensive? Well then I can hop over to *Mickey's Mart*, where I can buy Disney merchandise for $10 or less. Something for everyone.

But we're quite full of Disney and just want to get off our feet and eat. We feel the urge for something different. When we see Wolfgang Puck Cafe with what looks like seats available and no line-ups, after rubbing our eyes in disbelief, we leap at the opportunity.

Well we would leap if we could. Instead, we hoist ourselves up onto the high stools in front of the sushi chef. Neither of us have tried sushi before, but now seems like the perfect time. Once on the seats it will take a herculean effort to move us off.

Sushi is a Japanese specialty based on seasoned cooked rice that is topped with slices of various raw fish, or rolled in sheets of *nori* (seaweed) with fish, vegetables and wasabi. There's more to it of course, but we're stiff, tired novices willing to give it a go. There's a really nice bottle of wine to go with it, lots of people around and the opportunity to watch our dinner prepared in front of us. The place has atmosphere. No one is doing a high five with a Disney character either.

We're not really sure what we've ordered or what to do. As there's no one close to us we tempt fate and use our chopsticks. The green stuff on the side of the rolls looks interesting; we think we're supposed to eat this with the rolls.

Karen takes a huge bite of the green stuff. Apparently you're not supposed to eat wasabi in large quantities. Well at least not all at once. It's a Japanese horseradish that comes from grating the root of the wasabi plant (believed to kill germs on raw fish). Or it could be an imitation, depending on where you go. Depending on your tolerance for these things you can feel it's either warm, hot, stinging, or setting off a nuclear reaction inside your mouth. It's a sensation unto itself that makes your nose and mouth understand how hot it must be to land on the sun.

Karen's face suggests she's just landed. Like a true friend she suggests I should try some as I'll like it. The smoke is still coming out of her ears but stops about the same time as her eyes stop watering. Maybe she thinks the running has dulled my intelligence. I take about a tenth of what she's just experienced and get my own internal pachinko machine firing away inside me. A bonding moment.

When we wipe away yet more tears we agree that it tastes really good, but perhaps it would be best in smaller quantities. It certainly takes our mind off any stiffness or tired muscles. With the drama over we sit back and enjoy a brilliant dinner. Love the taste, love the relaxation, and love the ambience of the restaurant. Sometimes everything seems to click. It's not late when we leave, and we're not whooping it up celebrating with other marathoners, but it's a great way to end the day, and our Goofy adventure. Tomorrow we head home.

2007 Disney World Marathon Results				
Place	Name	Country	1/2 split	Finish
1st	Driano Bastos	Brazil		2:19:24
2nd	Matthew Dobson	United States		2:32.23
3rd	Roy Vargas	United States		2:33.43
4th	Sean Moore	United States		2:39.29
9,736th	Malcolm Anderson	New Zealand	3:02.18	6:32.12

Note: There were 10,940 finishers.

I talked to John Hughes, Disney's Race Director, after the marathon weekend. John acknowledges that Disney is seen as the Leader of the *Entertainment Marathons*. Who better to be a leader really, when you allow runners to run through the four biggest theme parks in the world? And, to John and the volunteers' credit, the races only minimally impinge upon the regular visitors to the park, even on race day.

As you can imagine, it takes an enormous amount of dedication and planning to pull off the logistical needs for something like this weekend. On top of the 30,000 runners who came for the weekend there were thousands of volunteers supporting our Disney experience.

Seven hundred volunteers helped with packet pick-ups for the weekend alone. There were 700 medical volunteers from Florida Hospital for the medical stations along the course. About 2,000 volunteers worked on the marathon at the start-line, aid stations, finish line and in a range of other capacities to ensure the event went as smoothly as possible, much of which we runners will never know about.

And then the Disney staff. As roads were being closed thousands of Disney staff still had to get to work. It would be bad form to have Goofy stuck in a traffic jam. What if we never high-fived, well alright, hugged, Cinderella because she couldn't get through the barriers? Just wouldn't be right.

It's a year-long process to plan the Marathon weekend event. Closer to the time, the week before, the parking lot for the start-line is closed and scaffolding, power, tents and portapotties are set up to the extent possible before race day.

January 2008 is the Disney Marathon's 15th Anniversary. Even though it's a leader it is still very much in the competition for marathoners. This, I find fascinating. What's the competition for Disney? The big ones like Chicago, New York and the Marine Corps Marathon in Washington DC. If you can only go to one or two of the big ones in a year, which one will you go to, and why?

We're not only runners, but consumers as well. Even just a few hundred runners descending upon a destination can make a huge impact on the local economy. Make it a few thousand competitors and there is a substantial dollar figure emerging. The consumer spending power of 400,000 finishers in the United States alone clearly represent a large, and as we know, expanding market. There is money to be made in a diverse range of ways.

Marathon running is becoming big business. It's not just the number of finishers either. Look at the socio-demographic profile of runners. We are older, with more spending power, and relatively affluent by and large with fewer financial commitments than the younger cohorts. Take us Disney marathoners, for example. On average we are well educated with the median income of each runner hovering around $75,000US.

And that's also why there is more and more sponsorship coming into marathons; because we have discretionary spending and companies like to be associated with feel good, healthy activities such as running. And well-to-do consumers.

With such commodification of essentially the natural act of running I'm wondering if I should open up a running business. I don't need much convincing because there seems to be so much opportunity out there for entrepreneurs to provide quality services and products that enhance the marathon running experience.

When I began training for the three marathons it seemed really important that I run a sub 4-hour marathon in Athens. I missed it by a minute. I'm convinced I would've broken four hours if I'd known what my times were through the race. I could have been shattered but I wasn't, because the satisfaction of finishing was immense. I realised then that the actual running was only part of the overall experience. I met wonderful people, learned more about how to run, and marathon running in general, almost got run over and saw some amazing places. I shared my experiences with others, and made long-lasting friendships. I have memories that will last forever. Although nice, the one-minute difference doesn't change anything else.

This odyssey, in fact, has led me to people and places, and continues to do so. I'm not the only one. Marathon running is very much about people and place. Among other things, it's real world human geography, and would make for a fascinating thesis study. And then there's the thousands of runners globally that also share their running experiences in different ways with others less fortunate. Like the purple people in TNT, who raise money and awareness to support charities around the world.

Disney Expo.
Take everything out
of this picture
and you have the
Athens Expo.

Karen and author.
(That's Karen beside
Woody.)

Runners waiting and
watching live band
play before start of
Disney marathon.

Author weight
training with
Disney medals.

34

Running Marathons For A Cause

In a 2006 research paper British sociologists Sarah Nettleton and Michael Hardey commented that the increase in fundraising through mass-participation running events is "emblematic of a series of issues pertinent to contemporary conceptualizations of health and illness". They go on to say that "active citizens can ostentatiously fulfil their rights and responsibilities by raising money for those in need". This draws attention to illness and enables the sharing of experiences with others.

In some of the larger marathons, such as the Flora London marathon, there are limited spaces available for runners and a lottery system is put in place. You may or may not get in. Charities, however, will buy a limited number of places and use these to attract runners who will then be able to run, and can also raise money for the charity.

Charity running, quite simply, is HUGE. The London Marathon Director David Bedford, himself a former world class runner, explains that the 2006 London Marathon alone raised 41.5 million pounds for charities. He says that there will be about 13,000 people running *directly* for a charity in the race. The charities themselves pay three hundred pounds for each entry, but they know that each charity runner will be able to get back over 2,000 pounds in donations and support which is fed directly back to the charity. Everyone wins. He says they have 'something like 100,000 UK applications' from people who want to run to raise money for a charity, adding, 'we've identified a new marketplace'.

Charities can buy 'Gold Bond' places in the London marathon, which will guarantee a runner a place without having to go in the ballot draw. Charities can also get charity places but require that runners reach certain fundraising levels – typically around 2,000 pounds. If you're one of the lucky runners who got in through the ballot system you can still opt to help raise money for a charity. In 2006 about 78% of the London marathoners were raising money for charity.

In 2005 there was a full-page advertisement in *Runner's World* that stated "Approx 60,000 runners will fail to win a place in the 2005 Flora London Marathon ballot so book your GUARANTEED ENTRY with the Victa charity. NOW! WE HAVE THE ENTRIES – WE NEED YOUR BODIES". This type of message is quite common around the London marathon event. The researchers Sarah Nettleton and Michael Hardey reviewed all the advertisements for the 2005 London Marathon in the August edition of *Marathon News*, the official monthly magazine of the London marathon. They found the same consistent structure throughout the ads – what they referred to from the academic literature as the *restitution narrative*. First, the scene – the details about the disease or illness are described. The 'characters of the plot' are then introduced and this is followed by a comment about how the problem can be addressed (for example, more research, or more staff etc). Then, the final statements about what can be done by the reader (runner). Nettleton and Hardey refer to this that "readers are lured by both goods with exchange value (a place in the marathon) and with the promise of satisfying their sense of communal responsibility".

Nettleton and Hardey comment that the Golden Bond scheme used by London has created a market now whereby the charities are essentially competing against one another for runners. It's a strange world isn't it, but in a way, it has some perfect internal logic to it. Where does it end though?

Well, all is not well necessarily. *The Guardian* newspaper in England reported in August 2007 that the smaller charities feel they are being squeezed out of the 'lucrative' London Marathon fundraising opportunities. They say the larger charities like Oxfam and Cancer receive too large a share of the available places. The larger charities may have dozens of entries available to them through the Golden Bond scheme (one has 100, for example). Although over seven hundred charities actually benefit from the scheme there are another five hundred on the waiting list. In fact a new Silver Bond scheme was introduced in 2007, which offers 550 charities one place every five years, but already that was oversubscribed for 2008 and 2009. One small charity was quoted as saying "The big charities are literally running away with the money, yet they already have vast reserves". Another charity commented "The event is fantastically organized, with military precision, but it is a closed shop. To me it just absolutely stinks of complete unfairness". The London

Marathon, however, states that many of the guaranteed places have been with charities that have been involved with the marathon for fifteen years.

The Guardian says that the dissatisfaction is prompting smaller charities to consider running a second London Marathon or build the profile of another race elsewhere in the country. The organizers, however, feel the criticism is unwarranted, pointing to the fact that 45 million pounds are raised with each London marathon, which is five times the amount raised in other major centres such as New York.

Running for charity can bring out the strangest in people and places. In the 2008 Flora London marathon Hannah Miller put on an egg suit to race against Therese Whitcomb-Eriksson who ran the marathon dressed as a chicken. This was to answer the age-old question, which comes first, the chicken or the egg?

And also to raise money for the Christian charity World Emergency Relief (WER) for its campaign to send laying hens to impoverished families in developing countries so that this would provide a sustainable source of eggs to eat and sell. By raising about 4,000 dollars they will have enough funding to buy 330 hens that could lay almost 40,000 eggs a year – what Therese referred to as an 'egg-cellent' result. Miller said "it's a cheap and easy way to make a real difference to the lives of people who are genuinely hungry and in need."

John Wallace is a school caretaker in London England. I met John in downtown London one evening after he'd finished work. He'd brought along his photograph album, medals, his son, and a huge trophy. We talked about his marathon achievements. John has been registering for marathons for many years as Clark Kent and runs in a Superman costume. Not the same costume all these years, as the photos show, but in the process he's raised over $100,000 this way over the course of his 250 marathons. Today there are other Supermen running but John was likely THE first one. Scooby-Doo is now often seen running marathons in the United Kingdom. Look around the start-line at any marathon and you'll usually see a costume of some sort. Osy, a Church caretaker in England, ran the London marathon dressed in a Polar Bear suit. That was in preparation for successfully running his 100th marathon at the North Pole.

Why run for a charity? You don't have to dress like an Egg or a Superhero to run for charity, but it is indeed a noble thing to be doing. It can give you a stronger sense of purpose in training, provides access to a support network that will give encouragement, and provide training plans and schedules, on-line discussion groups, pre and post-race parties and receptions, possibly t-shirts, a feeling of accomplishment, and a real sense of having done something meaningful for a worthwhile cause. Fundamentally, you are doing something to help people in need. Some would say it's more of a question of why you wouldn't run to raise money for a charity.

The John Hancock Boston Marathon Fundraising Program has a similar program to that in London. As it is the principal sponsor of the Boston Marathon it is able to provide select non-profit organizations with invitational marathon entries that are used to raise funds for them. Runners are typically asked to raise $3,000 for the respective charities. In 2007 the program raised $3.3 million for such organizations, including Horizons for Homeless Children, American Red Cross, and the Cystic Fibrosis Foundation.

And then there are those runners that command respect and awe for their individual commitment to causes. Tim Borland set off to raise money for ataxia-telangiectasia (A-T) research. A-T is a neurodegenerative disease that affects children. Tim ran the marathon distance 63 times in 63 continuous days. That's right, 63 in 63 days.

I talked to Tim the other day over the telephone. He raised money and awareness for the A-T Children's Project in their quest for a cure or life-improving therapies for ataxia-telangiectasia. A-T presents a combination of symptoms like cystic fibrosis, muscular dystrophy, cerebral palsy, and cancer. Although these children are born apparently healthy, they are usually dependent on wheelchairs by the age of ten and often do not survive their teen years.

For preparation – you have to ask how do you prepare for such a challenge, let alone your typical marathon event – Tim went to Stanford University to do a series of tests (aerobic capacity, VO2, bone density and muscle strength) to ensure he was physically up to the challenge. He'd run 15 marathons prior to the A-T CureTour. His training also included preparing himself mentally. He quit his job and he and his wife bought a camper van and took their two young children on what was to be the A-T CureTour across the United States.

So Tim, at age 31, started the A-T CureTour running the Disney (Anaheim) half-marathon twice then proceeded to run across the United States. He pushed an Axiom Racer (stroller) over the whole distance. At Day 40 he was running sub 4-hour marathons. On the 63rd day Tim ran the New York Marathon in a time of 3:29. He has since committed himself to running full-time in order to raise awareness and garner support for children's causes. A movie and a book are being produced that document Tim's achievements and the A-T cause.

Although we're not all like Tim, partly because many of us may not want to run across the US, we can, through our own individual efforts at running long distances, make a big difference in other people's lives – as well as our own.

35

End of An Odyssey... Or?

It doesn't seem right going back to the Canadian winter. Never does. Fortunately the flights are uneventful and I have enough leg room to prevent any serious cramping from occurring. They move the turbulence to another part of the sky which pleases Karen. What *really* doesn't seem right is driving back from the Toronto airport in the middle of the night in the Canadian winter. What *absolutely really* doesn't seem right is filling the car up with gas in the middle of nowhere in biting minus 20 degree Celsius temperature with a wind chill that makes the start-line at Athens seem like a heat wave. Sound familiar?

Once I finally get home and lie in bed I reflect on the few days with Donald, Mickey, Goofy and Karen. Not for too long though because I'm beat. I'm asleep before I can turn the light off.

Nothing spectacular happens over the next few days as

I get back into the groove of the Canadian winter, but in my mind things have changed forever.

Here I am – two months and 3 ½ marathons later, and wondering why people live in weather like this. I've visited places I've never been before, followed a training program (as best I could), met some wonderful people, and learned an enormous amount about marathon running. I feel extremely fortunate to have had this opportunity. My fitness level has improved, I'm healthier than I've been in twenty years, and I feel on the cusp of even greater levels of health and well-being. I feel like doing a mental lap of honour.

As special as this has been to me I realise that "special" is always relative. Dave Major, for example, ran his 200th marathon in Athens. It was, as Dave said, a special run for him. He and his wife Linda, and many other 100 Marathon club members, run a marathon or two every weekend. Other runners, Dane and Tim being extreme examples, have been raising money for charities. In Tim's case, his running passion has become completely interwoven with his life as he has dedicated himself to raising awareness and funds for children in need through his distance running. Other runners, meanwhile, are running marathons as an expression of triumph over serious illnesses such as heart attacks or cancer. Their running is inspirational.

John Dawson, a seventy-year old marathoner from England who got into marathon running after suffering a heart attack many years ago (and who has now run over 220 marathons) has, over the past year or so, been training a young man – Simon, who has Down Syndrome – to run a marathon. They successfully ran the London Marathon, were invited to 10 Downing Street as a result, and have been the source of inspiration for others – volunteers and those with Down Syndrome in Europe – who are now embarking on distance running, something they never thought was possible before. I've learned an incredible amount about the human condition from talking to John and others. (I first met John, as it turned out, in Athens, as he was one of Dave Major's friends running the marathon there.) Seeing what John and others like him have made possible in their lives has substantially increased my faith in humankind. My goal of three marathons in two months seems quite feeble in comparison. Then again, I suppose we all have to start somewhere.

I will have these memories forever. The future looks like a better place for me. Is all this made possible through running? How is it possible that something so simple can be so rewarding?

We have, perhaps, lost touch with the simple things in life. Lost touch with how to make ourselves feel good. I shouldn't talk on behalf of the rest of the world, I suppose, but for me at least, I know that the simple act of getting up and moving – getting out and running – even for 15-20 minutes, energises me and gives me a space to think. I'm made to move and not to sit at a desk in front of a computer. My body gets rejuvenated through the simple act of exercise. It functions better, and my mind is sharper.

It's not just about the running, though. There is a ripple effect. Because I want to increase my distance, or improve my ability at the longer distances, I've got to continually improve my eating habits, stretch more, and sleep more. The more I run, the stronger my cartilage-less knee feels. If I've worked less over the past 2 ½ months, I can categorically say I've worked better in less time. Quality work, not quantity work.

And so, in the two weeks following the completion of the Goofy Challenge, I start looking at new goals, thinking about the possible. A year ago on a New Zealand beach it seemed that running a marathon was 'remotely possible', but more likely, unlikely. But here I am; my confidence is high and I'm busy planning new goals.

I realise I'm one of those people that need goals. If I don't have goals how will I ever be able to achieve what I want in life? But they have to be realistic. By achieving what I set out to do here, my confidence in setting other goals has been made that much stronger. The 'challenge,' if that's the right word, is being committed to making those goals happen. Anyone can set goals, or make promises. That's easy. The hardest and most rewarding part is setting down a path towards making them happen. Faith in yourself is a powerful thing. Achieving goals makes that faith stronger.

At the same time, it's not all about achieving goals; it's also about enjoying the journey you take to achieve the goals. I've had a remarkable and unforgettable experience. So have thousands of others who have run marathons and gotten caught up in an unofficial social movement along the way. I'm like everyone else; the only difference is that I've decided to write about it.

It's January now. People in New Zealand are revelling in the summer; some are emailing to tell me how great the weather is on the other side of the world, and letting me know how concerned they are that snow and ice are a fact of life for me for the next three months. They're laughing of course, but that's okay because I'll be emailing them in June, July and August expressing my equal concern about their winter and telling them about the spectacular summers we have here in Ontario.

And I'll be running as well. It will likely be for an express purpose – running towards a goal or two. Maybe three, I don't know. The possibilities are endless.

I think that's one of the biggest things I've realised. When you have children you want them to be everything they can possibly be, and for them to be able to see that life offers enormous opportunities to satisfy their souls. We don't exactly speak like that to children, of course, but we don't want their world to be closed in. If we ourselves are fortunate enough, we offer them possibilities and create opportunities, and see what they can accomplish with them.

Maybe we lose sight of that as we grow up. Maybe the attainment of goals through running long distances puts the excitement back in life on physical, social, mental, emotional, and spiritual levels we've lost sight of. Whether we achieve the possible or not, the act of attempting to reach our goals – in my case getting up and moving – will still be better than to never have tried.

I'm now going way beyond what I set out to achieve with this book. The simple act of repetitively placing one foot in front of the other for a long period of time has brought me rewards I never thought possible a year ago, or even three months ago. I've discovered that there's nothing wrong with this addiction. And if this book has in any way made you think that running may be a good thing that you want to try, or do more of, then writing it has been worthwhile.

A social movement?

Absolutely.

I'm but one very small part of the bigger phenomenon. We don't typically call running a marathon a phenomenon, but I think we can when a million people worldwide are running marathons each year. Hopefully we are role models for each other, and hopefully we are role models for our children.

Why is marathon running a movement? It's healthy at every different level. It's inspirational. It's rewarding. It's fun. It's clean. It supports local economies. It provides employment, directly and indirectly. It introduces you to new places and new people; it makes this world a smaller place. While not everyone can run marathons – or want to for that matter – if they *really want to*, most people can train to run at least some distance, even if it's just around the block. And if running really isn't their thing, walking is a great substitute. The point, I suppose, is that at the core of this bigger social movement is movement itself at the individual level. No-one can make people move; they have to want to do it. And more of us seem to want to. As the numbers earlier in the book indicate, more people are certainly discovering the reward of running long distances.

I'm looking out the window. It's a dreary grey morning with some snow and ice on the ground and a cold wind blowing the branches of the leafless trees. Part of me thinks it's best I don't run today. But a much bigger part of me thinks it is best that *I do* run today. I look for excuses not to run, but really, they are not convincing.

And so I get changed into my running gear. No music. No running computer. No fuel belt. I'm happy to run with nothing but my own thoughts. That's another transition for me; I don't need the extras any more to enjoy running. Out 'there' I'll plan the day; I'll dream; I'll listen to my body; I'll take in the sights; I'll talk to the animals; I may sing. There's a great chance I'll get an idea I don't even know about. And I'll be better off for having run. Powerful stuff for me, and I can't imagine not having these moments in my life.

And I'll think of the people I've met over the past few months. The children cheering me along the Athens marathon route. The hugs from other runners, complete strangers, at the finish lines of each marathon. The runner in Disney World who talked to us excitedly about finishing every Disney marathon that had ever been run. The owner of the store in Athens who was hoping this book would be written in Greek. The bus driver in Orlando who couldn't understand why anyone would want to walk, let alone run, twenty-six miles. And all the volunteers in the Cayman Islands who stole from their sleep to come out at 4:00am on a Sunday to support a bunch of crazy people running in the darkness around their island.

These are the things that memories are made of, and I'll have them forever.

Epilogue

It's been several months now since I finished my odyssey. I've had the opportunity to go over all my notes from the period. I've continued running and developed enduring friendships with runners from around the world. I've learned a few things.

While the training books are extremely valuable and important, the biggest learning comes from simply getting out there and doing it; to get training, and to keep doing it. I've been very fortunate now to have run twenty-three marathons, including the amazing Comrades ultra marathon in South Africa. More memories.

This book has been a long time coming, in part, because running has continued to take me places since Disney, and life just seems to get in the way of writing. It takes time to put the words down in the right order.

Looking back I can say that when I started this odyssey I was very naive – a newcomer to marathon running who simply thought he could possibly do it, but wasn't sure. I thought three marathons in two months was 'out there,' on the fringe. Who would do such a thing?

I was wrong. Some people run a marathon every weekend, maybe two; others run one monthly, some have run dozens over their life, others hundreds. Members of the 100 Marathon Clubs around the globe simply amaze me. But they are not a fringe group of runners by any means. Regardless of nationality, they're just like you and me, and they are wonderful people who are passionate about running.

From talking and emailing with marathoners, looking at Internet sites and reading various publications, I've immersed myself in a world that previously I didn't know existed. This is no secret handshake society or mystical world in a wardrobe. If anything, the reality is more fascinating than that. Now exposed, I'm forever changed, and a better person because of it.

I've learned that the heart of the social movement of marathon running is the people. We run to achieve a common goal – to complete 26.2 miles, but our reasons for doing so are unique to each person. We can list the main reasons why people run, but ultimately it's our own context that defines our experience. I've run some portions of races with other people and have come away from the experience feeling like I have known them for a lifetime. I now look to run some marathons specifically so I can meet up with friends I've made at earlier marathons.

While there must be limits to what is possible, it's clear that running long distances has captured the eyes, ears, feet, and imagination of people around the world. Maybe we are all looking for something in this 'modern' world, the *tempo giusto* perhaps, and more and more of us are finding it running marathons.

We are social animals. We talk and we listen as we run. We listen to others, we listen to ourselves. And we listen to everything around us, be it thousands of spectators lining the streets, the silence of a desolate valley, a tree-lined trail filled with birds and animals, or the bustle of the concrete freeway or cobblestone streets that have been made available to us, the runners, for the marathon day.

We share the experience. We laugh. We think. We wonder. We dream. We remember. For many of us, life does not often afford us that kind of opportunity. When we are running we are also in control. For some of us having some sort of control in our lives seems impossible. But 'out there' the runner determines his or her pace. The runner decides where to run. The runner decides when to stop. The runner determines what to think about, if anything. The runner decides to listen to the world around, or listen to music, or both. Training and running marathons gives us all a chance to take some control of the rhythm of our own lives.

Why? Because, in part, it takes time to run a marathon, even if you're the world record holder. It takes time to train for a marathon. We are at one with our own thoughts (and at times with those with whom we run.) There is a growing movement worldwide to slow the pace of life; we have embraced too much speed in everything we do. Maybe this is having, and will have, serious negative effects for us and for our children. Running long distances can pull us away from the pace of life we impose upon ourselves or are presented with, as we take on more and more responsibilities, activities and commitments in the actual time we do have.

I've been extremely privileged to share in the remarkable stories of others. Some of my favourite runs have been out the back with Fred, or Callum and Jack, or with Karen along the trails or along the lake. My life has slowed down as a result of running. It has become very deliberate. I make the time to run, because I think not to run would be detrimental to my health.

My journey at the beginning of this book started off with a destination – a goal – but with no clear detailed road map. I didn't know what I would find in the process but I'm delighted to say I've found much more than I ever could have imagined. Along the way, I received a medal for completing the Athens Marathon. I received a medal when I melted in the Caymans. And I got my Goofy medal. Proud moments.

When I look back and see how naive I was, I'm almost embarrassed. My knowledge of marathon running increased exponentially. I've realised that the journey itself was the outcome all along. And it continues to this day. Hopefully it will continue for many days ahead. My boys, Callum and Jack, have started running five kilometre races with me and enjoy it. This feels really good.

Gordon the Hamster has not got stuck in his wheel for months. Fred still runs with me, and still stops to see if I continually run around the back yard track.

I did finally pay the Athens fine.

My earplug keeps falling out of my right ear.

Some things never change.

mja, 2008

About
the Author

Malcolm Anderson lives in Yarker, Ontario Canada. He is a left-handed, 47-year old who speaks with a funny accent. When he's not confusing people talking he's confusing himself trying to understand anything loosely called "technical". He took up running in 2006 in a bid to avoid technical things and to get into better shape. If he's not writing fiction or running, writing about running, talking about running or wishing he was running, or destroying music with his guitar and generally goofing off with friends and his children, Callum and Jack, he's conducting research at Queen's University. He has run over 20 marathons, including the 90km Comrades Ultramarathon in South Africa, and the Brathay 10 marathons in 10 days Challenge in the Lake District of England. His most important event was the recent 5km Wolfe Island race which he ran with Callum and Jack. He has his sights set on running longer distances, including more trail running, a 100-miler in 2009, qualifying for the Boston Marathon, and not getting a disabling, showstopper injury. His next book, out soon, is about runners who have completed 100 marathons or more, which he finds amazing.

PHEIDIPPIDES
BY ROBERT BROWNING
(1879)

First I salute this soil of the blessed, river and rock!
Gods of my birthplace, daemons and heroes, honour to all!
Then I name thee, claim thee for our patron, co-equal in praise
--Ay, with Zeus the Defender, with Her of the aegis and spear!
Also, ye of the bow and the buskin, praised be your peer,

Now, henceforth, and forever,--O latest to whom I upraise
Hand and heart and voice! For Athens, leave pasture and flock!
Present to help, potent to save, Pan --patron I call!
Archons of Athens, topped by the tettix, see, I return!
See, 'tis myself here standing alive, no spectre that speaks!
Crowned with the myrtle, did you command me, Athens and you,
"Run, Pheidippides, run and race, reach Sparta for aid!
Persia has come, we are here, where is She?" Your command I obeyed,
Ran and raced: like stubble, some field which a fire runs through,
Was the space between city and city: two days, two nights did I burn
Over the hills, under the dales, down pits and up peaks.

Into their midst I broke: breath served but for "Persia has come!
Persia bids Athens proffer slaves'-tribute, water and earth,
Razed to the ground is Eretria--but Athens, shall Athens sink,
Drop into dust and die--the flower of Hellas utterly die,
Die with the wide world spitting at Sparta, the stupid, the stander-by

Answer me quick,--what help, what hand do you stretch o'er
destruction's brink?
How,--when? No care for my limbs!--there's lightning in all and some--
Fresh and fit your message to bear, once lips give it birth!"

O my Athens--Sparta love thee? did Sparta respond?
Every face of her leered in a furrow of envy, mistrust,
Malice,--each eye of her gave me its glitter of gratified hate!
Gravely they turned to take counsel, to cast for excuses. I stood
Quivering,--the limbs of me fretting as fire frets, an inch from dry wood:
"Persia has come, Athens asks aid, and still they debate?
Thunder, thou Zeus! Athene, are Spartans a quarry beyond
Swing of thy spear? Phoibos and Artemis, clang them 'Ye must'!"

No bolt launched from Olumpos! Lo, their answer at last!
"Has Persia come,--does Athens ask aid,--may Sparta befriend?
Nowise precipitate judgment--too weighty the issue at stake!
Count we no time lost time which lags thro' respect to the Gods!
Ponder that precept of old, 'No warfare, whatever the odds
In your favour, so long as the moon, half-orbed, is unable to take
Full-circle her state in the sky!' Already she rounds to it fast:
Athens must wait, patient as we--who judgment suspend."

Athens,--except for that sparkle,--thy name, I had mouldered to ash!
That sent a blaze thro' my blood; off, off and away was I back,
--Not one word to waste, one look to lose on the false and the vile!
Yet "O Gods of my land!" I cried, as each hillock and plain,
Wood and stream, I knew, I named, rushing past them again,
"Have ye kept faith, proved mindful of honours we paid you erewhile?
Vain was the filleted victim, the fulsome libation! Too rash
Love in its choice, paid you so largely service so slack!

"Oak and olive and bay,--I bid you cease to en-wreathe
Brows made bold by your leaf! Fade at the Persian's foot,
You that, our patrons were pledged, should never adorn a slave!
Rather I hail thee, Parnes, --trust to thy wild waste tract!
Treeless, herbless, lifeless mountain! What matter if slacked
My speed may hardly be, for homage to crag and to cave

No deity deigns to drape with verdure?--at least I can breathe,
Fear in thee no fraud from the blind, no lie from the mute!"

Such my cry as, rapid, I ran over Parnes' ridge;
Gully and gap I clambered and cleared till, sudden, a bar
Jutted, a stoppage of stone against me, blocking the way.
Right! for I minded the hollow to traverse, the fissure across:
"Where I could enter, there I depart by! Night in the fosse?
Athens to aid? Tho' the dive were thro' Erebos thus I obey--
Out of the day dive, into the day as bravely arise! No bridge
Better!"--when--ha! what was it I came on, of wonders that are?

There, in the cool of a cleft, sat he--majestical Pan!
Ivy drooped wanton, kissed his head, moss cushioned his hoof;
All the great God was good in the eyes grave-kindly--the curl
Carved on the bearded cheek, amused at a mortal's awe
As, under the human trunk, the goat-thighs grand I saw.
"Halt, Pheidippides!"--halt I did, my brain of a whirl:
"Hither to me! Why pale in my presence?"! he gracious began:
"How is it,--Athens, only in Hellas, holds me aloof?

"My calf muscles felt like they'd just been pounded with a hammer, there was an angry alien trying to get out of my left knee, and someone was playing the cello with my Achilles tendon. The lungs once filled with air seemed to have simply given up. A strained contorted smile appeared on my face, indicating that an acupuncturist had put 26.2 pins inside my mouth. I couldn't go any further. It was the best of times. It was the worst of times. I'd started training.

'Training' is a bit of a stretch. But there I was. An image that still sends shivers through the bone fragments in my left knee. A beach in New Zealand. February, 2006. The sun streaming down, because there is no other way for it to go. Waves crashing upon the shore as the cool Pacific breeze, well, alright, gale actually, was doing everything to knock me down. People walking their dogs, smiling at me with a touch of pity in their eyes. Their owners were doing the same. Had they realized I'd just run the entire length of the country? That would've been nice. Truth was I'd just taken an extremely long and painful time to run a very short distance. My first fifteen minute run in years. 'My God', I thought. Has it come to this?

Apparently it had."

With minimal previous running experience the author applies himself to the task with determination and good humour, but like most of us he finds many distractions along the way. In fact, what I find most compelling about this book is the totally honest way in which Malcolm relates his concerns, difficulties, setbacks, experiences, discoveries and encounters with other runners as he progresses towards the completion of his goal.

It is always a huge pleasure to come across books or articles that renew my enthusiasm for the sport I have come to love and I was genuinely inspired on a couple of occasions to just go for a run "for the fun of it". It is no hardship to review a book like this and it deserves to be a great success.

– Jack Brooks, Secretary, 100 Marathon Club, United Kingdom
(The Running Club for runners who have run 100 marathons or more)